2 CHRONICLES

Readings: A New Biblical Commentary

General Editor
John Jarick

2 CHRONICLES

John Jarick

SHEFFIELD PHOENIX PRESS

2007

Copyright © Sheffield Phoenix Press, 2007

Published by Sheffield Phoenix Press
Department of Biblical Studies, University of Sheffield
Sheffield S10 2TN

www.sheffieldphoenix.com

All rights reserved.
No part of this publication may be reproduced or transmitted
in any form or by any means, electronic or mechanical,
including photocopying, recording or any information storage
or retrieval system, without the publisher's permission in
writing.

A CIP catalogue record for this book
is available from the British Library

Typeset by Vikatan Publishing Solutions, Chennai, India

Printed by Lightning Source

ISBN 978-1-905048-96-0 (hardback)
ISBN 978-1-905048-97-7 (paperback)

Contents

Preface

This reading of 2 Chronicles follows on from my earlier volume on 1 Chronicles in this commentary series, although the present volume can be read without reference to or knowledge of the former work if the reader is so minded. The Introduction sets out the reading strategy that I apply to the books of Chronicles, and presents a number of matters that might be borne in mind for the journey through the subsequent pages; whereas readers who have consulted the volume on 1 Chronicles need not be detained by the Introduction here, but may wish to proceed immediately to the commentary.

In between the initial publication of *1 Chronicles* (in 2002) and the appearance now of *2 Chronicles* (in 2007) together with a reprint of the earlier volume, the Readings series has undergone a change of publisher, Sheffield Phoenix Press having taken over the series from Continuum, which had earlier acquired Sheffield Academic Press, the original publisher. I wish to place on record my profound gratitude to the Directors of Sheffield Phoenix Press—David Clines, Cheryl Exum, and Keith Whitelam—and General Manager Ailsa Parkin, for their support for the series.

The two 'surveys' that appear in this volume have each had a previous airing in a different guise. The 'Survey of Solomon's Temple' began its life as a paper delivered to the Old Testament Seminar at the University of Oxford in June 2003 and was published under the title 'The Temple of David in the Book of Chronicles' in the volume *Temple and Worship in Ancient Israel*, edited by John Day (LHBOTS, 422; London and New York: T & T Clark International, 2005); and the 'Survey of Judah's Kings' began its life as a paper delivered to the 18th Congress of the International Organization for the Study of the Old Testament at the University of Leiden in August 2004 and is appearing in a short version under the title 'The Stings in the Tales of the Kings of Judah' in the volume *In Search of Philip R. Davies*, edited by Duncan Burns and John Rogerson (LHBOTS, 484; London and New York: T & T Clark International, 2008).

I am grateful to everyone who interacted with those two papers and who helped, also in other conversations, to stimulate my thinking on the books of Chronicles. I am particularly grateful to two of my graduate students, Angela Thomas (who transferred my lectures on King Solomon from tape to type) and Melissa Jackson (who transferred my Hebrew script into transliterated form), and to my colleague Andrew Davison (who made the calculations about solar and lunar years that appear in the final chapter of this volume, when I discuss the matter of the land enjoying sabbath for 70 years). And speaking of colleagues and sabbaths, I would also like to record my appreciation for the sabbatical term granted to me by St Stephen's House, in which I was able to further my engagement with the text of 2 Chronicles.

The more I have engaged with that text, the more I have seen that the compilers of these ancient Chronicles were consummate storytellers. They created a story-world that is much neater than the real world, because they tell a story in which just about everything ties together in a highly systematic way. I hope that I have detected a good number of the more intriguing tie-lines in my reading of the text, and I hope that you will enjoy the journey with me.

Oxford
October 2007

Introduction

Readers who are coming to this volume on 2 Chronicles after having read the companion volume on 1 Chronicles need not be detained by this Introduction; they may proceed immediately to the commentary sections of the present volume, unless they wish to have a reminder of the reading strategy employed in this particular approach to the books of Chronicles. But those who have not consulted the first volume will find here a number of things of a programmatic nature that are useful to have in mind before looking in detail at the stories that unfold across the pages of 2 Chronicles.

The first thing to note is that we are dealing here with the second part of a scroll entitled *dibrê hayyāmîm*, and of anonymous authorship. The work itself is generally referred to in English Bibles as 'Chronicles', and the putative author is generally styled 'the Chronicler' in scholarly discussions. However, I prefer to speak of 'The Annals' for the document and of 'the Annalists' for the people responsible for creating that document. The reason for my preference is not simply that many modern English translations render the expression *dibrê hayyāmîm* (when it occurs within the text of the scroll) as 'the Annals', such as the NRSV's 'the Annals of King David' for *dibrê hayyāmîm lammelek dāwîd* (in 1 Chron. 27.24), but also to suggest two aspects which may not be so ably signified by the designations 'Chronicles' and 'the Chronicler'.

Primarily I wish to signal that the book we have access to is not the product of a single author, not even in terms of that historical-critical model which postulates an original Chronicler upon whose foundation various levitical additions were laid or sundry priestly revisions were made. I rather think that the scroll from the first was the product of a collective enterprise of assembling, sifting, and refining certain Jerusalemite traditions; that is to say, that a community or guild of tradents was responsible for the composition of these Annals. I could of course speak of 'the Chroniclers' if the collective aspect of authorship was all that I wanted to imply for this work, but I am also attracted to the homonymous relationship between the word 'Annalists', as designating a school of chronographers, and the word 'Analysts', as designating professionals or others who apply analytical skills to their tasks. The people responsible for telling this version of the story of the kingdom of Judah through the pages of these Annals had exactingly analysed the events of the years under their scrutiny, and they put forward an account that scrupulously insisted on their line of analysis. This is an account which seeks to avoid any loose ends in the tale, and which brooks no alternative vision of the 'how' and the 'why' of it all. It does not sit easily alongside competing narratives. It demands to be read as the only scroll consulted on matters concerning the kingdom of Judah.

We of course have ready access to other scrolls purporting to tell of matters concerning that kingdom, since the ancient custodians of the Hebrew traditions decided not simply to accept the Annalists' account of matters, but bound those Annals in to a Bible that also included other accounts of the period, namely the books of Samuel and Kings. What the Annalists apparently sought to achieve looks to have been undermined by the later community of faith in its decision to preserve two competing versions of the events of those years. The Annalists created what to their minds should have stood unrivalled among the Judahite (or Judean) community as the definitive account of the nation's monarchical era, but there for all the world to see is its rival, the account in Samuel and Kings, superciliously agreeing with the Annals at times, stridently contradicting them at other times, and often enough diverting readers with tales of a northern kind, all the while winning the debate in certain quarters about what really happened and what it might have meant.

Yet we can, if we wish, set aside the scrolls of Samuel and Kings, and contemplate Chronicles without their interference. I don't say that these Annals ought to be contemplated without reference to any other ancient Hebrew documentation; since the Annalists seem to take as read a certain amount of Mosaic material, I do not suppose that they necessarily wished to replace or suppress writings which were concerned with other matters than specifically the events and protagonists of the monarchical period. But when it comes to the telling of the tale of the kingdom of Judah, I imagine that the Annalists would indeed have wished for no rival storytellers.

Accordingly, the commentary presented here seeks to discover what may be heard if one listens single-mindedly to the Annalists' account, tuning out the competing stories about the kings of Judah that might otherwise vie for our attention. Only in the two 'surveys' included in the present volume—the 'survey of Solomon's temple' and the 'survey of Judah's kings'—will it be useful to devote some brief comparative attention to the differences between the Annalists' presentation of matters and the presentation made in Samuel and Kings, the better to appreciate the Annalists' unique spin on the events of the monarchical years. But in the chapter-by-chapter commentary, the aim is to roll with the Annalists' account, to enter their story-world and to get a feel for the specific tales that they are telling. Any rival accounts of what may or may not have happened in the kingdom of Judah form no part of that reading.

This being so, the present study need not theorize about precisely when these Annals were written, or which other now-biblical scrolls were in existence at the time (references to other 'canonical' writings in the comments below should not be taken as implying that the Annalists knew those precise documents). Some of the traditions represented within the Annals may be very old ones indeed, while others may have been rather freshly devised by the compilers themselves. Perhaps there were other written accounts in existence by the time the Annalists set about their task, or perhaps they were working at more or less the same time as various teams of chroniclers were putting together their own accounts. They may have copied certain matters from the scrolls of Samuel and Kings, or both they and the compilers of Samuel and Kings may have copied certain matters from another scroll; it might even be that the Samuel–Kings scribes made some use of these Annals. Since our task is to read the Annals in their own right as a coherent piece of literature with its own life, we need not join such endless debates.

All that can be said with certainty about the date of composition of these Annals is that they were not compiled in their present form before the Persian conquest of Babylon (alluded to at the end of 2 Chronicles, and already assumed in a post-exilic settlers list that had been presented in 1 Chron. 9), and accordingly that the work could not have been completed before the late sixth century BCE. It is probably significantly later than that, and if the genealogy of Davidic descendants in 1 Chronicles 3 is anything to go by then the final touches to the document were not made until the late third century BCE. However, since there seem to be other considerations than strictly historical ones on the part of the

Annalists in setting out the number of generations that they do in their list of the direct line of descent from David (as commented upon in the previous volume), no firm grounds for dating the composition can be derived from such 'data'.

There are other scholarly debates, too, which this study similarly leaves alone. Some readings of Chronicles divide the work into segments that stem from 'the Chronicler' and other segments that stem from one or another source-document utilized by 'the Chronicler' and yet further segments that have been added to the work after the time of 'the Chronicler' by one or another tradent. It should be evident from what was said earlier that the present reading is not interested in such theorization, but is only concerned with the work of 'the Annalists' as we find it. But equally it might be noted in this context that the work in view here is the scroll that begins with name of the primeval human 'Adam' (1 Chron. 1.1) and ends with the decree of the Persian king Cyrus (2 Chron. 36.23), and no special attachment is made to the scroll of Ezra–Nehemiah, which some interpreters (though fewer nowadays than used to be the case) take as part of the work of 'the Chronicler'.

Perhaps talk of 'the Annals' alongside 'the book of Chronicles' and at the same time the designations '1 Chronicles' and '2 Chronicles' as two separate 'books' may seem to cloud the issue of exactly what document is under study here. But the matter is simple enough. The Hebrew scroll of Chronicles is a single document, running from Adam to Cyrus, as just mentioned, and it is this complete Hebrew document that forms the basis of this study, and so the present volume does not treat '2 Chronicles' as a book separate from '1 Chronicles' but rather understands them as one continuous work. But the ancient Greek translators found it useful—not least because their language in written form takes up more space on a scroll than does the Hebrew script—to divide the work into two, ending the first half of the account at the end of the reign of King David (1 Chron. 29.30) and beginning a second half with the story of King Solomon (2 Chron. 1.1); this divide has remained a useful practical device, and so the present volume takes up the story from the succession of Solomon through to the end of the kingdom and to the possibility of a new beginning that is opened up at the very end of the scroll.

Although the Hebrew document is in view, this study is presented in English, and many readers will have a standard English text alongside them. Since the NRSV (the New Revised Standard Version) is now a widely used text, the cadences of that version have been generally accepted in these pages, but not entirely. For one thing, the NRSV's designations for divinity have not been accepted here; where English readers may be used to seeing such expressions as 'the LORD his God was with him' (2 Chron. 1.1) or 'that night God appeared to Solomon' (1.7), in these pages they will see 'his god Yahweh was with him' and 'that night the deity appeared to Solomon', which arguably render the Hebrew more accurately though less piously than the traditional translations. In addition to the question of divine names and designations, there are also a number of other specific occasions where I have preferred an alternative rendering to that chosen by the NRSV panel, but in such individual cases attention is drawn to the difference between my rendering and the wording of the standard translation.

It might also be noted that there is a regrettable one-verse discrepancy between the English and Hebrew verse-numberings in two chapters of 2 Chronicles, namely chs. 2 and 14. This means that what appears as 2.1 in most English Bibles (such as NRSV) is 1.18 in the Hebrew Bible, 2.2 in English is 2.1 in Hebrew, 2.3 is 2.2, and so on. Similarly, what appears as 14.1 in most English Bibles is 13.23 in the Hebrew Bible, 14.2 in English is 14.1 in Hebrew, 14.3 is 14.2, and so on. The English numbering is used in this commentary.

The Annalists had begun their account (in 1 Chronicles) with Adam and the generations that were believed to have descended from him. In doing so, they alluded to the very beginnings of humankind and in turn to the beginnings of the great divisions of peoples in the known world and the beginnings of the Israelite people itself. They then devoted an inordinate amount of text to their story of King David as founder of the kingdom of Israel and planner of the temple of Yahweh, and now (in 2 Chronicles) they proceed to the story of the building and dedication of the temple by King Solomon. In these parts of their account they show that they are particularly interested in getting across a certain view of the beginnings of the regal and religious system they advocate. And when in due course they draw the Annals to a close with an invitation from the Persian king for people to 'go up', to return to Jerusalem after a period of exile, the Annalists end their epic tale with a new beginning—and an implied challenge for their community, to act in accordance with the way the Annalists envisaged things to have been constituted in the earlier beginning of the 'kingdom of Yahweh'. With this overarching frame, the Annals can truly be described as a 'book of beginnings'.

But here lies a rather uncomfortable aspect of the Annalists' agenda: if anyone might have been thinking that they wanted to establish Israelite or Judahite/Judean practice in some other way, or might have felt that a strict system in political and religious life of men receiving the mantle of royal or priestly office from their fathers is not necessarily the best way forward, the message of the Annalists is that the traditions are sacrosanct, even part of the divine cosmic plan, set up by the great David with the full blessing of heaven at the beginning of the Israelite kingdom, perfected by his worthy successor Solomon, interfered with by certain of the later kings at their peril, and championed once again with success and blessing by other monarchs in the line of succession. Only absolute commitment to a time-honoured system can bring about a perfect society, seems to be the underlying theme running through the columns of this scroll.

Of course it is only one group's telling of the story, and is 'history'-telling only of a certain propagandistic kind. There may be some particular historical groundedness to parts of the tale, but in many respects these Annals have a certain fantasy quality about them. They create an imaginary world in which things happen just so, and in which any potentially untidy loose ends in their narrative of the past are tied together in a highly systematic way. This is storytelling with the didactic purpose of inculcating a particular ideology, bombarding the reader with a kaleidoscopic procession of heroes and villains and presenting a frontierland of danger and opportunity. There is considerable artistry in the telling of the tale—including at times a distinctly musical language and a careful mathematical precision—yet that does not entirely mask the dark underbelly of the writing, with its persistent note of conformity to the political and religious system advocated by the Annalists. While appreciating the artistry of the ancient tradents, and enjoying many aspects of the literary world of the text, a modern reader cannot entirely put aside the notions that one brings to a reading of the text from a real world that has experienced the horrors of totalitarianism and fundamentalism.

Thus there is something decidedly uncomfortable, yet also fascinating, in handling a scroll that seems to claim for itself the distinction of being the authoritative account of how things were and how they should be. But it is precisely such a scroll that we are encountering when we read 'The Annals'. Let us proceed, then, with the second instalment: '2 Chronicles'.

SOLOMON

(2 CHRONICLES 1–9)

A Survey of Solomon's Temple

The book of Chronicles—especially when read in its own right and not emended to agree with readings in the books of Samuel and Kings—puts forward a picture of the temple in Jerusalem which is quite startling in a number of respects, and it is the purpose of this survey to explore some of those unique features.

By devoting a great swathe of text in their Annals to the preparations for and the planning of the temple by King David (in 1 Chronicles) and then to the building and dedication of it by King Solomon (in 2 Chronicles), the Annalists show that this structure has huge importance in the religious system that they advocate. But just what did they envisage in terms of this temple, and how does their vision sit with other biblical sources?

For one thing, the Annalists imagine a temple that reaches unambiguously heavenwards. Other storytellers in ancient Israel are content to picture a relatively low building, as in 1 Kings 6.2, where we are told that 'the house that King Solomon built for Yahweh was 60 cubits long, 20 cubits wide, and 30 cubits high'; in other words, the main structure is just half again as high as it is wide, and only half as high as it is long. But in 2 Chron. 3.3-4 we read that 'these were the dimensions Solomon established for building the House of God: the length, in cubits of the old standard, was 60 cubits, and the width was 20 cubits, and the length of the vestibule was the same as the width of the house, namely 20 cubits, and the height was 120 cubits'; in other words, the Annalists' temple appears to be a staggering six times higher than its width and twice as high as its length.

Setting the measurements out in this way may be open to some dispute, so it would be well to look at v. 4 more closely. Much hinges on how we construe the phrase concerning the vestibule, and whether we regard the following phrase concerning a measurement of height as referring to the vestibule alone or to the building as a whole, and indeed whether we are willing to accept that the Annalists intentionally set out such a statistic for the height of their temple. The Hebrew reads as follows: *wĕhā'ûlām*

ʾăšer ʿal-pĕnê hāʾōrek ʿal-pĕnê rōhab-habbayit ʾammôt ʿeśrîm wĕhaggōbah mēʾâ wĕʿeśrîm. The NRSV renders this as 'The vestibule in front of the nave of the house was 20 cubits long, across the width of the house; and its height was 120 cubits.' However, just four verses later (in v. 8), when the Hebrew says wayyaʿaśʾet-bêt-qōdešhaqqŏdāšîm ʾorkô ʿal-pĕnê rōhab-habbayit ʾammôt ʿeśrîm, the NRSV says 'He made the most holy place: its length, corresponding to the width of the house, was 20 cubits'. Admittedly the phrase ʾăšer ʿal-pĕnê hāʾōrek ʿal-pĕnê rōhab-habbayit does not appear quite as elegant as the phrase ʾorkô ʿal-pĕnê rōhab-habbayit, but in such close proximity they are most naturally seen as variations on a theme, and so something like the wording of the NJPS translation is to be preferred, namely (for v. 4) 'The length of the porch in front [was equal] to the breadth of the house—20 cubits' and (for v. 8) 'its length [was equal] to the breadth of the house—20 cubits'.

Accordingly, I am not persuaded that there is anything so alarming about the expression in v. 4 concerning the horizontal dimensions of the vestibule that we must begin emending the verse to fall more into line with readings in the book of Kings, as NRSV does by speaking of 'the vestibule in front of the nave of the house', which seems rather to be a translation of 1 Kings 6.3's phrase wĕhāʾûlām ʿal-pĕnê hêkal habbayit ʿeśrîm ʾammâ ʾorkô. While one can understand the NRSV translation panel's desire to bring the two texts into harmony, it seems to me that the Annalists' words, read within the context of their description of the temple, carry a different meaning from the phrasing in the Kings context. And so too I am inclined to accept the reading of mēʾâ wĕʿeśrîm, '120' cubits for the height of the structure, rather than feeling that it must be brought down to a lower figure in view of the height of just šĕlōšîm, '30' cubits for the temple depicted in 1 Kings 6.2. If our quest were for a real First Temple in Jerusalem, then we would doubtlessly prefer the figure given in the book of Kings. As Hugh Williamson rightly remarks, a height of 120 cubits is 'far too high for the first temple' (Williamson 1982: 206), but I would express matters a little differently from him in respect of his comment that 'a hundred and twenty cubits contradicts the expected thirty cubits, which was the height of the rest of the temple'. That 'the height of the rest of the temple' was 30 cubits can unquestionably be said in relation to the figures set out in the book of Kings, which indeed gives a figure of 30 cubits for the height of the temple, but the book of Chronicles gives no figure for the height of the temple other than this measurement

of 120 cubits. There is mention in 2 Chron. 3.15 that 'in front of
the house he made two pillars 35 cubits high, with a capital of
five cubits on top of each', and when we compare this with 1
Kings 7.15-16's contention that the pillars were each 18 cubits
high with a capital of five cubits on top of each, we might observe
that the Annalists' pillars plus capitals are not only 17 cubits
higher than their counterparts in Kings but are thus also ten
cubits higher than the height of the temple itself in Kings. Again,
if our quest were for the real First Temple in Jerusalem, we
would presumably prefer the pillar dimensions provided by the
book of Kings, but the consistently higher figures presented by
the Annalists are telling us something about how they imagined
the temple to be, and it would seem that the lower dimensions
conceived by the traditions represented in the book of Kings were
simply not high enough for the Annalists' grander vision of the
temple.

It is not clear, however, whether they imagine the entire temple
reaching to the grand heights of 120 cubits, or just the *'ûlām*, the
'vestibule' or entrance-hall being of that height. The punctuation
in the NRSV directs readers strongly towards the latter understanding, since it reads as follows: 'These are Solomon's measurements for building the house of God: the length, in cubits of the
old standard, was 60 cubits, and the width 20 cubits. The vestibule in front of the nave of the house was 20 cubits long, across
the width of the house; and its height was 120 cubits' (2 Chron.
3.3-4 NRSV). This suggests that it is the vestibule that reaches
towards heaven, while the main body of the temple is of an undisclosed height, though presumably constituting a less soaring
edifice than the entrance-hall. If we have an eye to the text of
Kings, then we might well imagine that the body of the temple is
indeed 30 cubits high. On the other hand, we might, in the more
immediate context of the Annalists' temple-measuring activities,
imagine a rather more consistently proportioned temple of 20
cubits in height above the nave and the holy of holies, given the
setting out of other dimensions in which 20 cubits in one direction
corresponds to 20 cubits in another direction, such as in the case
of the holy of holies, concerning which we are told that 'its length,
corresponding to the width of the house, was 20 cubits, and its
width was 20 cubits' (2 Chron. 3.8).

In some respects I am attracted to the thought that the
Annalists' temple might be constructed in cubes of 20 cubits,
since we are told of three segments to their temple, a holy of

holies plus a nave plus a vestibule, and we are told that the *bêt hā'ĕlōhîm* or 'House of God' was 60 cubits long and 20 cubits wide; accordingly, we might think of three 20-by-20 segments making up the ground plan, but the designation of the nave as *habbayit haggādôl* or 'the great house' rather suggests that the 60-cubit length ought to be applied to that part of the building by itself, with a 20-by-20 *bêt-qōdeš haqqŏdāšîm* or 'holy of holies' and an arguably 20-by-20 *'ûlām* or 'vestibule' being added to the back and front respectively of the *bayit gādôl*. The height of either the *bayit gādôl* or the *bêt-qōdeš haqqŏdāšîm* are then not explicitly expressed, but at least the *'ûlām* stands at 120 cubits.

Now it may be that the Annalists want us to think of the entire complex as reaching those grand heights. After all, their text reads *wĕ'elleh hûsad šĕlōmōh libnôt 'et-bêt hā'ĕlōhîm*, 'these were the dimensions Solomon established for building the House of God': *hā'ōrek*, 'the length' such-and-such; *wĕrōhab*, 'and a width' of such-and-such, with a vestibule of such-and-such; *wĕhaggōbah*, 'and the height' such-and-such. It is certainly possible to construe the Annalists' sentence structure as indicating the dimensions of the complete structure in their minds, and not pointing only to the height of the vestibule. However, this may be stretching our imaginations a little too far, even if we concede that we are dealing with an imaginary temple rather than one that really stood in this form on a Jerusalem hill around the turn of the first millennium BCE. It may strike us as more plausible that the creators of this text thought of a 20-cubit-square tower standing 120 cubits high at the front of a building stretching back a further 60 cubits and rising to a height of 20 or 30 cubits, rather than that they conjured up the even more imposing image of a building which rose to the height of 120 cubits along its full length of 60 cubits.

But whichever of these pictures most appeals to us, it is clear that a temple so conceived, a structure which reaches far higher than the extent of its length or breadth, expresses something that is dear to the hearts of many who conceptualize a space for divine-human encounter. The architects and stonemasons of mediaeval Europe would find nothing strange about the Annalists' conceptualization, and nor would the devout citizens of ancient Mesopotamia. Indeed, the book of Genesis records a vignette of the primaeval inhabitants of the land of Shinar saying to themselves, 'Come, let us build ourselves a city, and a tower with its top in the heavens, and let us make a name for ourselves; otherwise we shall be scattered abroad over the face of the whole earth', whereupon the deity comes down from heaven and scatters them abroad over the face of the whole earth (Genesis 11.4, 8).

The Annalists have the hubris to conjure up in the city of Jerusalem a tower with its top in the heavens, and they have Solomon stand in front of that tower and pray over and over that the deity may hear in heaven the prayers directed toward that place (2 Chron. 6.21, 23, 25, 27, 30, 33, 35, 39). His ultimate petition concerns the inevitable scattering of the people over the face of the earth: 'If they sin against you—for there is no one who does not sin—and you are angry with them and give them to an enemy, so that they are carried away captive to a land far or near; then if they come to their senses in the land to which they have been taken captive, and repent, and plead with you in the land of their captivity, saying, "We have sinned, and have done wrong; we have acted wickedly"; if they repent with all their heart and soul in the land of their captivity, to which they were taken captive, and pray toward their land, which you gave to their ancestors, the city that you have chosen, and the house that I have built for your name, then hear from heaven your dwelling place their prayer and their pleas, maintain their cause and forgive your people who have sinned against you' (2 Chron. 6.36-39).

And sure enough, in the unfolding of the Annals, the people are in time spread abroad; indeed, ironically the bulk of them are carried away to the same place where Genesis had sited the primaeval tower (compare 'therefore it was called *bābel*' [NRSV 'Babel'] in Genesis 11.9 with 'he took them into exile in *bābel*' [NRSV 'Babylon'] in 2 Chron. 36.20). But at the end, there is the new beginning, a way back from Babel/Babylon to Jerusalem, when King Cyrus of Persia proclaims that 'Yahweh, the god of heaven, has given me all the kingdoms of the earth, and he has charged me to build him a house at Jerusalem, which is in Judah. Whoever is among you of all his people, may his god Yahweh be with him! Let him go up' (2 Chron. 36.23). The Annalists dare to think that Yahweh's people on earth might reach again for the heavens. Perhaps they think or hope that it will be different next time, or perhaps they fear in their hearts that it will all turn out the same—'for there is no one who does not sin', as their Solomon said—but at least there is an opportunity for better times to come again, and for a rebuilt tower in Jerusalem to point once again to the deity.

The second feature that I wish to highlight is that the Annalists imagine their heavenward-reaching temple as standing on the top of a very special mountain. In itself this should not really surprise us, in that the ancient notion that the interface between heaven and earth was on mountain-tops is a familiar one, and the modern designation of 'the Temple Mount' in Jerusalem is frequently encountered in literature and in news bulletins. And yet these Annals do something with the traditions of ancient Israel that no other biblical writers do. We might almost overlook it, in 2 Chron. 3.1, where the claim is made that 'the house of Yahweh in Jerusalem' was built 'on Mount Moriah'.

Now the only other place in the Hebrew Bible where the place-name 'Moriah' occurs is in a particular part of the story of Abraham. Genesis 22.2 has the deity saying to Abraham, 'Take your son, your only son Isaac, whom you love, and go to the land of Moriah, and offer him there as a burnt offering on one of the mountains that I shall show you'. The unfolding of the story is well known: Abraham takes his son, his only son Isaac, whom he loves, to a mountain that the deity shows him, builds an altar there, binds Isaac and prepares to offer him as a burnt offering, only to hear an angelic voice cry out, 'Do not lay your hand on the boy or do anything to him; for now I know that you fear the divine, since you have not withheld your son, your only son, from me' (v. 12). Abraham then looks up and sees a ram caught in a thicket by its horns, and so he takes the ram and offers it up as a burnt offering instead of his son.

There can be no doubt that the Annalists are thinking of this story of Abraham's near-sacrifice of Isaac in crafting their own story of the beginnings of the temple in Jerusalem. It is not merely their unique claim that the temple was built on 'Mount Moriah'. It is also evident that, just as the Genesis narrative depicts a narrowly averted destruction of the people of Israel before they had even begun, so too the Annals depict a narrowly averted destruction of the people of Israel before the site of the temple is determined in response to the crisis. We read in the Annals that 'Yahweh sent a pestilence on Israel, and 70,000 persons fell in Israel. And the deity sent an angel to Jerusalem to destroy it; but when he was about to destroy it, Yahweh took note and relented concerning the calamity, and he said to the destroying angel, "Enough! Stay your hand."... David looked up and saw the angel of Yahweh standing between earth and heaven, and in his hand a drawn sword stretched out over Jerusalem' (1 Chron. 21.14-16). The angel commands David to go up and build an altar at the site; the king does so, and offers burnt offerings on the altar, and then says, 'Here shall be the house of the god Yahweh and here the altar of burnt offering for Israel' (22.1).

Let us note a certain similarity in Abraham's and David's angelic encounters. In the Genesis narrative, we find 'the angel of Yahweh' calling to him from heaven (Genesis 22.11), and we hear the angel speaking as though he is Yahweh himself, commenting—without any introductory formula such as 'Thus says Yahweh'—that 'now I know that you fear the divine, since you have not withheld your son, your only son, *from me*' (v. 12). Then we read (in v. 14): *wayyiqrā' 'abrāhām šēm-hammāqôm hahû' yahweh yir'eh 'ăšer yē'āmēr hayyôm běhar yahweh yērā'eh*. The NRSV is in two minds on the translation of this verse. The main text has it that 'Abraham called that place "The LORD will provide"; as it is said to this day, "On the mount of the LORD it shall be provided"'. An alternative rendering is given in a footnote: 'Abraham called that place "The LORD will see"; as it is said to this day, "On the mount of the LORD he shall be seen"'. The first alternative might seem preferable in view of Abraham's words earlier in the story, in answer to his son's question 'Where is the lamb for a burnt offering?', that *'ĕlōhîm yir'eh-lô haśśeh lĕ'ōlâ běnî*, which NRSV renders as 'God himself will provide the lamb for a burnt offering, my son' (Genesis 22.8), though I am attracted to the NJPS rendering, 'God will see to the sheep for his burnt offering, my son'. But it seems to me that the NRSV's second choices, 'the LORD will see' and 'he shall be seen', work particularly well when the story as a whole is viewed in connection with the analogous tale in Genesis 16. In that earlier narrative, Abraham's pregnant slave-girl Hagar encounters 'the angel of Yahweh' at a spring in the wilderness (v. 7), after which she 'called the name of Yahweh who spoke to her, "You are *'ēl rŏ'î*"', a name which appears to mean 'The God of My Seeing', and thus either 'the god who sees me' or 'the god whom I see' or both, and the storyteller has her express (although admittedly in words the later scribes seem to have had some difficulty in transmitting) her wonder that she has seen the One Who Sees. The Hebrew there (in Genesis 16.13) reads *hăgam hălōm rā'îtî 'ahărê rŏ'î*, which the NRSV translates as 'Have I really seen God and remained alive after seeing him?', but with a footnote remarking that the meaning of the Hebrew is uncertain. The NJPS prefers 'Have I not gone on seeing after he saw me?', though it too notes that the meaning of the Hebrew is uncertain. In any event, these two stories are clearly about 'seeing', and so Abraham's excursion into the land of *môriyyâ*—a name which itself might be taken to mean 'the seeing of Yah'—takes him to the mountain where Yahweh is to be seen: *běhar yahweh yērā'eh*.

And what do we find in the Annals? *Wayyāḥel šělōmōh libnôt 'et-bêt-yahweh bîrûšālaim běhar hammôriyyâ 'ăšer nir'â lědāwîd 'ābîhû*, 'Solomon began to build the House of Yahweh in Jerusalem, on Mount Moriah, where Yahweh had appeared to his father David' (2 Chron. 3.1). Note the word *nir'â*, 'he appeared' or 'he was seen', corresponding to the word *yērā'eh*, 'he will be seen' or 'he will appear' in the name Abraham had bestowed upon his mountain. And notice too the same slippage between 'the angel of Yahweh' and Yahweh himself is to be met in the Annalists' depiction of David's encounter with the divine as was noticeable in the Genesis narrative concerning Abraham (and also in the analogous narrative concerning Hagar). At first the Annals tell us that 'David looked up and saw the angel of Yahweh standing between earth and heaven' (1 Chron. 21.16), but then we are told that it was actually Yahweh who had appeared to the father of Solomon, just as Genesis had had Abraham speak of seeing Yahweh on the mountain of Moriah.

In Genesis, as Abraham presumably stood contemplatively for a time on the mountain, 'the angel of Yahweh called to him a second time from heaven, and said, "By myself I have sworn that, because you have done this, and have not withheld your son, your only son, I will indeed bless you, and I will make your offspring as numerous as the stars of heaven and as the sand that is on the seashore; and your offspring shall possess the gate of their enemies, and by your offspring shall all the nations of the earth gain blessing for themselves, because you have obeyed my voice"' (Genesis 22.15-18). Is it entirely coincidental that the Annalists speak of Solomon—who in their accounting stands uniquely before Yahweh on the same mountain—in terms that seem to echo certain aspects of that divine promise? They say of him that 'King Solomon excelled all the kings of the earth in riches and in wisdom, and all the kings of the earth sought the presence of Solomon to hear his wisdom, which the deity had put into his mind' (2 Chron. 9.22-23), and they have the queen of Sheba say to him, 'Happy are your people! Happy are these your servants, who continually attend you and hear your wisdom! Blessed be your god Yahweh, who has delighted in you and set you on his throne as king for your god Yahweh. Because your god loved Israel and would establish them forever, he has made you king over them, that you may execute justice and righteousness' (9.7-8).

Something of that assessment of Solomon's wisdom and wealth is also to be found in the book of Kings, but the idea that the king of Israel stood before the deity on the same mountain as that on which the patriarch of the Hebrews had stood with his son Isaac bound upon an altar is not something that remotely occurred to the compilers of that book. Indeed the writers of Kings do not explicitly state that the temple is on any hill at all; it might simply be on the same level as the rest of the city of David, as far as their account is concerned. One might even suspect that they deliberately avoid imagining the temple as being on a high place, since high places are associated with the worship of other gods. In 1 Kings 11.7-8 they tell us that 'Solomon built a high place for Chemosh the abomination of Moab, and for Milcom [or Molech] the abomination of the Ammonites, on the mountain east of Jerusalem, and he did the same for all his foreign wives, who offered incense and sacrificed to their gods', and in 1 Kings 20.23, 28 they tell us scathingly of the Aramaeans' apparent belief that the Israelite god is 'a god of the hills'. Accordingly, the curious failure of the compilers of Kings to situate the temple on a hill may tell us something of their discomfort about such matters. But for the Annalists matters are very different. Their Solomon builds no other temple or high place than the one dedicated to the name of Yahweh, and he builds it on the same high place that the compilers of Genesis had depicted as the site of Abraham's act of uncompromising faithfulness to the same god.

The Annalists speak of 'the mountain of the House of Yahweh' (2 Chron. 33.15), and they designate that mountain as the Mount Moriah of old (3.1); for them, nothing less than a special mountain could be the appropriate location for this place of interface between heaven and earth. Mount Sinai is not feasibly available to them, though this mountain can replace that one insofar as, 'when Solomon had ended his prayer [of dedication], fire came down from heaven and consumed the burnt offering and the sacrifices, and the glory of Yahweh filled the temple; and the priests could not enter the House of Yahweh, because the glory of Yahweh filled the House of Yahweh; and when all the people of Israel saw the fire come down and the glory of Yahweh on the temple, they bowed down on the pavement with their faces to the ground, and worshipped and gave thanks to Yahweh' (2 Chron. 7.1-3). The Annalists had already rehearsed this spectacle before the prayer, when the ark of the covenant is brought into the temple and placed in the holy of holies, for then too 'the House of Yahweh was filled with a cloud, so that the priests could not stand to minister because of the cloud, for the glory of Yahweh filled the House of God' (5.13-14). All of this is evidently calling to mind the depictions of Mount Sinai and the tabernacle in the book of Exodus, where we are told that 'when Moses went up on the mountain, the cloud covered the mountain; and the glory of Yahweh settled on Mount Sinai... Now the appearance of the glory of Yahweh was like a devouring fire on the top of the mountain in the sight of the people of Israel' (Exodus 24.15-17). And again, when 'Moses finished the work [of setting up the tabernacle], the cloud covered the tent of meeting, and the glory of Yahweh filled the tabernacle, and Moses was unable to enter the tent of meeting because the cloud settled upon it, and the glory of Yahweh filled the tabernacle... and the cloud of Yahweh was on the tabernacle by day, and fire was in the cloud by night, before the eyes of all the house of Israel at each stage of their journey' (Exodus 40.34-38).

The Annalists could hardly make it clearer that they regard the mountain and temple of Jerusalem as standing metaphorically on the ground that the mountain of Sinai and the tabernacle of the wilderness wanderings had once occupied. The compilers of Kings were moderately attracted to this notion too, in that they included in their work the notion of a cloud filling the temple on the occasion of the ark's deposition into its resting place in the sight of the priests (1 Kings 8.10-11), but only the Annalists bring into the picture the even grander spectacle of cloud and fire coming down from heaven in the sight of all the children of Israel after the dedicatory prayer of the king. This is in a sense Sinai transplanted, just as it is Moriah reconstituted, in the minds of the Annalists. No site for a temple could be more authentic and appropriate than this.

Now in the traditions of ancient Israel there was another place that had commanded respect as an authentic and appropriate site for 'The House of God', and that was the place that bore the very name 'Beth-El'. It too had drawn Abrahamic associations, as reflected in Genesis 12.8, where we are told that Abraham 'built an altar to Yahweh and invoked the name of Yahweh' at Bethel. But its great foundation legend claimed nothing less than the imprimatur of the eponymous ancestor of Israel, the patriarch Israel or Jacob himself, who, so the story

goes, 'came to a certain place and stayed there for the night...
And he dreamed that there was a stairway set up on the earth,
the top of it reaching to heaven; and angels of god were ascending
and descending on it' (Genesis 28.11-12). Yahweh speaks to
Jacob in the dream, promising him the land on which he lies and
offspring to populate it, so when Jacob awakes from his sleep,
he exclaims, 'Surely Yahweh is in this place—and I did not know
it! ... How awesome is this place! This is none other than the
House of God, and this is the Gate of Heaven' (vv. 16-17).

How could this fit into the worldview of the Annalists, who
surely imagine that 'the Gate of Heaven' is on their mountain in
Jerusalem, where David had seen the angel of Yahweh standing
between earth and heaven and where Solomon and all Israel had
seen cloud and fire come down from heaven and embrace 'the
House of God' erected there? The simple answer is that it does
not, and so the Annalists are studious in scrubbing Bethel from
their account. They breathe no word of Bethel's claims to be a
holy site, and they mention the place just twice, never with any
interesting narrative but merely within lists of towns and territories, first in a list of Ephraimite possessions and settlements
(1 Chron. 7.28) and later in a list of obscure towns that King
Abijah of Judah takes from King Jeroboam of Israel (2 Chron.
13.19). There is nothing special about the place in either case,
which stands in considerable contrast not only with the Genesis
legends but also with the twenty appearances of Bethel in the
book of Kings, where it features as a continuing rival to the
status of Jerusalem as Israel's holiest site.

One looks in vain for any Annalistic parallel to the colourful
tales told in Kings of the old prophet in Bethel who hoodwinks a
visiting prophet into accepting some hospitality from which he
does not return (1 Kings 13), or of the company of prophets in
Bethel who alert the great Elisha to the impending disappearance
of his master Elijah (2 Kings 2), or of the Assyrian-sponsored
priest who is sent to Bethel after the dissolution of the northern
kingdom in order to teach the new inhabitants how to worship
Yahweh (2 Kings 17.24-28). One even looks in vain for a denunciation of the temple at Bethel, along the lines of 1 Kings 12's account
of the breakaway king Jeroboam setting up a golden calf at Bethel
and appointing non-levitical priests to serve at the altar there.
Certainly the Annalists oppose such practices, as they show in a
vigorous speech that they place in the mouth of King Abijah of
Judah, shouting out to the northerners prior to battle, 'You think

that you can withstand the kingdom of Yahweh in the hand of the sons of David, because you are a great multitude and have with you the golden calves that Jeroboam made as gods for you; have you not driven out the priests of Yahweh, the descendants of Aaron, and the Levites, and made priests for yourselves like the peoples of other lands?' (2 Chron. 13.8-9). The diatribe goes on for some time, but the name 'Bethel' is never enunciated. Might the mention of the specific name in some way dignify Bethel's rival claim to that of Jerusalem?

In one respect, however, it does seem that the Annalists make a nod towards Bethel's claim to have been constituted in the patriarchal age as the definitive dwelling place of Israel's god, and they thereby imply that the claim of Jerusalem to be the true Bethel displaces that of the northern site. The allusion lies in King David's declamation of the temple site, in 1 Chron. 22.1: *zeh hû' bêt yahweh hā'ĕlōhîm wĕzeh-mizbēaḥ lĕ'ōlâ lĕyiśrā'ēl*. The NRSV translates this as 'Here shall be the house of the LORD God and here the altar of burnt-offering for Israel'. I have no strong quarrel with that translation in the context of a narrative sequence in which the temple is yet to be built on the site where David has as yet constructed only an altar for burnt-offerings, but I would point out that the phrases might more literally be rendered, '*This is* the house of the LORD God, and *this* the altar of burnt-offering for Israel'. I make a point of this in order to draw attention to a certain similarity of expression with the declamation of Jacob in Genesis 28.17, *'ēn zeh kî 'im-bêt 'ĕlōhîm wĕzeh ša'ar haššāmayim*, which NRSV renders as 'This is none other than the house of God, and this is the gate of heaven'. There too of course no temple had yet been built on the site, but only—if we accept the narrative sequence of Genesis as we have it—the altar that Abraham had constructed at the place two generations before. Jacob immediately takes the stone that he had been using as a pillow for the night and sets it up as a pillar, pours oil on the top of it, and vows that 'If the deity will be with me, and will keep me in this way that I go, and will give me bread to eat and clothing to wear, so that I come again to my father's house in peace, then Yahweh shall be my god, and this stone, which I have set up as a pillar, shall be the House of God' (Genesis 28.20-22). The phrase 'it shall be the House of God' is *yihyeh bêt 'ĕlōhîm*, and its presence shows that the earlier expression regarding the place as being already *bêt 'ĕlōhîm* does not at all imply that a temple already stands there. Thus I would probably prefer the expressions in 1 Chron. 22.1 to appear in English as 'This is the House of the LORD God' (or more literally 'This is the House of the God Yahweh') 'and this the altar of burnt-offering for Israel', to suggest more clearly to the English reader that the phrasing put into the mouth of David in these Annals appears to have been especially crafted by the Annalists to supplant the Bethelite contention that a founder of Israel's traditions had placed the stamp of authenticity on a shrine other than Jerusalem's temple site. The true *bêt 'ĕlōhîm* is at Jerusalem, and not at the so-called 'Bethel', is the Annalists' belief; David, and not Jacob, has it right in their eyes.

Sara Japhet has justifiably commented that, in the Mount Moriah text which was discussed earlier, 'Davidic authority' may be seen as superseding 'the ancient traditions of the Abrahamic cult' (Japhet 1993: 552). I might nuance matters a little differently, and say that the Annalists, in having David's vision of Yahweh take place on Mount Moriah, see him as building upon Abrahamic traditions; and I would like to add that they then, in having David mimic the declarative style of Bethel's foundation legend (a matter not raised by Japhet), see him as displacing the ancient traditions of the Bethel cult.

It is a thoroughgoing displacement, in that the Annalists have David do far more than Jacob's paltry little action of setting up his pillow as a pillar. Immediately after he has proclaimed the site for Yahweh's temple, David embarks on all the preparations necessary for the building of a suitable edifice and for the conducting of appropriate activities in and around the completed structure. He issues orders 'to gather together the aliens who were residing in the land of Israel' (1 Chron. 22.2); he provides 'great stores of iron...as well as bronze in quantities beyond weighing, and cedar logs without number' (vv. 3-4); he calls 'for his son Solomon' and charges him 'to build a house for Yahweh, the god of Israel' (v. 6); and he commands 'all the leaders of Israel' to help Solomon in the task, 'so that the ark of the covenant of Yahweh and the holy vessels of god may be brought into a house built for the name of Yahweh' (vv. 17, 19). None of this is to be found in the books of Samuel or Kings; it is entirely the contention of the Annalists that David designated the temple site and made all these preparations. The aging David we see in the Kings account is full of bitter and calculating advice to his son Solomon on whom to have executed from among the palace officials, the royal family and the local aristocracy (1 Kings 2.1-9), but the Annalists' David is tireless in nobler concerns, organizing the Levites for various kinds of service in the temple complex (1 Chron. 23–26), as well as seeing to the proper organization of a now-peaceful kingdom (ch. 27), and in particular handing over to Solomon a full set of plans for the construction of the temple (ch. 28) before finally blessing the name of Yahweh in the presence of the assembly of all Israel (ch. 29).

This is an infinitely superior character to that rogue in Genesis who had set up a pillar at Bethel, and it is an infinitely superior character to that rogue in the book of Samuel who commits wanton adultery and proves himself singularly unable to manage a smooth transfer of power to the next generation. The Annalists' David has a voice of singular authority—'This is the House of the God Yahweh, and this the altar of burnt offering for Israel!'—and the tower of David that inexorably rises up on the site that he designates and in accordance with the plans that he bequeaths to his successor Solomon is an edifice fully worthy of his inexhaustible efforts.

There are, however, some intriguing and disturbing unsung efforts that lie underneath this edifice, for the Annalists imagine a temple for the god of Israel that is built without Israelite hands.

What had the mighty David done immediately after designating the temple site? He 'gave orders to gather together the aliens who were residing in the land of Israel, and he set [them as] stonecutters to prepare dressed stones for building the House of God' (1 Chron. 22.2). And his successor follows the same policy, for we read some time later that 'Solomon took a census of all the aliens who were residing in the land of Israel, after the census that his father David had taken, and there were found to be 153,600; from these he assigned 70,000 as labourers, 80,000 as stonecutters in the hill country, and 3,600 as overseers to make the people work' (2 Chron. 2.17-18). The Annalists seem to have no embarrassment in portraying an invidious policy of slave labour under which some of the enslaved are placed in charge of enforcing the enslavement, and they make it explicit in numerical terms that every single one of the non-enfranchised residents of the kingdom are rounded up for the building work.

This represents a considerable variation on the picture in Kings, where we are told that 'King Solomon conscripted forced labour out of all Israel, and the levy numbered 30,000 men. He sent them to the Lebanon, 10,000 a month in shifts; they would be a month in Lebanon and two months at home... Solomon also had [a further] 70,000 labourers and 80,000 stonecutters in the hill country, besides his 3,300 supervisors who were over the work, having charge of the people who did the work... Solomon's builders together with Hiram's builders and the Giblites did the stonecutting and prepared the timber and the stone to build the house' (1 Kings 5.13-18 [vv. 27-32 in the Hebrew text]). In the Kings account it is forced labour, to be sure, but it is Israelite labour working together with a workforce from the friendly neighbouring kingdom of Tyre and a contingent of Giblites as well. The assertion in the Annals that the temple builders are the entire resident alien population of Solomon's kingdom, and nothing but the resident aliens, is a startling picture.

Actually, there are two small caveats to the position just described, in that the Annals do speak of Tyrian workers involved in cutting timber in Lebanon for dispatching to the Jerusalem temple project though not in bringing the cut timber across Israelite soil to Jerusalem (2 Chron. 2.8, and note v. 16), but one special worker is brought onto the temple site itself. The latter is the skilled Tyrian craftsman, Huram-abi, whom King Huram of Tyre dispatches to Jerusalem to oversee the engraving and carving work (2 Chron. 2.13-14; cf. 4.11-18). In the Kings account, Solomon sends for a man called Hiram to come from Tyre to take the same leading role in the project (1 Kings 7.13-45), and many other Tyrians also appear to be on site. But for the Annalists, their Huram-abi is the only exception to the rule that everyone working at the temple must be a conscripted resident alien; it seems that they are unable to conceive of the resident aliens as being capable of managing entirely from their own inexperienced ranks with the delicate and highly skilled work that Huram-abi is called upon to take charge of, but the project in general can be left in their hands.

Some readers may have a further objection to the idea that the Annals speak only of non-Israelite labour on the temple project, in that 2 Chron. 2.1-2 had earlier announced that 'Solomon decided to build a temple for the name of Yahweh, and a royal palace for himself. Solomon conscripted 70,000 labourers and 80,000 stonecutters in the hill country, with 3,600 to oversee them'. Are these not to be understood as Israelite subjects? Should we edit out the later insertion of resident aliens since this first citation alone is in keeping with the presentation of matters in Kings and so a repetition of the statistics with an alien twist makes for a clumsy text? I think not. On the basis of an approach by Raymond Dillard (Dillard 1987: 5-7, 17-18), it can be argued that this initial mention of the workforce without specification of their citizenship is deliberately taken up by the later application of these statistics specifically to the resident aliens, the two listings of the matter being placed before and after the setting out of the royal correspondence concerning the temple project. This matches the double arrangement also of the listing of Solomon's wealth, before and after the account of the temple's construction (2 Chron. 1.1-17 and 9.13-28). Just as the '12,000 horses' counted in at 1.14 are the same set of creatures as the '12,000 horses' counted out again in 9.25, so too the '70,000 labourers' counted in at 2.2 are the same set of workers as the '70,000' resident-alien 'labourers' counted out at 2.18. At first the unenviable status of the workforce was not specified, but it is underlined at the end.

Now readers with an awareness of the exodus traditions of ancient Israel cannot help but draw to mind a situation once depicted of the Israelites themselves. The book of Exodus begins by picturing the children of Israel, as resident aliens in the land of Egypt, being given the task of building for the 'new king' of that land, who 'set taskmasters over them to oppress them with forced labour; and they built supply cities, Pithom and Raamses, for Pharaoh' (Exodus 1.8, 11). We might imagine that part of the building project was the construction of a temple or two for the Egyptian gods. Well, the boot is most certainly on the other foot in the Annals. The 'new king' in Israel counts the number of resident aliens he has to hand in his kingdom, and he sets them to work on a grand building project in the land of Israel, the construction of the temple for the Israelite god. Perhaps the Annalists, who do refer to 'Yahweh, the god of Israel', bringing his people 'out of the land of Egypt' (2 Chron. 6.5), imagine that justice is thereby served.

The compilers of these Annals certainly appear to have no misgivings about depicting a tendency on the part of the Israelite kingdom to enslave foreigners, and to state that the temple-building project depends on the wealth that is forcefully taken from such peoples. Witness the accounts of David's wars of conquests against the surrounding nations in 1 Chronicles 18: 'He defeated Moab, and the Moabites became subject to David and brought him tribute' (v. 2); 'then David put garrisons in Aram of Damascus, and the Arameans became subject to David, and brought tribute' (v. 6); 'then he put garrisons in Edom, and all the Edomites became subject to David; and Yahweh gave victory to David wherever he went' (v. 13). Later, when the Ammonite capital city of Rabbah is added to the list of conquests, we are told that David 'brought out the booty of the city, a very great amount, and he brought out the people who were in it, and set them to work with saws and iron picks and axes; thus David did to all the cities of the Ammonites' (20.2-3).

The Annalists give no explicit reason why David should attack all these nations. Perhaps we are meant to think that each of these neighbouring peoples are warlike nations that deserve to be subjugated and have their wealth flowing into Jerusalem, but in any event it is seen as good for the temple of Yahweh, since materials that are thus brought in will be vital for its construction and outfitting. A note about that is already given not long after the delivery of the divine oracle that 'one of your sons...shall build a house for me' (17.11-12): it is noted (in 18.8) that 'David took a vast amount of bronze' from the cities that he had conquered, and 'with it Solomon made the bronze sea and the pillars and the vessels of bronze'. Thus we are told that Solomon will build the temple from the material that David accumulates in his wars of conquest, and accordingly in the midst of a narrative of warfare and death and destruction there is a note that the Warrior God who fights for David will himself directly benefit from all those conquests, in the building of his temple back in Jerusalem.

One more word on the resident aliens who are put to the hard labour of actually building the temple in these Annals: the compilers of the document are rather keen on statistics, and they tell us that 'Solomon took a census of all the aliens who were residing in the land of Israel, after the census that his father David had taken, and there were found to be 153,600', all of whom the king promptly set to work (2 Chron. 2.17). This can be compared with the figures given for the earlier census that David had taken of the Israelites themselves, for on that accounting 'in all Israel there were 1,100,000 men who drew the sword, and in Judah 470,000 who drew the sword' (1 Chron. 21.5). In other words, the Annalists' statistics imply that the adult male resident aliens represent ten per cent of the adult male population of the kingdom. It is an intriguing tithe that is given to Yahweh in the pages of the Annals, a slave-labour force of 70,000 labourers, 80,000 stonecutters, and 3,600 overseers to bend their backs in the raising up of a monument to the god of the land in which they lived as aliens. Intriguing, too, that David's census had led to the designation of the temple site, at the place where the angel of Yahweh stopped in his journey of vengeance against David for counting the Israelites, while Solomon's census led to the construction of the temple with no word of censure from Yahweh. It would appear that it is perfectly acceptable to conduct a census of aliens in order to arrange them into an effective workforce for building the temple, but it is problematic to have conducted a census of Israelite soldiers, perhaps because that would show a lack of faith in Yahweh fighting Israel's battles. Still, the outcome for Israel is a happy one in the Annalists' story-world, for David's bringing of guilt upon the nation led to the revelation of the place where heaven and earth intersected, and Solomon's marshalling of an alien army of slaves led to the erection of a grand edifice that required no drop of Israelite sweat or blood in its construction.

There is yet another way in which hands other than Israelite hands may be said to be responsible for the temple that reaches towards the heavens from the mountain of Jerusalem, and that is to be met with in David's words to his son Solomon (in 1 Chron. 28.19) that *hakkōl bikĕtāb miyyad yahweh ʿālay hiśkil kōl malʾăkôt hattabnît*. The NRSV translates this as 'All this, in writing at the LORD's direction, he made clear to me—the plan of all the works'. More literally, we might render *bikĕtāb miyyad yahweh* as 'in writing from the hand of Yahweh', and we might understand the phrase as putting forward a belief that the deity himself had inscribed the temple plans, as Exodus 31.18 says of the tablets of the covenant: *kĕtubîm bĕʾeṣbaʿ ʾĕlōhîm*, 'written with the finger of god'. It would be no surprise to find so elevated a view among the Annalists, and their repeated use of the term *tabnît* for the temple plans (1 Chron. 28.11, 12, 18, 19)—a word also used in Exodus (25.9, 40) with reference to the plans for the tabernacle—seems to strengthen the case. Nevertheless, that interpretive possibility should not be overstressed. 'The hand of Yahweh' might more modestly, though still fundamentally importantly in the Annalists' system, refer to divine inspiration on David as he himself personally drew up the plans that he then so carefully handed over to his successor who would be charged with the responsibility of carrying out those plans to the letter.

Needless to say, no such plans, whether written by Yahweh's hand or by David's, are to be seen in the Kings account. Nor is there in that document anything resembling the detailed accounting in the Annals of the divine determination and royal implementation of the roles to be played by various families of priests and Levites once the temple has arisen above the city of Jerusalem. Such organizational activity takes up several chapters of the Annals, as the venerable King David makes sure first of all that the priests are organized into 24 divisions (1 Chron. 24), so that 'their appointed duties' can be effectively managed (vv. 3, 19). The detail is given that they were all organized by means of 'lots' (v. 5), a selection process that appears again in the assigning of other levitical duties, namely the divisions of assistants to the priests (v. 31), the divisions of singer-musicians (25.8), and the divisions of gatekeepers (26.13). Thus the casting of lots is mentioned several times throughout the relevant chapters as the means of organising the cultic personnel. In this way an emphasis is made that it is not by the decree of the king but rather by the will of the deity that particular clans are assigned particular responsibilities. If a temple functionary finds that, as a Jakimite, he is in the twelfth division of the priests (24.12), and another finds that, as a Hothirite, he is in the twenty-first division of the singer-musicians (25.28), and yet another finds that, as a Shuppimite, he is a gatekeeper on the western side of the temple complex, 'at the gate of Shallecheth on the ascending road' (26.16), then each of them can be assured that their lot in life has been determined by divine will. We might say that the hand of Yahweh has written the destiny of each man born into the priestly and levitical families. In all matters concerning the functioning of the temple, the Annalists assert that it must be 'just so'.

In summary, then, the book of Chronicles puts forward a somewhat startling picture of the temple in Jerusalem. The temple described in these Annals is a tall and thin structure, six times higher than its width, reaching heavenwards from the very mountain where Abraham had been prepared to offer up his son Isaac to the heavens. Tradition (as represented in Genesis) had Abraham naming the place 'Yahweh will be seen'; the Annals narrate that King David indeed sees Yahweh there, whereupon he declares the place to be Israel's true Bethel and embarks on all the preparations necessary for the building of a suitable edifice and for the conducting of appropriate activities in and around the completed structure. Yet no Israelite hand is involved in the construction of this impressive edifice; the workforce is entirely (apart from a skilled Tyrian craftsman) non-Israelite slave labour under the watchful eyes of non-Israelite overseers, all working to an architectural plan seemingly written by the hand of Yahweh himself. Thus the book of Chronicles depicts a rather different temple from the one which competing Israelite traditions have handed down to us.

2 Chronicles 1:
The Validation of the King

When 2 Chronicles begins, 'Solomon son of David' (1.1) has the stage to himself. The narrative in 1 Chronicles had been preparing us for this moment for some time: attentive readers had known already since the third chapter of the Annals that it would be through Solomon that the Davidic legacy would be carried, since the 17th chapter that his destiny would be to build a temple for the god of Israel, and since the 23rd chapter that he officially succeeded his father David as king over Israel and took part in an elongated handover of the wherewithal for the temple project. Now, after the 29th chapter of the Annals had been brought to a close with a final accounting of the great David's accomplishments, what is commonly called 2 Chronicles can take up the story with the accomplishments of Solomon.

Solomon's own destiny, like the destinies of his various descendants after him, seems written in his very name. Indeed, in Solomon's case the Annalists made this understanding of matters uniquely explicit when they reported that there had been an oracle from Yahweh, the god of Israel, which had decreed what the child should be called and what it would betoken for the individual and the nation: 'See, a son shall be born to you; he shall be a man of rest, and I will give him rest from all his enemies on every side, for his name shall be Solomon (šĕlōmōh), and I will give peace (šālôm) and quiet to Israel in his days, and he shall build a house for my name' (1 Chron. 22.9-10). We might also note that there are aspects of 'wholeness' and 'completeness' about the Hebrew word šālôm, so that šĕlōmōh might be construed not just as 'his peace' (i.e. the one who symbolizes peace and well-being granted by the deity) but also as 'his completeness' (i.e. the one chosen to complete and perfect the work begun by the father, David), but it is the aspect of 'peace and quiet' after the days of warfare with which David had had to be engaged that the Annalists highlight.

Through such oracular language it had been made clear to those who consult these Annals that Solomon was the divinely ordained successor to the throne of all Israel. Without such assurances, we might have wondered quite how David's tenth-born son, being also the fourth-born son of David's seventh wife Bath-shua (1 Chron. 3.1-5), had come to occupy his father's throne. But David had also reported to the nation that 'of all my sons (for Yahweh has given me many sons) he has chosen Solomon my son to sit upon the throne of the kingdom of Yahweh over Israel: he said to me, "It is your son Solomon who shall build my house and my courts, for I have chosen him to be my son, and I will be his father"' (1 Chron. 28.5-6). Accordingly, in this story-world that fourth-born son of the seventh wife was singled out by the deity for King David to groom him to become his successor, and now, after elaborate, systematic, and smooth succession management on David's part (1 Chron. 22–29), the chosen one Solomon reigns supreme: 'his god Yahweh was with him, and made him exceedingly great' (2 Chron. 1.1).

Solomon's first act is to summon 'all Israel' to go to 'the Tent of Meeting with the Deity' which was at the high place in Gibeon (vv. 2-3). That 'all Israel' is with him echoes the experience of his father David, who had also had 'all Israel' with him when he became king (1 Chron. 11.1) and when he had marched to Jerusalem to make it the centre of the kingdom (1 Chron. 11.4). No one had opposed those developments, and so too now the nation stands fully loyal to the divinely endowed leader, who will move the place of meeting with the national god from this high place in Gibeon to the new national temple in Jerusalem when that is built. When David had brought the sacred ark into the new national capital he had 'left the priest Zadok and his kindred the priests before the tabernacle of Yahweh in the high place that was at Gibeon, to offer regular burnt-offerings to Yahweh on the altar of burnt-offering' (1 Chron. 16.39), but he knew, once the site for the temple had been determined, that the altar of burnt-offering for Israel must be there rather than in Gibeon (1 Chron. 21.29–30.1). David had never returned to Gibeon to 'seek' (*dāraš*, NRSV 'inquire of') the deity there after he had been stopped in his tracks by the sword-wielding angel of Yahweh (1 Chron. 21.30), but now his son Solomon feels that the time is right for the new king to go there and 'seek' his god (*dāraš*, NRSV again 'inquire', 2 Chron. 1.5). Given that the father had instructed the son that 'if you seek him (*dāraš*, where NRSV agrees with the translation 'seek'), he will be found by you' (1 Chron. 28.9), readers can be confident that Solomon will encounter Yahweh at the site.

To make sure that he gets the deity's attention, the new king burns a thousand animals on Yahweh's altar—a substantial number, but only a fraction of the numbers that he will send heavenwards when he dedicates the new altar and temple in due course (the destruction of 22,000 oxen and 120,000 sheep will be reported in 2 Chron. 7.5, without any sense of shame on the part of the humans engaged in the mass slaughter). The Annalists' god seems to approve of such carnage, and grants Solomon an audience with the divine; for these tradents, the king's willingness to sacrifice valuable livestock is an indication that he is seriously dedicated to seeking Yahweh, and that he is confident that the national god will bless the nation with fertility and wealth to more than replace the animals that have been turned into ash on his altar.

Quite how the audience takes place is not stated. The Annals simply record that 'that night the deity appeared to Solomon and said to him, "Ask what I should give you"' (1.7). The statement that the event took place at night might suggest that a dream is envisaged, but no dream is explicitly mentioned. In this storyworld the deity can appear to a king who is awake and can speak directly to him, it would seem, judging by the encounter of Solomon's father with the so-called 'angel of Yahweh' (1 Chron. 21.16) who, it will soon be revealed, was actually Yahweh himself (2 Chron. 3.1). Readers may also recall that the same King David was depicted as holding direct conversations with the deity on occasions when he sought divine guidance (1 Chron. 14.10, 14); we might postulate that the narrators in such cases want us to understand that the king made use of some kind of oracular device or that it was a prophet or an omen-reader to whom he put his questions and from whom he received a response that was believed to have come from the deity, but by declining to mention any intermediary the Annalists permit readers to imagine that the deity was speaking directly to his chosen king who had sought him with a true heart. Something like this will happen again after Solomon has dedicated the temple, for 'then Yahweh appeared to Solomon in the night and said to him, "I have heard your prayer..."' (2 Chron. 7.12). In that narrative too it will not be said as such that Solomon is dreaming, or that a prophet has come and proclaimed the divine message to the king, but it will be reported as if, after the long day of public ceremony has drawn to a close, the deity makes a personal appearance to the king and speaks directly to him. And so on this occasion as well, with the divinely-chosen Solomon having performed the requisite rituals at the Tent of Meeting with the Deity, the deity indeed meets with him, as it were face to face.

The deity's straight-to-the-point invitation to the new king, 'Ask what I should give you' (1.7), contains interesting echoes of the experiences of the two earlier monarchs. The quasi-king Saul, whose very name designated him ironically as 'the one who was asked for', had been a would-be ruler who asked the wrong sorts of powers for help—'he had consulted a medium, seeking guidance, and did not seek guidance from Yahweh, so Yahweh put him to death and turned the kingdom over to David son of Jesse' (1 Chron. 10.13-14)—and even the genuine king David, a ruler who in most respects proved himself to be a man after Yahweh's own heart, had been given on a particular occasion a difficult choice of what sort of divine gift he would take as punishment for his misbehaviour—'three things I offer you; choose one of them, so that I may do it to you' (1 Chron. 21.10). Readers can be confident that Solomon is no Saul, but will ask only of Yahweh, as he is here invited to do, and they can be equally confident that Yahweh is not offering him harsh things, as he had felt he needed to do with David after that king had apparently offended the deity's sensibilities. Nevertheless, there is a test here for the fresh-faced monarch with the evocative name that suggests he is the complete article: what will he ask for, given the deity's willingness to welcome him to the throne of Israel with a generous and open-ended offer?

The Annals had earlier quoted David, during the detailed succession-management operation that he had conducted, as saying to Solomon, 'Now, my son, may Yahweh be with you, so that you may succeed in building the house of your god Yahweh, as he has spoken concerning you; only, may Yahweh grant you discretion and understanding, so that when he gives you charge over Israel you may keep the law of your god Yahweh' (1 Chron. 22.11-12). The son has taken his father's words to heart, and, now that Yahweh has indeed given him charge over Israel and he is asked what the deity should give him, he says, 'Give me wisdom and knowledge to go out and come in before this people, for who can rule this great people of yours?' (2 Chron. 1.10). It is the perfect answer, and it pleases the deity immensely; the divine voice announces that wisdom and knowledge are indeed granted to the new king, and as a bonus, some other useful things that Solomon had not specifically requested are added to the gift-list. Yahweh notes that 'you have not asked for wealth, possessions, and honour, or the life of those who hate you, and have not even asked for long life' (v. 11), all of which are the kinds of things that one might have expected a newly-elevated monarch to have aspirations about; and Yahweh then pronounces that 'I will also give you'—in addition to the wisdom and knowledge that were requested—'wealth, possessions, and honour' (v. 12 [strangely, NRSV varies the vocabulary and word-order in the two listings of the three items, despite the Hebrew text's consistency]).

The divine bounty does not explicitly extend to those other two things that an emerging king might have sought, namely 'the life of those who hate you' and 'long life'. In the former case, the category of 'the life of those who hate you', we are presumably to imagine that in this story-world no one hates the golden child who has had the destiny of succeeding his father to the throne of Israel upon him for many years of peaceful transition, unlike such later situations as those of the boy-king Joash who can only come to the throne upon the death of the hateful Athaliah (23.15) and Joash's son Amaziah who has to begin his reign by executing the murderers of his father (25.3). There are also several cases of Yahweh delivering the lives of very many enemy combatants into the hands of Judahite kings (e.g. Abijah at 13.15-17 and Jehoshaphat at 20.22-24), but no enemies seem to fight against Solomon (he captures a city in 8.3 and he conscripts non-Israelites as forced labour in 8.8, yet there are no tales of him needing to inflict any casualties in war). And in the latter case, the category of 'long life', it may be that the deity holds back from saying that he will grant such a blessing to this king because Solomon is not in fact the longest-serving monarch in the pages of the Annals: the record is held by Manasseh with 55 years (33.1), followed closely by Uzziah with 52 years (26.3). Nevertheless, the Annals will give Solomon the nicely rounded figure of a 40-year reign (9.30) to match that of his father David (1 Chron. 29.27), so he is certainly not depicted as a short-lived king in these pages, even though it would not have been accurate for the Annalists to have included 'long life' among the aspects 'such as none of the kings had who were before you, and none after you shall have the like' (v. 12); it is in 'wisdom and knowledge' and in 'wealth, possessions, and honour' that Solomon unquestionably outshines every other monarch in the Annals.

That this would be the case had already been foreshadowed in the narrative of the final stages of David's reign. The Annalists had said, before they even reported David's death, that 'Yahweh highly exalted Solomon in the sight of all Israel, and bestowed upon him such royal majesty as had not been on any king before him in Israel' (1 Chron. 29.25). And of course they had reported a divine promise concerning the glories of David's son in several passages (as noted earlier, those passages are 1 Chron. 17.11-14; 22.9-10; 28.5-6), so their child of destiny has much to allude to when he says to his god Yahweh, 'let your promise to my father David now be fulfilled' (2 Chron. 1.9). He also alludes to promises made, according to other Hebrew legends, to the distant ancestors of the nation as a whole, when he continues that sentence with the words, 'you have made me king over a people as numerous as the dust of the earth' (both Abraham and Jacob are promised by Yahweh that he will make their offspring as numerous as 'the dust of the earth' in the stories recorded in Genesis [13.16 and 28.14]).

The Annalists will not in the end be satisfied with rating Solomon as the greatest of the kings of Israel, but will draw their account of him towards a close with even greater hyperbole, claiming that 'King Solomon excelled all the kings of the earth in riches and in wisdom' (2 Chron. 9.22). In fact the compilers of this account are so keen to give us the impression that their hero outshone everyone else that they provide us with essentially the same listing of his wealth on two occasions, both here in ch. 1 within their initial evaluation of this king and again in ch. 9 within their closing account of his unsurpassed reputation. The later passage (9.25-28) repeats almost word for word what is said already here in the present passage (1.14-16); there are some variations between the two texts, not least in that this first description has appended to it an additional claim about Solomon running a clever import–export angle on horses and chariots (1.17) while the later description includes within it a claim about Solomon ruling over a vast territory (9.26), but the essential message is the same in both places, and its reiteration helps to emphasise the matter for readers: in these Annals, the Golden Age for Jerusalem was the reign of Solomon, who 'made silver [and gold] as common in Jerusalem as stone, and cedar as plentiful as the sycamore of the Shephelah' (1.15; 9.27). With such wealth at his disposal, this greatest of all imaginable monarchs is perfectly poised to bring about the task for which he is destined, the establishment of 'a temple for the name of Yahweh' (2.1 in English Bibles, although that verse's position as the ultimate verse of ch. 1 in the Hebrew text [1.18] perhaps more clearly demonstrates that, in the Annalists' picture, Solomon's wealth and possessions are primarily to be deployed to that purpose).

2 Chronicles 2–4:
The Preparation of the Temple

Chapter 2

Solomon now sets about the task for which the deity has appointed him. By translating the opening phrase as 'Solomon decided to build a temple', NRSV perhaps suggests that the idea was a new one in the new king's mind at this time, whereas in this story-world Solomon had for some time been privy to the information that his destiny was to build the temple (1 Chron. 22.6-16), and he had been handed the plans by his father David a good while before (1 Chron. 28.11-19), so there is no question of him only now 'deciding to build a temple'; it is rather a matter of him now being ready to begin the work or of issuing instructions for the project to begin, and so the Hebrew verb '*āmar* might be rendered as 'Solomon *was fully determined* to build a house for the name of Yahweh' or 'Solomon *gave orders* for the building of a house for the name of Yahweh'. That he is obligated to build such a house is written into the very contract that Yahweh had made with David: the deity would 'build David a house', which is to say that he would arrange for a Davidic dynasty to be established, and in return the son of David would 'build a house for Yahweh' (1 Chron. 17.10-12), so that is precisely what Solomon will do. To be sure, he will also build a new house for himself—or more literally, 'a house for his kingdom' (2 Chron. 1.1, 12), which might be taken to be simply an administrative building were it not for the later phrasing 'the house of the king' (7.11)—but much greater prominence is given in the unfolding narrative to the deity's house.

The first arrangement set in place is that 'Solomon conscripted 70,000 labourers and 80,000 stonecutters in the hill country, with 3,600 to oversee them' (2.2), and at first glance this impressively sized workforce may seem simply to be an appropriate enough gathering of manpower. Yet at the end of the chapter further details are given about precisely who constituted this workforce, when it is said that the king had taken 'a census of all

the aliens who were residing in the land of Israel', that the total
number of these resident aliens was 'found to be 153,600' (v. 17),
and that they were assigned in the same numbers as had been
set out in v. 2. Thus it is made clear that Solomon's arrangement
was that every single one of the non-enfranchised residents of
his kingdom was rounded up for the temple-building work. This
appears to be nothing short of an invidious policy of slave labour,
and one under which some of the enslaved are placed in charge
of enforcing the enslavement. But it is in keeping with the
example set by David, who immediately after designating the
temple site had given orders 'to gather together the aliens who
were residing in the land of Israel, and he set [them as] stonecutters to prepare dressed stones for building the House of God'
(1 Chron. 22.2).

In another respect, the Solomonic experience here contrasts
intriguingly with a Davidic experience, in that Solomon's census
was taken 'after the census that his father David had taken' (2
Chron. 2.17), yet there is no divine anger about this later census.
Presumably the deity had been upset about David's census (1
Chron. 21.7) because it had been a counting of the people of
Israel for military preparedness and thus smacked of a lack of
faith in Yahweh as the one who fought for Israel, whereas the
deity has no complaints about Solomon's census because it is a
counting of the resident aliens for temple-building purposes and
thus evidences the new king's faithfulness towards the god of
Israel. No Israelite hands will be necessary to build Yahweh's
temple, just as no Israelite hands are apparently necessary to
fight Israel's battles. The Warrior God who fought for David
would seem to be the Victor also over these particular non-
Israelite people, who must now bend their backs in the raising
up of a monument to the god of the land in which they lived as
aliens.

There are further non-Israelites whose assistance the king of
Israel needs for the project, namely Lebanese timber-cutters and
a skilled artisan for leading the work in metals and fabrics for
the temple furnishings. For this he calls upon the king of the
city-state of Tyre, whom he notes had been of assistance to David
when David had built his cedar-wood palace in earlier days (2
Chron. 2.3, alluding to 1 Chron. 14.1). When the David story had
been told, the Tyrian king's name was given as 'Hiram' (1 Chron.
14.1), but in the Solomon story the narrators style him as 'Huram'
(2 Chron. 2.3, 12), yet it is evidently meant to be the same

individual. Such a slippage in spelling between the letters *vav* (yielding 'Huram') and *yod* (yielding 'Hiram') is a common scribal error in Hebrew manuscripts, and certain scribes in the trans-mission history of the scroll of Chronicles have written the *vav*-form in the margin at 1 Chron. 14.1 to indicate their preference for 'Huram' in both accounts. There is some further slippage in Tyrian names in the development of the present narrative, in that the Lebanese king refers to the skilled artisan that he sends to Israel as 'Huram-abi' (2 Chron. 2.13), but later the Annalists refer to him as just 'Huram' and then immediately as 'Hiram'—though the scribes again place 'Huram' in the margin—and then soon afterwards as 'Huram-abi' again (4.11, 16). It is as though the skilled artisan so represents the Tyrian monarch and citi-zenry that his name is interchangeable with the name of the king himself, and indeed the lengthier form of the craftsman's name, 'Huram-abi', means 'Huram is my father' and thus desig-nates him as the quintessential representative of his nation. Evidently the craftwork of Tyre is regarded by the storytellers as the finest in the region, and only the best will do for the House of Yahweh, though the Annalists are no doubt pleased to record that this exceptionally talented individual deployed by King Huram for the purpose has an Israelite mother, descended from the tribe of Dan (2.7).

In this, and in the matter of supplying various kinds of fine timbers from the Lebanese forests, the king of Tyre is happy to cooperate with Solomon's venture. He does not even take offence at Solomon's undiplomatic contention that 'our [Israelite] god is greater than other gods' (v. 5), but goes along with the idea when his reply includes the words 'Blessed be Yahweh, the god of Israel, who made heaven and earth' (v. 12). Perhaps the Annalists want us to imagine that the king of Tyre recognized the god of David and Solomon as more than a national god for Israel, on account of all the victories that had been granted to David—one might note that Huram refers to 'my lord, your father David' (v. 14) as though Tyre too had been under Davidic control or influence—and on account of all the magnificence that had been bestowed upon Solomon—one might further note that Huram speaks of the new king of Israel as being 'endowed with discre-tion and understanding' (v. 12)—but it could equally be read as the clever phrasing of a ruler who sought good neighbourly rela-tions between the Yahweh-devoted land to his south and his own non-Yahwistic state, or who simply knew a good deal when he saw one and was willing to pander to his customer's view of the world in order to seal the lucrative arrangement of supplying him with the timber he wanted. Jerusalem has become an immensely wealthy city in this story, and so it can pay handsomely for the natural resources that the king of Tyre has at his disposal. He has much to gain by pandering to his new customer with such words as 'Because Yahweh loves his people, he has made you king over them' (v. 11, a phrasing that will be echoed by the queen of Sheba in 9.8).

Solomon's intentions for the temple are that it will be even better than any temples that the Lebanese artisans may have crafted in their own land. 'The house that I am about to build will be great', he boasts (in 2.5), and he repeats and expands this aspiration with the words 'the house I am about to build will be great and wonderful' (v. 9). The scene has been fully set for a matchless building to be constructed.

Chapter 3

The site for the temple is now delineated as being 'on Mount Moriah, where Yahweh had appeared to [Solomon's] father David' (3.1). This brief phrasing is immensely significant, for the Annalists appear to be asserting that the House of Yahweh is being built on the very mountain on which Abraham had once prepared his son Isaac for sacrifice to Yahweh (although that tale is not related within these Annals as such), and that King David had beheld the deity himself and not a heavenly intermediary (as a certain tale that is related within the Annals might have suggested) at the same sacred site. A full discussion of these interpretive details was set out in the 'Survey of Solomon's Temple' earlier in this volume (see especially pages 13-17), so there is no need to repeat the discussion here. Suffice it to say that in the Annalists' world-view nothing less than a very special mountain could be the appropriate location for the place of unique interface between heaven and earth that Solomon's temple is to be.

The dimensions of the temple are then delineated as being 60 cubits in length and 20 cubits in width, and with at least part of the structure being 120 cubits high (vv. 3-4). Given that a cubit is about half a metre (whether 'of the old standard' [v. 3] or of the new), we have here a building that is about 30 metres long and 10 metres wide, and rising to a height of 60 metres. Again a full discussion of the interpretive details was set out in the

'Survey' section (see especially pages 9-13 on the shape of the
temple pictured by the Annalists), so the discussion need not be
repeated here, except to note that this structure, being six times
higher than its width and twice as high as its length, reaches
unambiguously heavenwards.

For some readers, one of the more intriguing aspects of the
tale is that Solomon has carvings made throughout the temple:
'he carved cherubim on the walls' (v. 7), 'in the most holy place he
made two carved cherubim' (v. 10), and he 'made the curtain of
blue and purple and crimson fabrics and fine linen, and worked
cherubim into it' (v. 14); and he also has palm-trees engraved
around the walls of the nave of the temple (v. 5) and pomegranates engraved on the chains encircling the pillars at the front of
the temple (v. 16). All of these carvings within the temple are
then supplemented by castings of twelve oxen just outside the
temple, holding up a large water-receptacle known as 'the sea'
(4.2-4). These hundreds of carved images and the twelve cast
images sit perhaps a little oddly against the later condemnatory
talk about 'the carved image' that King Manasseh set up in the
temple (33.7) and 'the carved and the cast images' that his
grandson King Josiah then removed (34.3-4). Nevertheless, the
different judgments upon images between the present passage
and those later stories might be explained by the Annalists
seeing Solomon's figures as representing service of Yahweh (in
the case of flying cherubim and water-bearing oxen) or bounty
from Yahweh (in the case of palm-trees and pomegranates) and
holding Solomon and his contemporaries as being immune from
any danger of worshipping cherubim or venerating palm-trees as
if those things were divine, whereas Manasseh and his contemporaries were seen as worshipping carved and cast images.

Even so, a reader knowledgeable about wider Hebrew traditions could point out that the Israelite law-codes seem to be
insistent that Israelites should never make images, 'whether in
the form of anything that is in heaven above, or that is on the
earth beneath, or that is in the water under the earth' (Exodus
20.4; Deuteronomy 5.8), on account of the human propensity to
bow down to such images and worship them. At the very least,
Solomon's twelve oxen (one ox for each member of the heavenly
zodiac, or is it one for each Israelite tribe?) on open display
outside the temple seems a potentially dangerous example to be
setting, even if ordinary members of the public never get to see
or venerate the great pair of cherubim within the most holy

place. But the Annalists show no concern about any of this; in fact they have already explicitly indicated that it has divine approval when they had recounted how 'David gave his son Solomon the plan...of the temple...and the plan of all that he had in mind...also his plan for the golden chariot of the cherubim that spread their wings and covered the ark of Yahweh's covenant—all this, in writing at Yahweh's direction, he made clear to me: the plan of all the works' (1 Chron. 28.11-19). Accordingly, readers of the Annals need have no misgivings about the abundance of carvings in the House of Yahweh: it is not against his will at all, but is exactly in accordance with the detailed plans that he himself had drawn up for David to instruct the young Solomon in what was required. Solomon is carrying out the plans to the letter.

Perhaps a word or two is in order about 'cherubim', lest any reader unfamiliar with ancient Hebrew mythology might think of the kind of sweet little chubby-faced children that can be seen in the western art tradition. The NRSV tries to steer English readers away from such imaginings by using the Hebraic plural form 'cherubim' rather than the English plural form 'cherubs', but what exactly is a 'cherub' in the context of the House of Yahweh? Anyone searching for biblical cherubim can encounter them already in Genesis 3.24, where they serve as frightening guardians of the way back into the paradise from which Yahweh had expelled the primeval human couple. They are also to be found in the psalms of ancient Israel, in such pictures as 'he [i.e. Yahweh] rode on a cherub, and flew; he came swiftly upon the wings of the wind' (Psalm 18.10); and 'he [i.e. Yahweh] sits enthroned upon the cherubim; let the earth quake' (Psalm 99.1); and 'you who are enthroned upon the cherubim, shine forth' (Psalm 80.1). For the most elaborate pictures of cherubim in the biblical writings one can turn to the prophet Ezekiel, particularly his tenth chapter read in relation to his first, but even without Ezekiel's strange imaginings it is clear that cherubim were thought to be awesome heavenly creatures who operated as the henchmen, bodyguards, and palanquin-bearers of the deity. In Ezekiel's visions a cherub has four wings and four faces (Ezekiel 1.6; 10.21), not to be confused with the six-winged seraphim of Isaiah (Isaiah 6.2, where the NRSV is happy to use the English plural form 'seraphs'), but the Solomonic style of cherub described by the Annalists has just two wings (2 Chron. 3.11), and presumably just one face, since the cherubim in the most holy place are said to be 'facing the nave' (v. 13) rather than facing in all directions at once. No ordinary mortal may approach the divine throne; the fearsome cherubim are there to ensure that. It seems that these strange beings were such a firmly established part of ancient Hebrew tradition that the Annalists cannot but include them in their temple account.

So too they include another intriguing detail, namely that 'he set up [two] pillars in front of the temple, one on the right and the other on the left, and the one on the right he called Jachin, and the one on the left Boaz' (v. 17). Here again there might be a possibility of simple folk regarding these items as worthy of veneration or worship in their own right, as representing deities or spirits so named, but the Annalists betray no fears about such matters. In their minds there can be no doubt that the two names, 'Jachin' ('he establishes', an element that we will meet again in the name of King Jehoiachin ['Yahweh establishes', 36.9]) and 'Boaz' ('in him is strength', the same name as that borne by David's great-grandfather [1 Chron. 2.12; Ruth 4.21-22]), proclaim aspects of the character of Yahweh, whose house this building is. Anyone passing between the two pillars or regarding them from a distance is to be reminded that the god of Israel is the one who has established this kingdom, and that it is from him alone that the people of Israel must draw their strength.

Chapter 4

The final details of the temple's furnishings and equipment are set out in this chapter. Among other details, we are told that just outside the temple stood a bronze altar which was '20 cubits long and 20 cubits wide' (4.1), the same dimensions as the most holy place (3.8); and a round container called 'the sea' which was '10 cubits from rim to rim' (4.2) and which was intended 'for the priests to wash in' (v. 6). There are ten basins for washing the implements used in burnt-offerings, ten golden lampstands 'as prescribed', and ten tables; there are hundreds of smaller basins, pots, shovels, forks, tongs, snuffers, ladles, firepans, and all sorts of things 'in great quantities'; and there are various decorations on different parts of the temple building. Among it all are a good number of items made 'of purest gold', and others 'of burnished bronze'.

All in all, this grand temple is a building well fit for purpose, even if the primary purpose of the courtyards seems to be as a slaughter-house complex for the dispatching of countless animals, as the large altar and many of the itemised implements remind us. But there are less violent functions too, such as 'the tables for the bread of the Presence' and 'the lampstands and their lamps...to burn before the inner sanctuary' (vv. 19-20). The Tyrian artisan variously known as 'Huram', 'Hiram', and 'Huram-abi' (vv. 11, 16)—name-changes commented upon earlier under ch. 2—has been an indefatigable craftsman, and in due course he has 'finished the work that he did for King Solomon on the House of God' (v. 11). All is now in readiness for the king and his people to inaugurate the life of the splendid complex that has risen on Mount Moriah.

2 Chronicles 5–7:
The Dedication of the Temple

Chapter 5

The great building project is now 'finished' (5.1) after an undisclosed but suitably lengthy period of time. We had been told that Solomon had begun the project 'on the second day of the second month of the fourth year of his reign' (3.2), and some time after the dedicatory ceremonies and related happenings have been narrated we will be told about what the king goes on to do 'at the end of 20 years, during which Solomon had built Yahweh's house and his own house' (8.1), so we are to imagine that Solomon devoted about half of his 40-year reign (9.30) to the building of the temple and the royal complex in Jerusalem. And now, to inaugurate the grand edifice that is the House of Yahweh, the king and the nation devote at least a full week and perhaps two full weeks to dedicatory festivities. The precise amount of time taken up here depends on whether one construes the expression in 7.9 that 'they had observed the dedication of the altar for seven days and the festival for seven days' as referring to concurrent activities or to two contiguous weeks; the note in that same verse that 'on the eighth day they held a solemn assembly', taken with the introductory verse in the present chapter which says that 'all the Israelites assembled before the king at the festival that is in the seventh month' (5.3) might suggest concurrency, but the later story of King Hezekiah keeping a festival for two whole weeks with the note that 'since the time of Solomon son of King David of Israel there had been nothing like this in Jerusalem' (30.26) seems to indicate that contiguity is in the Annalists' minds when they speak of 'seven days' of altar-dedication as well as 'seven days' of festival-observance.

The Annalists do not name 'the festival that is in the seventh month' (5.3), but it would seem to be a seven-day festival (7.9) that allows people to return to their homes 'on the 23rd day of the seventh month' (7.10). That would be the case if we assume that the festival observance followed the week-long altar dedication, as the order of phrasing in 7.9 implies, whereas if we worked on the assumption that the people assembled first for the festival, as the wording of 5.3 implies, and followed that with an altar-dedication week after the festival's normal conclusion, then we would be reckoning with a festival that normally finished a week earlier than that '23rd day'. As it happens, Hebrew tradition has generally spoken of a particular festival as running up to that day, the legislation in the book of Leviticus being phrased as follows: 'On the 15th day of this seventh month, and lasting seven days, there shall be the Festival of Tabernacles to Yahweh: the first day shall be a holy convocation, and you shall not work at your occupations; then for seven days you shall present Yahweh's offerings by fire, and on the eighth day you shall observe a holy convocation and present Yahweh's offerings by fire—it [too] is a solemn assembly, and you shall not work at your occupations' (Leviticus 23.34-36). Under this legislation, the people are twice assembled in holy convocation, with regular offerings to Yahweh being conducted in the intervening days, so it fits reasonably well with the Annalists' reportage that the king sent the people away to their homes on the 23rd day of the seventh month, even if it fits less well with their seeming wish to suggest that on this unprecedented occasion everyone spent two weeks in celebratory mood in the national capital. Accordingly, it would seem that the Festival of Tabernacles is the festive occasion that the Annalists have in mind for their Festival of Dedication, even though they do not mention it by name at this juncture (only referring to it later, in 2 Chron. 8.13, as one of 'the three annual festivals' that are commanded by Moses).

The first thing to be done to institute the life of the temple is to bring the ark of the covenant into the place that has been prepared for it, 'in the most holy place, underneath the wings of the cherubim' (5.7). When David had brought this sacred box into his new capital city of Jerusalem, he had done so with the enthusiastic agreement of 'the whole assembly of Israel' (1 Chron. 13.2) and with 'all Israel' present in the parade (1 Chron. 13.5; 15.3, 28); so now his son is accompanied by 'all the Israelites' (2 Chron. 5.3) and 'all the congregation of Israel' (v. 6) as he relocates the ark to its permanent enclosure. David had ensured that the appropriate functionaries, both of a priestly and of a levitical kind, were involved in moving this sacred object and performing appropriate music and songs for the occasion; so now Solomon has the priests as the bearers of the ark (v. 7) and the levitical singers and musicians as the accompanists to the grand occasion (vv. 12-13). They are all 'arrayed in fine linen' (v. 12), so it is an impressive spectacle as well as an impressive musical occasion, with the ringing refrain of praise to Yahweh, 'For he is good, for his steadfast love endures forever' (v. 13, the same refrain as had been used at David's earlier ceremony in 1 Chron. 16.14, and will be used again later in Solomon's festive occasion in 2 Chron. 7.3).

Yahweh is well pleased with the majestic arrival of the ark of his covenant—so called, it is revealed here, because it contained 'the two tablets that Moses put there at Horeb, where Yahweh made a covenant with the people of Israel after they came out of Egypt' (v. 10)—and he demonstrates his approval of matters by filling the building with a cloud, with the result that 'the priests could not stand to minister because of the cloud, for the glory of Yahweh filled the House of God' (v. 14). There will be a repeat performance with an even more spectacular display from the heavens after the king's prayer of dedication, when we will be told that 'fire came down from heaven and consumed the burnt offering and the sacrifices, and the glory of Yahweh filled the temple; and the priests could not enter the House of Yahweh, because the glory of Yahweh filled the House of Yahweh' (7.1-2). Some more can be said about the significance of all this on that later occasion, but it is already clear here in ch. 5 that the Annalists are alluding to the Hebrew tradition which held that, when Moses finished the work of setting up the nomadic temple-like structure known as the tabernacle, 'the cloud covered the tent of meeting, and the glory of Yahweh filled the tabernacle, and Moses was unable to enter the tent of meeting because the cloud settled upon it, and the glory of Yahweh filled the tabernacle' (Exodus 40.34-35). Yahweh is thus to be seen as placing his stamp of approval on Solomon's edifice as the right and proper home for Israel's god, the symbol of his presence among his people.

Chapter 6

With the ark now installed inside the temple and 'all the assembly of Israel standing' (6.3) in front of the building, the king is positioned before the altar on 'a bronze platform five cubits long, five cubits wide, and three cubits high' (v. 13) to deliver the official pronouncements on this grand occasion.

First of all he declares the building well and truly built. 'I have built you [i.e. Yahweh] an exalted house, a place for you to reside in forever', he declares to the deity (v. 2); and then to the people he declares, 'I have built the house for the name of Yahweh, the god of Israel, and there I have set the ark, in which is Yahweh's covenant that he made with the people of Israel' (vv. 10-11). The king similarly pronounces a blessing upon the people (v. 3) and also proclaims that the deity's name is blessed (v. 4). He provides another account of the divine oracle that had been given to his father David—an oracle first reported in 1 Chron. 17.3-15 and subsequently paraphrased in 1 Chron. 22.8-10 and 28.3-7—and represents it as now fulfilled in the sight of all Israel.

The king then 'knelt on his knees in the presence of the whole assembly of Israel, and spread out his hands toward heaven' (v. 13). There then follows in the remainder of the chapter a great prayer of dedication, in which the king requests of the deity that he be attentive to all subsequent prayers that are directed to him at his temple. Again and again Solomon asks of Yahweh, 'may you hear from heaven' (vv. 21, 23, 25, 27, 30, 33, 35, 39), whether that be in response to prayer in general (v. 21) or specifically to people required to swear oaths before the altar (v. 22), to the nation in a state of siege (v. 24) or drought (v. 26) or under diverse conditions of suffering (vv. 28-29), to the prayers of foreigners drawn to the Jerusalem temple (v. 32), to the soldiers of Israel needing to fight away from Jerusalem (v. 34), and to Israelites taken captive away from their land (vv. 36-37). The last situation is a particularly significant one in the context of the Annals, for the story told in these pages is leading inexorably to just such an outcome; Solomon's prayer is proclaiming on behalf of the Annalists that even in their captivity the people of Israel can turn again to their god, who will not forget them. But it is also interesting to note the Solomonic word for 'foreigners, who are not of your people Israel' but who 'come from a distant land because of your great name and your mighty hand and your outstretched arm' (v. 32); it may be difficult to credit such magnanimity to foreigners on the part of someone who has reportedly enslaved the entire non-Israelite population of his own land (2.17-18), but this king's interest in more distant lands is also on record in the Annals (e.g. 1.14-17; 8.17-18) and it will be said that 'all the kings of the earth sought the presence of Solomon to hear his wisdom' (9.23), so it is only right that he should pray also on behalf of this influx of intrigued visitors from other lands.

All of the sundry prayer-inducing crisis situations that are itemized in the dedicatory prayer are encompassed by the requests that Yahweh be ever alert at the new temple: 'May your eyes be open day and night toward this house' (v. 20) and 'Let your eyes be open and your ears attentive to prayer from this place' (v. 40). And in due course the deity will specifically assent to this request, when he declares to the king in a private audience after the public ceremony has closed that indeed 'my eyes will be open and my ears attentive to the prayer that is made in this place' (7.15). But meanwhile the public pronouncement from the king is drawn to a close with the poetic grandeur of a call for Yahweh to ensconce himself in his temple, served by his priests and bestowing blessing upon the king and the nation (vv. 41-42, in words that echo those of Psalm 132.8-10). This is truly an occasion, despite all the cataloguing of misery and suffering that the dedicatory prayer has contained, for the king to include a hymnic word about 'your faithful ones rejoicing in your goodness' (2 Chron. 6.41). This is, after all, a god who 'keeps covenant in steadfast love with your servants who walk before you with all their heart' (v. 14), and on this day of inauguration of the full functions of the temple, Israel is at the height of its devotion to its god, in the estimation of the Annalists.

Chapter 7

After the prayer comes fire! 'Fire came down from heaven and consumed the burnt-offering and the sacrifices, and the glory of Yahweh filled the temple; the priests could not enter the House of Yahweh, because the glory of Yahweh filled the House of Yahweh' (7.1-2). This spectacular divine endorsement of what Solomon has instituted, building upon the earlier display (in 5.13-14) in which 'the House of Yahweh was filled with a cloud, so that the priests could not stand to minister because of the cloud, for the glory of Yahweh filled the House of God', evidently calls to mind the depiction of the covenant-giving occasion in the legends of Israel, for certain traditions tell us that 'when Moses went up on the mountain, the cloud covered the mountain; and the glory of Yahweh settled on Mount Sinai... Now the appearance of the glory of Yahweh was like a devouring fire on the top of the mountain in the sight of the people of Israel' (Exodus 24.15-17; note also the text concerning the cloud of glory in Exodus 40.34-35 that was quoted above in the discussion under ch. 5 of the Annals). The Annalists could hardly make it clearer that they regard the Temple Mount of Jerusalem as replacing the covenant-instituting summit of the deep south. The Annalists' Mount Moriah (2 Chron. 3.1) is in a sense Mount Sinai transplanted; no site for a temple could be more authentic and appropriate than this.

The pyrological display also evidently reflects an earlier episode in these Annals, for when David had first built an altar on the site that would become the location of the temple, and had presented burnt-offerings there and called upon the name of Yahweh, the deity had 'answered him with fire from heaven on the altar of burnt-offering' (1 Chron. 21.26). Accordingly, the second such manifestation of heavenly firepower now underlines what had already been indicated on that former occasion, namely that the deity unreservedly approves of sacrifices made to him on this particular spot.

Readers had not been told in the Davidic episode quite how many animals Yahweh burned to a cinder at that time, but in the Solomonic dedication ceremony we are given a figure of '22,000 oxen and 120,000 sheep' (2 Chron. 7.5) who are offered up to and gratefully accepted by the god of Israel. The latter figure of 120,000 neatly computes—if the word 'neatly' can be used in reference to such mass slaughter—to 10,000 sheep for each of the twelve tribes of Israel, while the former figure of 22,000 is less straightforwardly configurable, but perhaps indicates 2,000 oxen for each of the eleven non-levitical tribes. These rituals are conducted over seven days (according to v. 8), or perhaps over two weeks (if the reference in v. 9 is taken to mean that; see the discussion of this matter under the comments to ch. 5). If they are confined to one week's activity, and assuming that the actual slaughtering is conducted in daylight hours and that the sabbath-day is kept free from this work, then the Annalists are imagining something like 6 oxen and 30 sheep being dispatched every single minute of the working week—one sheep every two seconds and one oxen every ten seconds. This is killing on a hugely industrial scale, but it is apparently not the extent of the Annalists' imaginations, for they had earlier said that, when the sacred ark was being brought to the temple, the king and his people were 'sacrificing so many sheep and oxen that they could not be numbered or counted' (5.6). Readers might well wonder if there were any animals left alive in the entire kingdom after this enormous slaughter-fest.

But the Annalists raise no questions about either the economics or the theology of the scene that they have pictured. Theirs is a god who rains fire from the skies to consume powerless animals, and he is to be held in awe and fear. Various Hebrew traditions with which they were presumably familiar had spoken of his occasional predilection for consuming human beings by such means ('fire from Yahweh' was said to have burnt several people to death in pentateuchal stories such as Leviticus 10.2 and Numbers 16.35), and indeed his character had even been encapsulated in such an image ('Your god Yahweh is a Devouring Fire', according to Deuteronomy 4.24). The Annalists see their god as one who wants an endless stream of animals to be burnt for him 'regularly, morning and evening, according to all that is written in the law of Yahweh that he commanded Israel' (1 Chron. 16.40), and so the incredible number of sacrificial victims that they offer to him in their story of the dedication of the temple is, for them, only as it should be.

In further heavenly recognition of Solomon's good work in overseeing the elaborate dedication ceremony, after having overseen the construction and outfitting of a peerless temple at which such massive sacrificial activities could take place, Yahweh grants a divine appearance to Solomon and confirms that he has indeed 'chosen this place for myself as a house of sacrifice' (2 Chron. 7.12). This is the deity's second appearance to this favoured king, and, as was also the case with the first occurrence, it happens 'in the night' (cf. 1.7's 'that night the deity appeared to Solomon'), which might be taken as implying that a royal dream is the vehicle of divine communication, though the Annalists might have specified that— or indeed that a prophet came to the king and proclaimed the divine message to him—if they had wished us to think in such terms. Equally plausible in their story-world, particularly in view of Solomon's having just dedicated the temple on the site where 'Yahweh had appeared to his father David' (3.1), is that we are to read this narrative as an account of the deity making a personal appearance to the king and speaking directly to him, as it were face to face.

Yahweh's words are a reassurance and a warning. The reassurance is that, as Solomon had requested in his prayer in the previous chapter, Israel's god will indeed 'hear from heaven, and will forgive their sin and heal their land' (7.14) whenever the people of Israel humble themselves and seek their god at this temple; and further, Yahweh categorically states that his intention in choosing and consecrating this temple is that 'my name may be there forever, and my eyes and my heart may be there for all time' (v. 16), with the Davidic monarchy ruling over Israel forever. But the warning is stark: if the king and his people 'turn aside and forsake' their god's instructions, 'then I will pluck you up from the land that I have given you; and this house, which I have consecrated for my name, I will cast out of my sight, and will make it a proverb and a byword among all peoples' (v. 20). Yahweh's speech ends with the ominous words, put in the mouths of later observers witnessing the utter destruction of the once magnificent structure that Solomon had erected, of *kol hārā'â hazzō't*—'all this calamity'. Readers know that the present Annalistic paradise of a perfectly appointed and perfectly functioning temple will not last forever after all. Nevertheless, they can bask for a moment or two yet in the account of the Golden Age of Solomon, as the Annals continue in the next two chapters to sing the praises of the temple-builder and dedicator.

2 Chronicles 8–9:
The Reputation of the King

Chapter 8

After spending the first half of his reign ('20 years' in 8.1 over against a total of '40 years' in 9.30) on constructing the religious and royal buildings at the heart of his kingdom, Solomon can now look further afield, taking full advantage of the blessings that his god bestows upon him, in accordance with the divine undertaking to give the temple-builder 'wealth, possessions, and honour, such as none of the kings had who were before you, and none after you shall have the like' (1.12).

Accordingly, Solomon turns his attention to other towns of his kingdom, including a number that he has apparently been gifted by that old friend of the kingdom, King Huram of Tyre, the man who had been so cooperative with the building projects of both David (1 Chron. 14.1) and Solomon himself (2 Chron. 2.3-16), and who will be seen again later in economic partnership with Solomon (8.18; 9.10, 21). The reference now to 'the cities that Huram had given to him' (8.2), together with the later inclusion of Lebanese areas as one of the territories falling under Solomon's governance (v. 6), has subtly shifted some richly-forested areas from simply being a source of timber for the Israelite king's building projects to being part of his dominion. The details of such a transaction between the kingdoms of Tyre and Israel are not spelled out, but the Annals are happy to report that the king of Israel's construction expertise is applied now to these towns: the 'building' (*bānâ*, v. 2) that he causes to happen may be the construction of new Israelite towns where there had been no towns before, or may be a 'rebuilding' (as NRSV postulates) of what had previously been non-Israelite towns. If the towns were regarded by the Annalists as pre-dating the influx of Israelites under Solomon, then perhaps they thought of them as having fallen into depression and being no longer regarded as useful by the Tyrian kingdom, so that Huram could cede them to Solomon in a mutually convenient arrangement, and Solomon could then give them a much-needed wealth-injection from his overflowing coffers.

It may even be that the Annalists regard these territories as having been given to Solomon as spoils of victory, for they do make one reference to a military venture on that king's part in the very next verse: 'Solomon went to Hamoth-zobah, and captured it' (v. 3). The region mentioned there is one that had been in the frame of the David stories, for among the various places and peoples that David had conquered we were told about how he had 'struck down King Hadadezer of Zobah, towards Hamath' (1 Chron. 18.3) and had extracted significant items of wealth from that territory. In view of the earlier story, Solomon could be seen here, in the one explicit military venture attributed to him in the Annals, as simply bringing back into line a city that had once been brought under Israelite control by his father but may have rebelled against continuing Israelite control in Solomon's time. But with the Lebanese towns, which are not said to have been taken by force of arms, the king of Israel is expanding the areas where his people live and from which they can contribute to his unparalleled economic success story. Solomon's expansion of the kingdom accordingly appears to be by peaceful means, and not by the kinds of conquests with which David had been preoccupied. The successor to the Davidic legacy has a strong standing army stationed throughout his territory— witness 'all the towns for his chariots and the towns for his cavalry' (2 Chron. 8.6)—and he presumably has a considerable imperial-style force at his disposal, if the later report that 'he ruled over all the kings from the Euphrates to the land of the Philistines, and to the border of Egypt' (9.26) is brought into the picture (unless the Annalists want us to suppose that this hyper-bolically large realm was of its own volition under Solomon's wing simply because 'all the kings of the earth sought the presence of Solomon' on account of his wisdom, as 9.23 expresses matters). In any event, apart from the single case of needing to recapture Hamath-zobah, Solomon does not have to deploy his troops in anger, as his father David had so often done against sundry enemies. After the warrior has come the man of peace, building various 'storage towns' (8.4, 6) and 'fortified cities' (v. 5) throughout his rich realm.

Part of the secret of Solomon's success in being able to build 'whatever [he] desired to build...in all the land of his dominion' (v. 6) is the scheme of conscripting the resident aliens in Israel as 'forced labour' (v. 8). Such a policy had been recounted at the beginning of the temple-building project, when we were told that the king had taken a census of all the resident aliens and had set every single one of them to work as labourers or stonecutters or overseers (2.17-18). Readers might have anticipated that this servitude would be for that project alone, and that the system would be dissolved once that special task had been completed, but now we learn that the king and his Israelite subjects were so comfortable with it that it was maintained beyond the central project of Solomon's reign.

Indeed the Annalists claim that this system of forced labour 'is still the case today' (8.8). The phrase appears to indicate that the Judahites (or Judeans) of the Annalists' own time maintained a system of non-Judahite forced labour, or at least a system of profound inequality between a ruling class and a serving class, although it might rather indicate only what the Annalists wished could be the case in their time. Either way, they show no embarrassment about the king of Israel virtually enslaving various non-Israelite peoples, or at least those whom the Israelites had not simply exterminated (vv. 7-8). For modern readers the notions of ethnic cleansing and enslavement are rightly obnoxious, but evidently the Annalists were not uncomfortable with such matters, so long as they were among the beneficiaries of such inhumane practices and were not the ones being ethnically cleansed or enslaved by others. What would have made them uncomfortable is any suggestion that Solomon might have enslaved Israelites, and so they are quick to add the emphatic note that 'of the people of Israel Solomon made no slaves for his work; they were soldiers and officers and commanders' (v. 9). This will become an important caveat for us to bear in mind when Solomon's reign has drawn to an end and certain rebellious Israelites will step forward and try to claim that he had 'made our yoke heavy' (10.4); readers of these Annals who have noted the clear distinction made in the account of Solomon's reign between his conscription of 'the people who were left of the Hittites, the Amorites, the Perizzites, the Hivites, and the Jebusites, who were not of Israel' (8.7) and his absolute avoidance of making 'slaves for his work' of anyone who was 'of Israel' (v. 9), will not give credence to the words of the nefarious Jeroboam son of Nebat and other Israelites under his sway when they make the accusation that Solomon had put them under 'hard service' (10.4). The Annalists' Solomon cannot be accused of doing anything but good for his fellow Israelites, even if non-Israelites might not be so blessed under his rule.

Two particular non-Israelites seem to fare reasonably well under Solomon's aegis, though they too are kept in their place, as it were. The first of these is mentioned in a brief episode as follows: 'Solomon brought Pharaoh's daughter from the city of David to the house that he had built for her, for he said, "My wife shall not live in the house of King David of Israel, for the places to which Yahweh's ark has come are holy"' (8.11). There is considerable story-potential here in a picture of a princess from the greatest empire and most cultured civilisation of the time coming to this new city that has been rising in the hill country of the land of Canaan, but the Annalists are not distracted into such avenues; for them, it is enough to mention her as an example of Solomon's grandeur—and to carefully keep her away from Yahweh's business. They do not give her a name, and they do not derive the line of Israelite kings from her union with their Hebrew hero. They do, however, trace that line from Solomon's marriage to another foreign woman, whose name they do record, and that is 'Naamah the Ammonite' (12.13), who has the honour of becoming the mother of Solomon's son and heir, Rehoboam. Yet beyond that genealogical distinction they have nothing to relate about Naamah either; readers must simply assume that she was treated similarly to her Egyptian counterpart, accommodated in the new fine palace complex just outside the old 'city of David'.

There will also be a third woman who features in Solomon's life, and she will be the subject of a longer story (in 9.1-12), even allowed to speak and interact with the great man and yet—like Pharaoh's daughter—not given a name of her own, and that is the 'Queen of Sheba'. But whatever we make of her character, she does not marry Solomon or remain in his kingdom, so we are dealing in these Annals with just two wives for the great Hebrew king, one from the world power of Egypt but unable to provide the kingdom of Israel with an heir, and one from the neighbouring nation of Ammon (which had been incorporated into the Israelite sphere by the all-conquering David [1 Chron. 20.1-3]) who does bear a son for Solomon. That all-conquering David had been much more active in accumulating wives and fathering sons, according to the Annals—he produced no less than 19 sons from seven wives and an undisclosed number of further sons from an undisclosed number of concubines (1 Chron. 3.1-9)—but the peaceful Solomon is not depicted by the Annalists as replicating his father's efforts in this respect.

Where Solomon does follow his father's example is in his assiduous efforts to ensure that the functioning of Yahweh's temple is precisely as it should be, 'according to the ordinance of his father David', or in other words entirely as 'David the godly man had commanded' (2 Chron. 8.14), all of which is also 'according to the commandment of Moses' (v. 13). Any reader who might have been a little worried about that Egyptian princess or that Ammonite noblewoman potentially sullying the purity of temple functions by living in the royal compound of Jerusalem, perhaps along the lines of the wickedness that a later foreign princess will bring (21.6; 22.2-3, 10; 23.12-15), can be reassured by the Annalists' description of absolute fidelity to the ways of Yahweh on the part of Solomon and those exercising duties under him. 'They did not turn away from what the king had commanded the priests and Levites regarding anything at all' (8.15). Solomon's very name denotes perfection or completion, and so it is fittingly recorded that 'all the work of Solomon (*šĕlōmōh*) was accomplished' and that the House of Yahweh 'was finished (*šālēm*) completely' (v. 16). Monarch and deity are in perfect harmony, and the nation flourishes, even to the extent—normally unheard of in Israelite tales—of successful maritime trade bringing in ever-greater wealth to the kingdom (vv. 17-18). It seems as if everything Solomon touches turns to gold.

Chapter 9

In a story-world that mostly has to do with kings and other male figures, it is refreshing to have a female character step forward. Even if she remains somewhat veiled behind the generic title of 'the queen of Sheba' (9.1) and is not given a personal name by the storytellers, nonetheless she is given some words to speak and she appears as a worthy dialogue-partner and trading-partner for Solomon, holding discussions with him and exchanging valuable commodities, though the narrative is careful to depict the Israelite hero as the superior party in both the dialogue and the trading.

The Annalists do not clarify which particular nation or tribe or clan known as 'Sheba' it is that they have in mind in this story. The genealogies with which the Annals had begun had presented no less than three groups that went by this same name (*šĕbā'* in Hebrew), all in 1 Chronicles 1: one in v. 9 (not to be confused with the similarly-named tribe of Seba [*sĕbāʾ*] earlier in that same verse), another in v. 22, and a further group in v. 32. The first of these peoples was catalogued as a sub-group of the Cushite nation, under the Hamite or great southern branch of humanity as conceptualized by the Annalists (vv. 8-16), but the second and third sets of Shebans were placed under the Shemite or Semitic branch (vv. 17-54), and were presented as related to the Israelites, the one group somewhat distantly and the other rather closely. The distant relatives are the descendants of Sheba son of Joktan son of Eber; they, like the Israelites, are members of the Eberite (Hebrew) peoples, though from the opposite side of the great Hebrew divide, since the Israelites are seen as descendants of Eber's other son Peleg (vv. 19-34). The closer relatives are the descendants of Sheba son of Jokshan son of Abraham, and they are not far removed from the descendants of Israel son of Isaac son of Abraham (vv. 32-34); in other words, the eponymous Israel is seen in the Annalists' scheme set out in 1 Chronicles 1 as a cousin of the third eponymous Sheba, and hence those latter people of Sheba are regarded as a kindred group to the people of Israel.

Accordingly, the 'queen of Sheba' that the Annalists now bring forward in 2 Chronicles 9 might be the queen of a Hebrew (Eberite) people with a certain affinity towards the Israelite nation, or she might be the queen of a Cushite people carrying a certain exotic quality in the imaginations of these Israelite story-tellers (perhaps analogous to the frisson caused in another Hebrew story when the Israelite leader Moses married a Cushite woman [Numbers 12.1], though in the present story about Solomon and the queen of Sheba there is no suggestion of marriage). But we can at least rule out one further possibility that the English text of the Annals might suggest, and that concerns the clan of Sheba mentioned among the Israelite tribe of Gad in 1 Chron. 5.13. That particular eponymous ancestor has a slightly different name in Hebrew, being *šebaʿ* (ending in the letter *ayin* rather than *aleph* and having a different vocalization in the reading tradition than *šĕbāʾ*), so he is not a contender here; but in any case it would be difficult to imagine that an Israelite clan would have had its own 'queen' who could come to Jerusalem as a kind of peer to the King of All Israel and exchange stupendous gifts with him before returning 'to her own land' (2 Chron. 9.12).

This majestic woman arrives in style, with 'a very great retinue and camels bearing spices and very much gold and precious stones' (9.1), and before she leaves she presents to Solomon '120 talents of gold, a very great quantity of spices, and precious stones—and there were no spices such as those that the queen of Sheba gave to King Solomon' (v. 9), so the Annals present her land of Sheba, whether it be populated by Shemitic or Hamitic peoples in their reckoning, as a wealthy territory and one particularly associated with the unmatched quality of its spices. Nonetheless, Sheba under its anonymous queen is no match for Israel under its wondrous King Solomon, for the latter is able to grant to the former a cornucopia of gifts 'well beyond what she had brought to the king' (v. 12).

This queen stands as exemplar for the contention of the Annals that 'all the kings of the earth sought the presence of Solomon to hear his wisdom, which the deity had put into his mind' (v. 23), in that she is presented as having come to Jerusalem 'to test him with hard questions' and to discuss with him 'all that was on her mind' (v. 1). His god-endowed mind is fully able to meet any challenge that her own royal mind could concoct, and so we find that he 'answered all her questions, and there was nothing hidden from Solomon that he could not explain to her' (v. 2). She is completely won over, and on behalf of all the kings of the earth she proclaims that the people of Israel are especially favoured, in that their god Yahweh has shown great love for them in setting the incomparable Solomon upon the throne of this kingdom (9.7-8). This panegyric partly echoes earlier words expressed by King Huram of Tyre (2.11-12), and indeed the very same Huram is brought into the picture again here in two notes about Solomon's ongoing trading activities (9.10, 21—actually the Hebrew text has 'Hiram' in v. 10, but this is presumably another of those scribal slippages between the letters *vav* and *yod* that we have observed several times in the Annals, and not least within the earlier mentions of Huram/Hiram). Having a non-Israelite royal personage express these sentiments before the temple-building project began and another such individual repeat the sentiments after that project has been completed is a well-rounded way of driving home to the Israelite readers of the Annals that King Solomon is to be regarded as utterly peerless, not only making Jerusalem wealthier than any other king of Israel could achieve (v. 27) but also 'excelling all the kings of the earth in riches and in wisdom' (v. 22). Or in other words, not only was Solomon bringing about things 'the like of which had never been seen before in the land of Judah' (v. 11)—and, we might add, would never be seen again in that land after him—but he was also bringing into fruition things 'the like of which were never made in any kingdom' whatsoever (v. 19).

The narrators list a number of things that they regard as outshining the accomplishments of Solomon's peers, from the splendid algum-wood steps that he supplied for both the temple and the palace (v. 11) to a great ivory throne overlaid with pure gold and fashioned with two lions at the sides of the throne itself and twelve further lions flanking the steps leading up to the throne (vv. 18-19). 300 golden shields, each containing 300 shekels of gold, and countless drinking vessels of pure gold, are to be seen in 'the House of the Forest of Lebanon' (vv. 16, 20), presumably a grand hall for spectacular regal occasions, probably constructed with the best quality timber from Lebanon and perhaps furnished with pillars and roof-beams that artistically replicated the appearance of a forest. The name of this structure, 'the House of the Forest of Lebanon', might also be intended to suggest the expansion of Solomon's realm into the area of Lebanon (an expansion mentioned in 8.2, 6). But Solomon's arms reach in a sense as far as the known world: in concert with those consummate seafarers the Tyrians—'the servants of Huram'— 'the king's ships went to Tarshish' (9.21), the farthest point west in the ancient Hebrew conception of the world (one might compare the efforts of that comic character Jonah to sail away to Tarshish in order to escape his responsibilities [Jonah 1.3]), and from such exotic climes 'once every three years the ships of Tarshish used to come bringing gold, silver, ivory, apes, and peacocks' (v. 13).

With the fruits of the whole world flowing to Jerusalem, it is little wonder that 'King Solomon excelled all the kings of the earth in riches', in addition to his fabled wisdom (v. 22). But that is still not enough for these Annals to claim. They also state that 'he ruled over all the kings from the Euphrates to the land of the Philistines, and to the border of Egypt' (v. 26). This is perhaps not too surprising an expanse of territory within the context of the Annals, for the picture had already been painted of an all-conquering David subduing the Philistines and the Moabites and the Edomites and the Ammonites and the Amalekites and the Arameans (1 Chron. 18–20); Solomon is simply maintaining control over these nations that had been bequeathed to him by his father. And in doing so, the Solomon depicted in these Annals just happens to be seen as exercising Israelite dominion over a region that certain Hebrew legends had delineated as having been promised to the descendants of Abraham (witness Genesis 15.18-21: 'On that day Yahweh made a covenant with Abram, saying, "To your descendants I give this land, from the [border] of Egypt to the great river, the river Euphrates"'). At the same time Solomon is depicted as having achieved in his reign a situation which certain Hebrew prophetic traditions dream of as taking place in the future, a magical time in which Jerusalem is seen as the centre of the earth and people from all the nations are seen streaming into it to drink from its wisdom and to marvel at its splendours (Isaiah 2.2-4; Micah 4.1-4). The Golden Age of Solomon was such a time, the Annalists appear to be saying; and perhaps they are also wanting to suggest that such an age can come again, if enough people will take up the closing challenge of the Annals to 'Go up [to Jerusalem]!' (2 Chron. 36.23) and will commit themselves to follow the examples of David and Solomon and to reject the policies and behaviours of the motley band of kings that came after Solomon.

The heights of Solomonic splendidness will never quite be scaled again in the Annals, despite the efforts of even such marvellous monarchs as Hezekiah and Josiah. That the Golden Age cannot last is already hinted at in the reference to 'the visions of the seer Iddo concerning Jeroboam son of Nebat' (9.29); it will not be long after Solomon is laid to rest that that prophesied character will step forward and seek to do what he had been unable to do so long as the wisest of all kings was on the throne in Jerusalem, namely to undermine the extent of the royal and religious system that David had so exhaustively instituted and that Solomon had so masterfully perfected. But even the incomparable Solomon is not immortal. After a perfectly rounded 40 years at the helm (v. 30), replicating the length of reign of his father David, the time comes for Solomon to 'sleep with his ancestors' and to be 'buried in the city of his father David' (v. 31). The two giant figures of the nation-builder David and the temple-builder Solomon have both now passed from the scene, and things will never be the same again.

REHOBOAM TO ZEDEKIAH

(2 CHRONICLES 10–36)

A Survey of Judah's Kings

A fundamental aspect of my reading of the book of Chronicles is
the observation that the storytellers responsible for setting out
this account of events in the reigns of the kings of Judah indulge
in a certain playfulness with the names of each of those kings. It
seems to me that the Annalists take delight in crafting an appropriate allusion to the royal name that almost always rebounds in
an unfavourable light on the monarch in question.

The discovery of such patterns in the literary world presented
in these Annals should perhaps come as no surprise. After all,
wordplay on the names of characters in a story is a significant
feature of storytelling in several places within the Hebrew Bible,
as indeed it is in many other literatures. The book of Genesis has
several splendid examples of such a literary feature, among
them the incident when the matriarch Sarah sees the son of
Hagar isaacking (in English: 'playing' or 'laughing') and resolves
that 'The son of this slave woman shall not inherit along with
my son Isaac!' (Genesis 21.9-10); or the incident when the
bumbling Esau complains about his sharper twin brother, 'Is he
not rightly called Jacob? For he has jacobbed me (in English:
'he has supplanted me') twice now!' (Genesis 27.36). These are
examples of clear punning that a Hebrew reader cannot miss.
But the charming little book of Ruth offers examples of how
names can play a role in the story-world without it being spelled
out as such. There the character Naomi, embittered by a threefold bereavement, says to her kinsfolk, 'Do not call me Naomi
any more' (Ruth 1.20); Hebrew readers do not need to be told that
the name 'Naomi' means 'pleasant' and is for that reason no
longer considered an appropriate designation for herself by its
holder. Similarly, when the hero appears on the scene, he is
simply introduced as Boaz (Ruth 2.1); Hebrew readers do not
need to be told that the name 'Boaz' means 'strength' and is for
that reason to be considered the perfect designation for the big
strong hero. And of course the name Ruth itself, pronounced
(though not fully spelt) in the same way as the Hebrew word for

'female companion', has a clear application in the tale of a young widowed woman who remained in solidarity with the said Naomi and became the perfect match for the said Boaz.

Examples of such a narrative technique can be found in many places in the Hebrew Bible. And indeed there are two particular cases in 2 Chronicles that are often brought forward as instances of wordplay on the name of a character. The first of these is the description of Bad King Asa consulting physicians—a pun that depends on a knowledge of the Aramaic language, in which the word ʾāsāʾ denotes a 'healer'. And the second instance is the description of Good King Jehoshaphat appointing judges—an allusion to his name that can readily be noticed by all readers of Hebrew, for the element šāpaṭ has to do with 'judging'. But Asa and Jehoshaphat are only two characters in the long sequence of nineteen kings of Judah whose tales are told one after the other in these Annals. To my mind there are many more examples of the tellers of the tales playing with the royal names, and including in the stories certain matters that bounce off the names or run up against them in an intriguing way. Before exploring the tales themselves, it is first necessary to establish whether the names have meanings that a Hebrew storyteller or writer could work with, and also whether Hebrew listeners or readers could be expected to perceive the playfulness that was being demonstrated, if indeed such artistry was deployed by the storytellers.

As it happens, the vast majority of the names of the kings of Judah present no problems on this score. Most of these names are simple compounds of a divine element and a verbal element. The divine element is an abbreviated form of the name of the national god, Yahweh, taking the form 'Yeho' or 'Yo' when it is the opening element of the compound human name, and the form 'Yahu' or 'Yah' when it is the concluding element. The other constituent of these royal names, the verbal element, expresses an activity for which the deity is praised or which it is hoped he will perform.

In accordance with this pattern, the name of the fourth king of Judah is Jehoshaphat, or in Hebrew yĕhôšāpāṭ —composed of the abbreviated divine name 'Yeho' (i.e. Yahweh) and the verb šāpaṭ which means 'to judge'; thus that royal name is a proclamation that 'Yahweh judges'. Similarly, the successor to that king is called Jehoram, or in Hebrew yĕhôrām (sometimes also found in the shorter form yôrām—evidently a conjoining of the divine element and *rām* which means 'to be exalted'; and so the national piety that 'Yahweh is exalted' is expressed in the monarch's name. So too we find that the tenth king is called Jotham, or in Hebrew *yôtām*—that is, 'Yo' plus *tām* which means 'to be complete or whole or perfect'; thus that name asserts that 'Yahweh is perfect'.

Towards the end of the monarchy, three kings in a row carry names consisting of 'Yeho' plus a verb. The sixteenth king of Judah is Jehoahaz, or in Hebrew *yĕhô'āḥāz*—and since the verb *'āḥaz* means 'to grasp or seize', then we have an expression claiming that 'Yahweh seizes', perhaps asserting that the national god takes hold of the king or that he acts dynamically through the king. The seventeenth king is Jehoiakim, or in Hebrew *yĕhôyāqîm*—the *yāqîm* part is the *hiphil* imperfect (that is, the continuing-action, causitive form) of the verb *qûm*, 'to get up or arise', and so the whole carries the meaning 'Yahweh raises up'. And the eighteenth king is Jehoiachin, or in Hebrew *yĕhôyākîn*—here the *yākîn* part is the *hiphil* imperfect of the verb *kûn*, 'to stand upright', and so this name proclaims that 'Yahweh establishes' or 'Yahweh makes firm'.

As it happens, the Annals are not consistent on the names of the three kings just mentioned. The name Jehoahaz appears in the brief story told in 2 Chronicles (36.1), but in the genealogical list in 1 Chronicles (3.15) the man is styled as Johanan, or in Hebrew *yôḥānān*—which couples a shorter divine element with the verb *ḥānan*, 'to be gracious', and thus proclaims that 'Yahweh is gracious'. His successor is mostly called Jehoiakim, but on one occasion (in 2 Chron. 36.4) he is called Eliakim instead, or in Hebrew *'elĕyāqîm* —which employs the pan-semitic designation of the deity while retaining the verbal element *yāqîm*, thus asserting that it is 'El [who] raises up'. And while Jehoiachin's story is told in 2 Chronicles (36.8-10), again the genealogical list in 1 Chronicles (3.16-17) styles things differently, this time reversing the elements of the name to give us Jeconiah, or in Hebrew *yĕkānyâ*—but leaving us with the same fundamental meaning of 'Yahweh establishes'.

Having mentioned the form Jeconiah, which places the divine element after the verb, we may list the other occurrences of that pattern. The sixth king of Judah is Ahaziah, or in Hebrew *'ăḥazĕyāhû*—that is, *'āḥaz*, 'to grasp or seize' plus 'Yahu': 'Yahweh seizes', exactly the same meaning as the name of Jehoahaz even though the constituent parts of the phrase are reversed (in fact the form 'Ahaz-Yah' rather than 'Yeho-ahaz' represents the normal order of things in a Hebrew sentence, but that is of no consequence when it comes to names welding together the verb and the subject into a compound form). Consider also the eighth king, Amaziah, or in Hebrew *'ămaṣĕyāhû* —evidently composed of the elements *'āmaṣ*, 'to be strong' and 'Yahu', and yielding the clear message that 'Yahweh is strong'. And similarly, the twelfth king, Hezekiah, or in Hebrew *yĕḥizĕqîyāhû*, links the so-called imperfect or forward-looking form of the verb *ḥāzaq*, 'to strengthen' with the divine element to express the confidence or the hope that 'Yahweh strengthens' the monarch and the nation.

A variation on these patterns can be seen when the divine element is matched with a nominal rather than a verbal element. Thus we find that the second king of Judah is called Abijah, or in Hebrew *'ăbîyâ* —that is, *'ăbî* ('my father') and 'Yah', thus asserting that 'Yahweh is my father' and calling to mind the words of the coronation psalm: 'I will tell of Yahweh's decree: he said to me, "You are my son; today I have begotten you"' (Psalm 2.7). The name of the ninth king, Uzziah, or in Hebrew *'uzzîyāhû*, proclaims that 'Yahu' (i.e Yahweh) is *'uzzî* ('my strength'); and the last reigning monarch over Judah, Zedekiah, or in Hebrew *ṣidĕqîyāhû*, bears the designation '"Yahu" (or Yahweh) is *ṣidĕqî* ("my righteousness")'.

All of the royal names mentioned so far are quite clearly combinations of the divine name Yahweh (or in one case El) with another well-known Hebrew word. But there is a smaller number of royal names among the kings of Judah which do not carry a divine element, and there are one or two cases in which no well-known Hebrew word is to be detected.

Those without a divine element but still with a clear verbal meaning are the first, eleventh, and thirteenth on the list, namely Rehoboam, Ahaz, and Manasseh. In the case of Rehoboam, or in Hebrew *rĕḥab'ām*, we see the verb *rāḥab* ('to become wide or large, to expand') coupled with *'am* ('people' or 'nation'); this can be read as 'the nation expands' or as 'he expands the nation', with the 'he' understood as the unnamed deity or as the king himself. In the case of Ahaz, we simply have the verbal expression *'āḥāz*, 'he grasps or he seizes', the same element as we have combined with a divine name in both Ahaziah and Jehoahaz; since here there is no divine name coupled with the expression, we might understand it as an unnamed deity taking dynamic action through the king or as the king himself being designated as one who acts dynamically. And in the case of Manasseh, or in Hebrew *měnaššeh*, we have the *piel* or intensive participle of the verb *nāšâ* ('to forget'). This latter name was not a new one in Israel; it had of course already been carried by an eponymous tribal ancestor, and its meaning had been specified in Genesis: 'Joseph named his first-born son Manasseh, "For", he said, "the deity has made me forget all my hardship and all my father's house"' (Genesis 41.51).

Four royal names remain, and two of those appear to resonate with non-Hebrew words. The third king of Judah, Asa or *'āsā'*, has a name that is not evidently Hebrew but is identical to the Aramaic word for 'physician' or 'healer'; and the fourteenth king, Amon or *'āmôn*, has a name which might be Hebrew (more on this later) but which is in any event identical to the Hebrew transliteration of the Egyptian god Amun, as seen in Jeremiah's oracle: 'See, I am bringing punishment upon *'āmôn* of Thebes, and Pharaoh, and Egypt and her gods and her kings' (Jeremiah 46.25).

That just leaves us with the onomastic uncertainty of the seventh king, Joash, and the fifteenth, Josiah. In Hebrew these are *yô'āš* and *yō'šiyāhû* respectively, and they appear to carry the same verbal element, perhaps the verb *'āšâ* but not indisputably so. Readers may wish to note that the English versions of the names mask the common verbal element by having no equivalent to the Hebrew letter *aleph* and by transliterating the Hebrew letter *shin* as 'sh' in the case of Joash but as 's' in the case of Josiah. But matters are already difficult enough in Hebrew, since one of the three root-letters of the verb is not evident in the form utilized for the name, and also because the name *yô'āš* is often spelt with a *vav* following the initial *yod*, which makes it look like the divine element 'Yo'. Indeed on several occasions in the book of Kings (though never in the book of Chronicles) the name is given in the form *yěhô'āš*, which indisputably opens with the divine designation. If the fullest spelling is accepted as the proper form of the name of the seventh king of Judah, *yod-he-vav-aleph-shin*, then the name would appear to be making the proclamation or expressing the hope that 'Yeho' does whatever action is denoted by the verb *'āš*. This would be the same expression, in reverse order, as that set forth in the name of the fifteenth king, *yō'šiyāhû*, which similarly is saying that 'Yahu' does whatever action is denoted by the verb *'āš*, there in the imperfect or forward-looking formation. The other possibility for *yô'āš* is that it too is the imperfect formation of *'āš* rather than being the divine element plus *'āš*, and that the shorter spelling of *yod* (for the imperfect) and then *aleph* and *shin* is to be accepted. In this case, the name Joash is simply stating that 'he *'āš*-es or 'may he *'āš*' without specifying whether it is the deity or the monarch who does the *'āš*-ing.

But what does it mean to speak of someone being called upon to *'āš* or being known for such an activity? The form *'āš* could derive from a hollow verbal root *'ûš* or from an initial-*vav* root *wā'aš* (or such a root transmogrified into an initial-*yod* stem *yā'aš*) or from a duplicated root *'āšaš* or from a final-*he* root *'āšâ*. Unfortunately none of these possible roots is commonly used in Biblical Hebrew, and so we moderns cannot say for certain what resonance there may have been in ancient Hebrew ears when they heard the names *yô'āš* and *yō'šiyāhû*. Of the possibilities just listed, only the verb *yā'aš* is to be found explicitly in the biblical literature, four times in a *niphal* or reflexive form and once in a *piel* or intensive form, neither of which give us the *qal* or simple active meaning that we might wish for the usage in these royal names; if nonetheless we were to accept as relevant here the presumed basic meaning of that particular root and apply it to the designations of the monarchs in question, we would have something like 'Yahweh despairs', a most unlikely name for royal parents to have bestowed upon the heir to the throne. Meanwhile a possible form of the verb *'āšaš* exists in one obscure instance in the Hebrew Bible, and that in the *hitpolel* or reflexive form, so a clear meaning for *'āš* can hardly be determined from that. There has been speculation among lexicographers about the possibility of a verb *'ûš*, which has been variously postulated to mean either 'to be strong' or 'to give', and if indeed a name like Josiah means 'Yahweh is strong' or 'Yahweh strengthens', then it would be analogous to the royal names Amaziah and Hezekiah, which yield such meanings through their verbal elements of *'āmas* and *hāzaq* respectively; or if indeed Josiah is a proclamation that 'Yahweh gives', then it is a similar kind of name to that of his son Johanan, whose name proclaims that 'Yahweh is gracious' through its verbal element of *hānan*.

But I am attracted to the suggestion of Wilhelm Gesenius and Martin Noth that we are to reckon with a verbal root *'āšâ*, which has not come down to us in Biblical Hebrew but which the lexicographers relate to a cognate Arabic root meaning 'to heal'. This would make it the Hebrew equivalent of the Aramaic root *'āsā'* that we have noted as resonating in the name of the third king of Judah, and would deliver a meaning of 'he heals' for the seventh king of Judah and the fuller proclamation that 'Yahweh heals' in the case of the fifteenth king. We will see in due course whether such a meaning can be seen as resonating in the tales of King Joash and of King Josiah told by the Annalists.

With some caution, then, regarding a very few of the names to be found on the king-list of Judah, we can confidently assert that almost all of the royal names would have easily carried a significance to the Hebrew reader, one that a Hebrew writer need not have to spell out to the audience for them to grasp. It is evident that, if an English-language play is called 'The Importance of Being Ernest', an English-speaking audience is already tuned to hear the resonance between the name and the character. Or when the proverbial Englishman of a previous generation heard accounts of the imperial successes of Queen Victoria, he could be expected to have the national prayer that God would 'send her victorious' resonating in his mind. But equally, if a British historian were to write about a great defeat suffered by the army of Queen Victoria, that writer need not necessarily spell out for readers the clear irony to be seen in the event over against the royal name. Or similarly, if an English storyteller were telling a story about a little girl called Joy and painted a picture of her as a sad and lonely figure, we English listeners or readers would clearly see the irony of the name within that story without any need for the writer to tell us what the name 'Joy' is supposed to convey.

It is my contention that just such a utilization of the names of each of the kings of Judah is discernible in the storytelling artistry of 2 Chronicles, not just in the cases previously identified by scholarship (namely Jehoshaphat appointing judges and Asa consulting physicians) but arguably in each and every case of all nineteen monarchs. If we work our way systematically through the list—from the first king, Rehoboam, to the last king, Zedekiah—with an eye to the specific royal names within the contexts of the particular royal stories, we find that the third and fourth kings on the list are not alone in the treatment they receive from the tellers of the tales.

Beginning, then, with the tale of Rehoboam (2 Chron. 10.1–12.16), the reader witnesses the great irony of the name 'Expanding Nation' being borne by the man under whose stewardship ten of the twelve tribes of Israel are lost to the kingdom. It all comes about because 'the king did not listen to the people (*hā'ām*)', and thus, 'when all Israel saw that the king would not listen to them, the people (*hā'ām*) answered the king, "What share do we have in David? We have no inheritance in the son of Jesse. Each of you to your tents, O Israel! Look now to your own house, O David!" So all Israel departed to their tents, and Rehoboam (*rĕḥab'ām*) reigned [only] over the Israelites who were living in the cities of Judah' (10.15-17). Yet despite this enormous shrinking of the nation under his rule, King Rehoboam does his bit to increase his people through vigorous procreative activity, for we read that 'he took 18 wives and 60 concubines, and became the father of 28 sons and 60 daughters' (11.18-23). All of these figures are considerably in excess of any other king of Judah in these accounts— and certainly far more wives and concubines than his father Solomon, who according to these Annals had modestly contented himself with just two wives, an Egyptian princess (8.11) and an Ammonite noblewoman (12.13), plus a dalliance with the Queen of Sheba (9.1-12). Thus no-one comes close to Rehoboam's efforts to expand the royal household, even as he shrinks the kingdom.

The major incident in the tale of Abijah (13.1-22) is a decisive battle between the northern Israelite forces and his own Judahite troops, and before the battle the King of Judah gives a rousing speech which ends with the call, 'O Israelites, do not fight against Yahweh, the god of your fathers!' (v. 12), exactly the kind of saying that ought to be attributed to a man living under the designation 'Yahweh is My Father'. The storytellers then relate that Yahweh 'defeated Jeroboam and all Israel before Abijah and Judah. The Israelites...were subdued at that time, and the people of Judah prevailed, because they relied on Yahweh, the god of their fathers' (vv. 15-18).

The tale of Asa (14.1–16.14) begins well, with the kingdom enjoying peace for several decades, but then, 'in the thirty-ninth year of his reign Asa was diseased in his feet, and his disease became severe; yet even in his disease he did not seek Yahweh, but sought help from physicians' (16.12). The storytellers do not spell out that the name 'Asa' is a term for 'Healer' or 'Physician' in the Aramaic language, though the story does bring this disease upon the king as a consequence of his having made an alliance with the king of Aram. One imagines that the early readers of this tale, presumably knowing the Aramaic language reasonably well and perhaps having consulted an *'āsā'* from time to time themselves, would have chuckled at this pun that juxtaposes the Aramaic word for 'physician' (the king's name *'āsā'*) with the Hebrew word for 'physicians' (*rōpě'îm*), and they would hardly have missed the irony of a so-called physician who cannot heal himself and cannot even find healing from others who are termed physicians, but instead sinks to an ignominious death.

The story of Jehoshaphat (17.1–20.37) is full of positive notes, including a reflection of his name 'Yahweh Judges' in a particular policy initiative: 'He appointed *judges* (*šōpěṭîm*) in the land in all the fortified cities of Judah, and said to the *judges* (*šōpěṭîm*), "Consider what you are doing, for you *judge* (*šāpaṭ*) not on behalf of human beings but on behalf of *Yahweh*; he is with you in giving *judgment* (*mišpāṭ*)..."' (19.5-7). However, despite his good sense in that matter, some time later 'King Jehoshaphat of Judah joined with wicked King Ahaziah of Israel in building ships to go to Tarshish, ...but [the prophet] Eliezer...prophesied against Jehoshaphat, saying, "Because you have joined with Ahaziah, Yahweh will destroy what you have made"; and the ships were wrecked and were not able to go to Tarshish, and Jehoshaphat [died] and was buried' (20.35–21.1). Thus did Yahweh decisively judge the Yahwistic judge-maker for joining with the apostates of the north.

The tale of Jehoram (21.1-20) demonstrates that the man does not match the sentiment of his name, 'Yahweh is Exalted', for we are told that 'when Jehoram had ascended the throne of his father and was established, he put all his brothers to the sword, and also some of the officials of Israel... He walked in the way of the kings of Israel, as the house of Ahab had done, for the daughter of Ahab was his wife. He did what was evil in Yahweh's sight' (vv. 4-6). Accordingly, 'Yahweh struck him in his bowels with an incurable disease, and in the course of time, at the end of two years, his bowels came out because of the disease, and he died in great agony' (vv. 18-19).

The account of the reign of Ahaziah (22.1-9) is a brief one. He is said to have reigned for just one year, 'walking in the ways of the house of Ahab, for his mother [Athaliah from the house of Ahab] was his counsellor in doing wickedly. He did what was evil in Yahweh's sight, as the house of Ahab had done; for after the death of his father they were his counsellors, to his ruin' (vv. 1-4). He certainly does come to a ruinous end, and indeed his name, 'Yahweh Seizes', symbolizes his fate, for 'it was divinely ordained that the downfall of Ahaziah should come about through his going to visit [his relative King Jehoram of Israel, son of King

Ahab]... Jehu son of Nimshi, whom Yahweh had anointed to destroy the house of Ahab, was executing judgment on the house of Ahab, and he [killed]...Ahaziah's nephews, who attended Ahaziah, and [then] he searched for Ahaziah, who was captured while hiding in Samaria and was brought to Jehu, and put to death' (vv. 7-9). We might say that the man called 'Yahweh Seizes' was comprehensively seized by Yahweh's anointed one.

The tale of Joash (22.10–24.27) begins with a non-Davidic interregnum during which the young boy is kept safe from the marauding Queen Athaliah. Then his own reign begins promisingly enough, but, after the death of his mentor Jehoiada the priest, Joash becomes a dishonourable king, and eventually he suffers a catastrophic defeat at the hands of 'the army of Aram'; this is Yahweh's doing, say the storytellers, 'because [the people of Judah] had abandoned Yahweh, the god of their fathers. Thus [the army of Aram] executed judgment on Joash. When they had withdrawn, leaving him severely wounded, his servants conspired against him because of the blood of the son of the priest Jehoiada, and they killed him on his bed' (24.24-25). This story too appears to be developing a certain ironic spin on the king's name, for, as we have seen, 'Joash' may mean 'He [i.e. the deity] Heals', whereas in fact the deity does not heal him after he is left severely wounded by the foreign forces, on account of his not having listened to the divine word that had been preached to him by the son of his former mentor. In all of this there are marked parallels with the name and fate of his descendant Josiah, as we shall see in due course.

But meanwhile the account of the reign of Amaziah (25.1-28) notes that 'he did what was right in Yahweh's sight, yet not with a true heart' (v. 2). Indeed later in his reign he compromises himself, in that 'he brought the gods of the people of Seir, set them up as his gods, and worshipped them, making offerings to them. Yahweh was angry with Amaziah and sent to him a prophet, who said to him, "Why have you resorted to a people's gods who could not deliver their own people from your hand?"' (vv. 14-15)—in other words, the king had forgotten what his very own name proclaimed, namely 'Yah[weh] is Strong'. The lesson that the god of Israel is indeed stronger than the gods of Seir is taught to King Amaziah through Yahweh determining 'to hand [Judah] over [to Israel], because they had sought the gods of Edom. Thus King Joash of Israel went up and faced King Amaziah of Judah in battle at Beth-shemesh, ...and Judah was defeated by Israel' (vv. 20-21). And for good measure, 'from the time that Amaziah turned away from Yahweh they made a conspiracy against him in Jerusalem, and he fled to Lachish; but they sent after him to Lachish, and killed him there' (v. 27).

The next king is listed in the Davidic genealogy in 1 Chronicles (3.12) as Azariah, but the account of his reign in 2 Chronicles (26.1-23) calls him Uzziah. The change of names is not explained, but presumably we are meant to think of this individual as having adopted a new name upon his accession to the throne, and it does seem that the throne-name 'Yahweh is My Strength' has more metaphorical force in the story of his reign than does the presumed childhood-name 'Yahweh Helps', for we read of the king's ill-advised attempt to perform a priestly act in the temple of Yahweh, with disastrous consequences: 'When the chief priest...and all the priests looked at him, he was leprous in his forehead. They hurried him out, and he himself hurried to get out, because Yahweh had struck him. King Uzziah was leprous to the day of his death, and being leprous lived in a separate house, for he was excluded from the house of Yahweh' (vv. 20-21). The moral of the story is to be found in the note that 'he had set himself to seek the deity in the days of Zechariah, who instructed him in the fear of the divine; and as long as he sought Yahweh, the deity made him prosper... But when he had become strong he grew proud, to his destruction, for he became false to his god Yahweh' (vv. 5, 16). If only he had remained true to his throne-name, 'Yahweh is My Strength', rather than thinking 'I myself am strong', things could have been very different in this story-world.

The story of Jotham (27.1-9) is a brief one, but it is a tale which befits a monarch called 'Yah[weh] is Perfect'. Such a one 'did what was right in Yahweh's sight' (v. 2) and 'became strong because he ordered his ways before his god Yahweh' (v. 6); the storytellers evidently believe that not much more needs to be said.

The tale of Ahaz (28.1-27) depicts a king who practised all 'the abominable practices of the nations whom Yahweh had driven out before the people of Israel', such as 'making cast images for the Baals', and 'making offerings in the valley of the son of Hinnom, and making his sons pass through fire', and 'sacrificing on the high places, on the hills, and under every green tree. Therefore', the narrators declare, 'his god Yahweh gave him into the hand of the king of Aram, who defeated him and took captive a great number of his people...and he was also given into the

hand of the king of Israel, who defeated him with great slaughter'
(vv. 1-5). All of this is appropriate for a king named 'He [i.e. the
deity] Seizes', and one might compare the similar destinies of his
ancestor Ahaziah and of his descendant Jehoahaz, both of whose
names connect the *ahaz* component with the specific divine name
Yahweh and accordingly mean 'Yahweh Seizes', and both of
whom are indeed seized by a divinely ordained act.

The tale of Hezekiah (29.1–32.33), in contrast to that of his
father, tells us that 'he did what was right in Yahweh's sight,
just as his ancestor David had done' (29.2). The name 'Yahweh
Strengthens' comes into significance in two episodes in his story.
The first is when King Sennacherib of Assyria invades Judah,
and King Hezekiah's response is to strengthen the fortifications
of Jerusalem and to encourage his people with the words, '*Be
strong (ḥizĕqû) and of good courage...for our god Yahweh is with
us*' (32.7-8)—and the narrators add that indeed 'the people were
encouraged by the words of *Hezekiah* (*yĕḥizĕqîyāhû*) King of Judah'
(v. 8). The second resonance with his designation as someone
whom Yahweh strengthens comes sometime after the Assyrian
threat has been thwarted by Yahweh's intervention: 'In those
days Hezekiah became sick and was at the point of death; he
prayed to Yahweh, and he answered him and gave him a sign'
(v. 24), with the eventual outcome that 'Hezekiah prospered in
all his works' (v. 30).

The account of the long reign of Manasseh (33.1-20) tells us at
first that 'he did what was evil in Yahweh's sight, according to
the abominable practices of the nations whom Yahweh had
driven out before the people of Israel. For he rebuilt the high
places that his father Hezekiah had pulled down, and erected
altars to the Baals, made sacred poles, worshipped all the host of
heaven, and served them' (vv. 2-3)—in other words, this man
who bears the name 'Forgetting' has forgotten all the lessons
that have been taught over many generations in this story-world
and not least in the contrast between his father's and grandfather's reigns. He will need to be reminded, and so we find that
'Yahweh spoke to Manasseh and to his people, but they gave no
heed. Therefore Yahweh brought against them the commanders
of the army of the king of Assyria, who took Manasseh captive in
manacles, bound him with fetters, and brought him to Babylon.
While he was in distress he entreated the favour of his god
Yahweh and humbled himself greatly before the god of his
fathers. He prayed to him, and the deity received his entreaty,

heard his plea, and restored him again to Jerusalem and to his kingdom. Then Manasseh knew that Yahweh indeed was divine' (vv. 10-13). He embarks on a new career of faithfulness, and is rewarded with a lengthy reign.

The account of the rather shorter reign of Amon (33.21-25) tells us that 'he did what was evil in Yahweh's sight, as his father Manasseh had done. Amon sacrificed to all the images that his father Manasseh had made, and served them. He did not humble himself before Yahweh, as his father Manasseh had humbled himself, but this Amon incurred more and more guilt, so his servants conspired against him and killed him in his house' (vv. 22-24). That is almost the entire account of Amon's brief reign in the Annals, and it seems to belie the meaning of his name in Hebrew, which is 'Craftsman' (so used in Proverbs 8.30's depiction of Wisdom as the 'Amon' or 'craftsman' at Yahweh's side during the creation of the world). More likely, then, in the context of these Annals is that we should think of this particular Israelite king's name in its Egyptian guise as the name of a certain deity, one which coincidentally happens to appear in a rather pertinent way in an Israelite oracle recorded in the book of Jeremiah: 'Yahweh of hosts, the god of Israel, has said: "See, I am bringing punishment upon Amon of Thebes, and Pharaoh, and Egypt and her gods and her kings, upon Pharaoh and upon those who trust in him. I will hand them over to those who seek their life"' (Jeremiah 46.25-26). In serving those non-Yahwistic images and not humbling himself before Yahweh, only to be killed by conspirators seeking his life, King Amon of Judah has fitted rather neatly into the pattern of that prophetic word from outside the Annals.

The tale of Josiah (2 Chron. 34.1–35.27) begins well, with the new king doing 'what was right in Yahweh's sight' (34.2). However, he suddenly embarks on the disastrous policy of confronting Pharaoh Neco of Egypt, whereupon 'Neco sent envoys to him, saying, "What have I to do with you, king of Judah? I am not coming against you today, but against the house with which I am at war; and heaven has commanded me to hurry. Cease opposing the one who is with me, so that he will not destroy you." But Josiah would not turn away from him, but disguised himself in order to fight with him. He did not listen to the words of Neco from the mouth of the deity, but joined battle in the plain of Megiddo. The archers shot King Josiah; and the king said to his servants, "Take me away, for I am badly wounded". So his servants...brought him to Jerusalem, and there he died' (35.20-24). Once again this is a story that appears to contain an ironic spin on the king's name 'Josiah', for the name may mean 'Yahweh Heals', whereas in fact the deity does not heal him after he is left severely wounded by the archers, on account of his not having listened to the divine word that had been proclaimed to him by the pharaoh. The parallels with his ancestor Joash, whose name seems to use the same verbal element as that in Josiah but leaves the name of the deity unexpressed (simply 'He Heals') and whose fate is remarkably similar, are too marked to be entirely coincidental in this story-world.

Josiah's firstborn son is called Johanan ('Yahweh is Gracious') in the genealogical list in 1 Chronicles (3.15), but in the telling of the tale in 2 Chronicles (36.1-3) he carries the more appropriate name of Jehoahaz ('Yahweh Seizes'), for after a mere three months on the throne the young man is unceremoniously deposed and carried off to Egypt.

The story of Jehoiakim (36.4-8) sees him elevated to the throne in the following way: 'The king of Egypt made [Jehoahaz's] brother Eliakim king over Judah and Jerusalem, and changed his name to Jehoiakim' (v. 4). These two forms of his name—'El Raises Up' and 'Yahweh Raises Up'—both express confidence in the divine choice of this ruler, yet after a decade-long reign he is deposed by the Babylonian imperial authorities. Thus Yahweh brings down the one whom he had raised up, since the king 'did what was evil in the sight of his god Yahweh' (v. 5), including various 'abominations' and other matters that were 'found against him' (v. 8).

The penultimate king of Judah also carries two different names in the Annals: when first listed in the Davidic genealogy in 1 Chronicles (3.16-17) he is styled as Jeconiah, but when it later comes to a description of his brief reign in 2 Chronicles (36.9) he is styled Jehoiachin. Readers are left to suppose that this may be an analogous case to that of his father, concerning whom it is reported that 'the king of Egypt...changed his name' (v. 4), but in any case the two names appear to be simple variations on each other, since they each contain the two elements that make up the meaning 'Yahweh Establishes' or 'Yahweh Makes Firm'. However, expressing such a hope in two different ways does the new eight-year-old king no good; he reigns for a mere 'three months and ten days in Jerusalem' before 'in the spring of the year King Nebuchadnezzar sent and brought him to

Babylon, along with the precious vessels of the house of Yahweh, and made his brother Zedekiah king over Judah in Jerusalem' (vv. 9-10).

Finally, the tale of Zedekiah (36.11-21) brings the reign of the house of David to an end. The last king of Judah bears the name 'Yahweh is My Righteousness', yet this king 'did what was evil in Yahweh's sight, did not humble himself before the prophet Jeremiah who spoke from the mouth of Yahweh', and refused to 'return to Yahweh' (vv. 12-13). Indeed, under his reign, according to the storytellers, the people of Judah 'were exceedingly unfaithful, ...polluted the house of Yahweh, ...[and] kept mocking the deity's messengers, despising his words and scoffing at his prophets, until Yahweh's wrath against his people became so great that there was no remedy' (vv. 14-16). And so it is that the righteous Yahweh terminates the reign of Zedekiah and indeed suspends the kingdom of Judah altogether.

This swift survey through the accounts in the Annals concerning the kings of Judah has demonstrated that for each king there is something of a play-on-words or an ironic twist to the royal name, such that the designation of the monarch turns out to be related to a specific aspect of his reign. This literary device is in fact considerably more prominent in these Annals than it is in the parallel stories to be found in the book of Kings, to the extent that it appears to have been a deliberate feature of the Annalists' telling of the tales.

The scholars who have already pointed out the puns on the names of Jehoshaphat (the king who appoints judges to judge on Yahweh's behalf) and Asa (the king who seeks help from physicians) have noted that neither of those puns are to be found in the book of Kings. The whole episode of Jehoshaphat and the Yahwistic judges is absent from Kings; and of Asa's end it is simply said that 'in his old age he was diseased in his feet, and Asa slept with his fathers and was buried with his fathers in the city of his father David' (1 Kings 15.23-24)—there is nothing in that matter-of-fact telling about seeking help from physicians or anyone else; only the Annalists put the sting in his tale by having a chuckle about the so-called physician who cannot be healed.

If we look to the further twists that I have identified in the Annalists' storytelling concerning the names of the other kings of Judah, it can be observed that these twists too are not to be found (or at least not in the same developed way) in the book of

Kings. The major incident in the Annalists' tale of Abijah, wherein King 'Yahweh is My Father' delivers that stirring speech urging the Israelites not to fight 'against Yahweh, the god of your fathers', is completely absent from the book of Kings. So too the stirring speech of Hezekiah, in which King 'Yahweh Strengthens' encourages his people with the words 'Be strong and of good courage...for our god Yahweh is with us', can only be heard in the Annals. The framing of the tale of Jehoram, in which King 'Yahweh is Exalted' puts all his brothers to the sword and Yahweh in turn strikes him in his bowels and has him die in lingering great agony, plays no part in the narrative of Kings. The particular irony of the reign of Amaziah, whose name proclaims that 'Yahweh is Strong' but whose actions proclaimed that the gods of Seir were a match for the god of Judah, is not set out in the Kings account. Similarly, Kings does not spell out that so long as King Uzziah remained true to his name 'Yahweh is My Strength', Yahweh made him prosper, but as soon as he thought 'I myself am strong' and became false to Yahweh, Yahweh demonstrated the divine power. And the great turn-around in the fate of Manasseh, with notorious King 'Forgetfulness' being brought to his senses by a spell in a Babylonian dungeon, remembering the god of his fathers and acknowledging Yahweh throughout the rest of his now-restored reign, is such a contrast with the account of the completely unrepentant and thoroughly castigated King Manasseh in the book of Kings that one can hardly imagine that the two versions of events are talking about the same character.

Matters are even clearer when consideration is given to the kings of Judah who share a key element in their names. In the survey of the kings in sequence, it was noted that there is a remarkable parallel in the fates of King Joash and King Josiah, both of whose names have the key element of 'āš, quite possibly from the root 'āšâ and therefore plausibly meaning 'he heals'. In the Annalists' telling, both Joash and Josiah ignore a clear word from Yahweh and are thereupon wounded in battle and are manifestly not healed by Yahweh. The book of Kings makes no such connections between these two monarchs: neither of them receives and ignores any word from Yahweh that would make their respective fates deserved under a scheme of divine retribution, and indeed King Joash is not wounded in battle at all, but is the victim of a nefarious conspiracy within the royal household. It seems that the Annalists have conformed the dénouements of these two kings to parallel each other on the basis of their names having the same essential meaning. Indeed it is interesting to note that an incidental similarity that the book of Kings has between the deaths of King Josiah and King Ahaziah, namely that both those monarchs received a fatal blow at Megiddo and were then carried back to Jerusalem in their chariot, is not to be found in the Annals. Ahaziah's name is quite distinct from Josiah's name, and so Ahaziah is not in Megiddo and he does not have a chariot-journey back to Jerusalem, as far as the Annals are concerned.

But Ahaziah does share the key element of his name with two other kings of Judah, namely Ahaz and Jehoahaz, and so it is with those two that he is to be compared in the Annals. Accordingly we find that the crucial expression in the Annalists' version of the tale of Ahaziah, making it clear that the capture and execution of King 'Yahweh Seizes' was from the hand of the deity himself rather than simply by the hand of the multiple-king-slayer Jehu, is unique to the Annals. So too the crucial expression in the Annalists' version of the tale of Ahaz, making it clear that the devastating defeat of King 'He Seizes' (i.e. 'The Deity Seizes') was the work of the deity himself in giving Judah over into the hand of the king of Aram and the hand of the king of Israel, is only to be seen in the Annals. In the case of Jehoahaz, the storytellers are so keen to get him out of the way in one short verse that no spelling out of Yahweh standing behind events is felt necessary, and so this King 'Yahweh Seizes' is simply swept off the stage by the king of Egypt.

A small number of the other kings also have such short tales that the telling seems not to have space to draw out the meaning of the name with great deliberation. For Jotham, the Annalists simply add (over against the even briefer tale in Kings) that he received great amounts of tribute from the Ammonites and that he 'became strong because he ordered his ways before his god Yahweh' (2 Chron. 27.6). For Amon, the small addition is that 'he did not humble himself before Yahweh, as his father Manasseh had humbled himself, but this Amon incurred guilt more and more' (33.23). And in the cases of Jehoiakim and Jehoiachin, the narrative in the Annals becomes breathlessly briefer than the narrative in the book of Kings, as we rush headlong towards the supreme irony of Yahweh's ultimate overthrow of the kingdom reigned over by monarchs bearing such names as 'Yahweh Raises Up' and 'Yahweh Makes Firm'.

The very last monarch to reign over this kingdom is called Zedekiah, and here the Annalists pause, to spell out (as the book of Kings does not) that King 'Yahweh is My Righteousness' 'stiffened his neck and hardened his heart against turning to Yahweh, the god of Israel; and all the leading priests and the people likewise were exceedingly unfaithful, following all the abominations of the nations, and they polluted the house of Yahweh which he had hallowed in Jerusalem...and they kept mocking the messengers of the deity, despising his words, and scoffing at his prophets, until Yahweh's wrath against his people became so great that there was no remedy' (36.13-16). In the Annalists' telling, then, the most unrighteous of kings brings the kingdom of Judah to a horrid end. The all-righteous Yahweh simply must act to wipe out such pollution; the last royal name ironically implies that nothing less could be expected.

But also in the Annals the last royal name is set up at the very beginning of the story of the kingdom of Judah as a separate realm, in the tale of Rehoboam. We have seen that Rehoboam's name means 'Expanding Nation', yet he presides over the defection of the northern tribes to leave little Judah to its own affairs. That particular irony is also to be found in the book of Kings, although the Annalists' extra touch concerning Rehoboam's expansion of the royal household is not part of the Kings account. And the Annalists in fact work in to the tale of Rehoboam an allusion to the final royal name, when the first king of Judah and his officers humble themselves and say, 'Yahweh is righteous' (*ṣadıq yahweh*) (2 Chron. 12.6). The narrators lay down the message, 'Because he humbled himself, Yahweh's wrath turned from him, so as not to destroy them completely' (v. 12). If only King 'Yahweh is My Righteousness' had taken the same attitude in that respect as had King 'Expanding Nation', Yahweh would not have felt the need to destroy the nation completely in the time of the nineteenth king of Judah.

This survey has looked at the nineteen kings of Judah. But of course the Annals also tell the tales of a number of other monarchs, namely a Queen Athaliah who reigns in Judah for a few years and three kings who predate the kingdom of Judah, namely Saul and David (whose tales are told in 1 Chronicles) and Solomon, so something should perhaps also be said about those monarchs.

Athaliah need not detain us for too long, since she is spoken of as an interloper who is not rightfully reigning, a daughter of an apostate kingdom who seizes the throne for a time before the true heir can be brought out of hiding to take his rightful seat. She evidently carries a Yahwistic name, in Hebrew ʿătalĕyāhû, but since the verb ʿātal is not known in Hebrew, little more can be said. Perhaps the Annalists would prefer us to think that she is really quite foreign to Hebrew thinking, and cannot—or indeed should not—be dignified with any puns or playfulness on her name.

This is not the case, though, when it comes to a consideration of the first king of all Israel, and in this discussion of the Annalists' name-spinning it is very instructive to make a comparison of the two versions of the downfall of Saul. In Hebrew this name is šāʾûl—a name that takes the form of the passive participle of the verb šāʾal, and accordingly carries the meaning of 'the one who is asked for', one who is very much wanted by his parents, or by a nascent nation looking for a regal figure to lead them into a bold new future. The book of Samuel ventures a pun on this name in its account of Saul's undoing: we are told that 'when Saul (šāʾûl) inquired (šāʾal) of Yahweh, Yahweh did not answer him, not by dreams, not by Urim, nor by prophets; then Saul said to his servants, "Seek out for me a woman who is a medium, so that I may go to her and inquire of her"' (using in the latter case of 'inquire' the verb dāraš) (1 Samuel 28.6-7). The story goes on to tell of Saul using a medium at Endor to bring up from the ground the departed prophet Samuel, in order to ask him what the king should do about the Philistine enemy that is pressing hard against him; and of course Saul is not pleased with the answer he receives, just as the storytellers are not at all pleased with the practice of necromancy in which Saul is indulging.

Now when we compare the Annalists' version of Saul's downfall, we read that 'Saul (šāʾûl) died for his unfaithfulness; he was unfaithful to Yahweh in that he did not keep Yahweh's command, and moreover he inquired (šāʾal) of a medium, seeking guidance (šāʾal), and did not seek guidance (dāraš) from Yahweh' (1 Chron. 10.13-14). There is more here than simply a decision on the part of these narrators to use šāʾal as well as dāraš for Saul's directing of an inquiry towards the world of the dead: the writers have fashioned the expression in such a way that the infinitive construct form šĕʾōl appears, where a finite form of the verb would have worked just as well. The choice of verb-form, as well as the choice of verb itself, suggests a further play-on-words is intended at this point. In part the wordplay is as it is in the book of Samuel, namely that Saul, 'the one who was asked for', is being depicted as a sauler, one who asks questions that ought not to be asked, or at least asks the wrong people. But if that were the extent of the wordplayfulness in the Annals, the perfect tense of the verb would have achieved the objective. In fact, though, a double pun is achieved through the use of the form *šĕ'ôl* in the description of where the king directed his oracular inquiry: he sought through a medium to gain answers from the world of the dead, that shadowy underworld known in Hebrew precisely as Sheol.

Incidentally, this wordplay in the Annals on the Hebrew name of the underworld suggests the intriguing possibility that the designation Sheol might actually mean 'a place to which questions are put', and thus that that noun had arisen from ancient necromantic practices considered anathema by the official Hebrew cult. At least it shows—together with the frequent use of the cognate verb *šā'al* to denote the consulting of oracles—that *šĕ'ôl* can readily be understood in that way. But for our present purposes, all we need to take from the episode is the evidence that the Annalists out-pun the book of Samuel when it comes to making a stinging rebuke of the failed King Saul. Saul has not only wrongly sauled, as he did in that other account of his failure, but he has sheoled a medium; he looked to the realm of the dead to give him guidance, instead of to the heavenly realm, to Yahweh—and 'therefore Yahweh put him to death' (1 Chron. 10.14). He who had sought Sheol, goes to Sheol.

Turning to the successful King Solomon, there is no sting to be found in the account in the Annals—rather, readers find that any rebuke of Solomon that may be made or implied in the book of Kings (such as his legendary multiple marriages and tolerance of non-Yahwistic devotion alongside the temple of Yahweh) is studiously avoided. But an explicit and entirely positive outworking of the meaning of his name is made in the Annals, whereas no such thread is played upon in the other account. In the thoroughly peaceful transfer of power from David to Solomon that is to be observed in the Annals—as opposed to the murderous court intrigues laid bare in the succession narrative of Samuel and Kings—the retiring monarch proclaims to his young successor, 'My son, I had planned to build a house to the name of my god Yahweh, but the word of Yahweh came to me, saying, "You have shed much blood and have waged great wars;

you shall not build a house to my name, because you have shed
so much blood in my sight on the earth. See, a son shall be born
to you; he shall be a man of rest, and I will give him rest from all
his enemies on every side, for his name shall be Solomon (*šĕlōmōh*),
and I will give peace (*šālôm*) and quiet to Israel in his days"'
(1 Chron. 22.7-9). Now nothing quite like this is expressed in the
famous dynastic oracle of 2 Samuel 7 (nor indeed in the parallel
reporting of the oracle in 1 Chronicles 17); there the prophet
Nathan is represented as proclaiming on Yahweh's behalf that
'when your days are fulfilled and you lie down with your ancestors, I will raise up your offspring after you, who shall come
forth from your body, and I will establish his kingdom, and he
shall build a house for my name' (2 Samuel 7.12-13). The name
of this offspring is not prophesied, although there is some talk
about the necessary rest that is required in the nation's affairs
to allow for Yahweh's house to be built: thus the prophet declares
that 'I will appoint a place for my people Israel and will plant
them, so that they may live in their own place, and be disturbed no
more, ...and I will give you rest from all your enemies' (7.10-11).
Interestingly, the Annalists do not have Nathan report the divine
words as 'I will give you rest (*wahănihôti lĕkā*) from all your
enemies', but rather 'I will subdue (*wĕhikĕna'ĕtî*) all your enemies';
instead, in the Annals at a considerably later time David reports
the deity as having said 'I will give *him* rest' (*wahănihôti lô*) and
'he shall be a man of rest' (an *'îš mĕnûhâ*), as well as spelling out
that 'his name shall be *šĕlōmōh*, and I will give *šālôm* and quiet to
Israel in his days'.

Clearly the Annalists have tied the specific name of Solomon
to their account of his reign in a way that the compilers of Samuel
and Kings did not. Indeed depicting Solomon's reign as a reign of
peace is not sustainable in the account in the book of Kings, since
there we find not only a bloodthirsty beginning to his reign in
the removal of sundry individuals who might threaten his accession to the throne, but also far-from-peaceful latter days to his
reign in the invasions of sundry kings, chieftains, warlords and
rebels. However, styling *šĕlōmōh* as the very embodiment of *šālôm*
is highly effective in the fundamentally different picture painted
in the Annals, wherein none of those considerably negative
incidents are to be found. At least the translation panels of the
RSV and NRSV think that it is an excellent literary device in the
book of Chronicles; they are so captivated by the ploy that they
bring it in for the Hebrew text's usages of *nûah* and *mĕnûhâ* as

well as *šālôm*, thus gushing rather repetitively that 'he shall be a man of peace, [and] I will give him peace from all his enemies on every side, for his name shall be Solomon, and I will give peace and quiet to Israel in his days'. But we need not go to the extent of those renderings to observe that Solomon's name has been made to resonate powerfully in the Annalists' telling of his tale.

Of course in the case of that monarch, whom the Annalists have evidently portrayed as the uniquely blessed builder of the temple of Yahweh, it is not a question of any 'sting in the tale', as it is in the case of the kings of Judah, and as it is in the case of the initial quasi-king Saul. Although the northern tribes draw away from the Davidic monarchy as soon as Solomon is no longer on the scene, and they make an accusation that Solomon had 'placed a heavy yoke' upon them (2 Chron. 10.4), it is not evident in the Annalists' narrative that the reader ought to give any credence to the accusation; rather it might be deduced that the northerners, under the influence of the rebellious Jeroboam son of Nebat and 'certain worthless scoundrels [who] gathered around him' (13.7), were engineering a contrivance to break away from 'the kingdom of Yahweh in the hand of the sons of David' (v. 8). Hence there is discord after the time of Solomon in the Annalists' narrative, but there is no irony in their book's depiction of the kingdom under Solomon himself being a peaceful and quiet kingdom.

And so too in the case of the incomparable David, the Annalists have avoided the kind of ironic twist that they seem to enjoy giving to the names of the lesser mortals whose reigns they describe. And in this case alone, the boot is on the other foot insofar as a comparison with the telling of the tale in the book of Samuel is concerned, for it is the other account that appears to make some play with the meaning of the name David, while the Annals have none of those instances. The narrative in Samuel frequently speaks of people loving David. 'And David came to Saul and entered his service, and Saul loved him greatly...and sent to Jesse, saying, "Let David remain in my service, for he has found favour in my sight"' (1 Samuel 16.21). 'When David had finished speaking to Saul, the soul of Jonathan was bound to the soul of David, and Jonathan loved him as his own soul' (18.1). 'Now Saul's daughter Michal loved David, and Saul was told, and the thing pleased him' (18.20). 'David had success in all his undertakings, for Yahweh was with him; so when Saul saw that he had great success, he stood in awe of him, and all Israel and Judah loved David, for it was he who marched out and came in leading them' (18.14-16).

Now all of these instances, and others besides, employ the common Hebrew verb for love in all its guises, namely the verb *'āhab*. This is not of course the verb *dûd*, which underlies the name David, but that is because strictly verbal forms of *dûd* are not generally used in Biblical Hebrew; various derivatives from it, like *dôd* ('lover'), *dôdîm* ('love-making'), and *dûdā'îm* ('love-apples' or 'mandrakes'), are used in the Hebrew Bible, but the verb itself seems not to have been available to narrators to use in their narratives, whereas *'āhab* was apparently in everyday use as the verb to describe the full panoply of love. However, we should note the phrasing that the book of Samuel uses after the birth of David's heir, for we are told that 'Yahweh loved him [i.e. the baby Solomon], and sent a message by the prophet Nathan; so he named him Jedidiah, because of Yahweh' (2 Samuel 12.24-25). The name Jedidiah, or in Hebrew *yĕdîdĕyâ*, is evidently composed of the imperfect or forward-looking form of the verb *dûd* plus the divine element Yah, and is clearly taken to mean 'Yahweh loves' or 'Beloved of Yahweh'. Since the verb in the accompanying phrase 'Yahweh loved him' is *'āhab*, the narrators show that the single constituent element of David's name and the repeated talk of David being the object of the verb *'āhab* is to be connected. David too is 'beloved', by everybody who encounters him, it seems, and by the entire nation. Although he himself is not styled as Jedidiah, it is clear that he has incontrovertibly found favour in Yahweh's sight. He is the golden boy, the quintessential charismatic hero, loved by the king and the king's son and the king's daughter and by all Israel and Judah.

Incidentally, an intriguing aspect of the book of Samuel is that it never quite seems to say that David actually loves anybody. Did he love Saul or just give him the grudging respect that a king should receive? Did he love Jonathan or just appreciate Jonathan's selfless love for him? Did he love Michal or just regard her as the reward for his victories over the Philistines? Did he love the nation or just see it as his destiny to reign over the children of Israel? Even where our English translations want to say that he loved someone, in the line of lamentation 'I am distressed for you, my brother Jonathan; greatly beloved were you to me' (2 Samuel 1.26), the Hebrew text of Samuel employs neither *'āhab* nor *dûd*, but instead says *nā'ămĕtā lî mĕ'ōd*, 'you were very pleasant to me'. Similarly, the lament has David speak of 'your love for me' (*'ahăbātĕkā lī*), but not of 'my love for you' (which would be *'ahăbātî lĕkā*). But I digress somewhat; the point is that David's name means 'beloved', so he does not have to love, he merely has to be loved, to live up to his name. And in the book of Samuel he certainly does live up to it.

Yet in the Annals there is no wordplay on the belovedness of the great king. He is David, pure and simple, and the verb *'āhab* makes not a single appearance in the telling of his story. To be sure, the same divine favour is upon him—'David became greater and greater, for Yahweh...was with him' (1 Chron. 10.9; cf. 2 Samuel 5.10)—but in the Annalists' account he is single-minded in his work for Yahweh, so stories about his relation-ships with sundry mortals encountered along the way find no place here. It is of no consequence in the Annals whether Saul or Jonathan or Michal or indeed any other individual loved David; what is of consequence is that David worked tirelessly in the cause of Yahweh, establishing the kingdom and then making all the preparations necessary for the building and subsequent functioning of Yahweh's temple. In the Annalists' account, David's first words (in 1 Chron. 11.6) are an exhortation to the Israelites to seize Jerusalem, and his last words (in 29.20) are an exhorta-tion to the Israelites to 'bless your god Yahweh'. On this telling, then, all the acts of King David, from first to last, are devoted to the glory of Israel's god through the founding of a political and religious system that sweeps all before it. This is simply too grand an enterprise to be distracted by talk of 'love'.

David stands alone, then, in the Annals, in having no puns or playfulness surrounding his name, even though the book of Samuel alludes on several occasions to the meaning of that particular name, and not necessarily with a positive connotation. Solomon somewhat similarly stands with his head held high in the Annals, in that, although the book does introduce a kind of pun on his name, it carries an entirely honourable nuance and it is not undermined in the telling of the tale. But when it comes to the tales of the other kings, while the writers of the book of Kings rarely indulge in name-spinning, the scribes that worked on the Annals seem to have taken delight in crafting an appropriate allusion to the royal name that almost always appears to rebound in an unfavourable light on the monarch in question.

It can, then, be concluded that the giving of ironic twists to the royal names is a deliberate feature of the telling of the tales in these Annals. It is a further indication of the systematization of accounts and the tying up of loose ends that characterizes the work of the Annalists. Throughout the entire parade of nineteen kings of Judah that pass before us on the pages of 2 Chronicles, from the story of Rehoboam 'the Enlarger' who shrinks the kingdom to the story of Zedekiah 'the Righteous' who profanes the divine name, each of the kings has a 'sting in his tale'.

2 Chronicles 10–12:
Rehoboam 'the Enlarger'

Chapter 10

The son of the all-wise King of All Israel shows himself to be a singularly inadequate successor, achieving the exact opposite of what his optimistic name had proclaimed as his father's aspiration for the kingdom. Solomon had captured and fortified new areas of territory (8.3-6), had brought various non-Israelite groups under firmer control (8.7-8), and had expanded his trading ventures into far-flung realms (8.17-18; 9.14, 21). The kingdom which was bequeathed to his son Rehoboam was said to extend hyperbolically 'from the Euphrates to the land of the Philistines, and to the border of Egypt' (9.26). In bestowing the name 'Expanding Nation' (Hebrew *rĕḥabʿām*, more precisely 'the nation expands' or 'he expands the nation') upon his successor, Solomon may be presumed to be calling upon the heavens to continue through his son the golden age of ever-increasing prosperity and success that the people have witnessed under Solomon's own rule. This child is intended to be the one to continue the good work, and to carry the Davidic blessing even further than has been achieved so far.

But alas, Rehoboam does not begin his reign as his father had done, with an act of devotion to the national deity (Solomon's first act at 1.2-6), nor do we see him praying a prayer like that of Solomon when he had ascended to the throne: 'O Yahweh...you have made me king over a people as numerous as the dust of the earth; give me now wisdom and knowledge to go out and come in before this people, for who can rule this great people of yours?' (1.9-10). Instead we see Rehoboam presume that the kingdom is his to do with as he pleases, and that the people may be treated as harshly as he wishes. But Yahweh has other ideas.

The scene begins with 'all Israel' assembled at Shechem in the central north of the kingdom 'to make [Rehoboam] king' (10.1). It seems reminiscent of those earlier scenes in which 'all Israel were of a single mind to make David king' (1 Chron. 12.38) and 'all the leaders and the mighty warriors, and also all the sons of King David, pledged their allegiance to King Solomon, and Yahweh highly exalted Solomon in the sight of all Israel' (1 Chron. 29.24-25). But on this occasion 'all Israel' includes a certain individual, 'Jeroboam son of Nebat' (2 Chron. 10.2), whose machinations at the ceremony cause things to unravel.

This individual had been mentioned at the end of the story of Solomon, in a brief reference to the existence of 'visions of the seer Iddo concerning Jeroboam son of Nebat' (9.29). In that verse it might also be inferred that there was a 'prophecy of Ahijah the Shilonite' that similarly concerned the said Jeroboam, but in any case later here in ch. 10 it is made clear that there was a word of Yahweh 'which he had spoken by Ahijah the Shilonite to Jeroboam son of Nebat' (v. 15). Readers of the Annals are not let in on what the prophet Ahijah had said to Jeroboam, nor what Iddo the seer had said about him, but we are told that he had been 'in Egypt, where he had fled from King Solomon' (v. 2), and that he returned now to Israelite territory only upon the death of Solomon, ready to cause trouble for Solomon's successor. The inference that the Annalists invite us to make is that Jeroboam son of Nebat was a known trouble-maker in Solomon's time, that various seers had prophesied that he would seek the kingdom for himself, and that he had had to flee in order to save his skin and to plot his eventual grab for power.

Jeroboam's stratagem at Rehoboam's coronation is to have the people say to the fresh-faced monarch, 'Your father made our yoke heavy; now therefore lighten the hard service of your father and his heavy yoke that he placed on us, and we will serve you' (v. 4). Such talk of a heavy Solomonic yoke is an outrageous accusation within these Annals. The Annalists had made it clear that although Solomon had 'conscripted forced labour' from various Canaanite ethnic groups that 'were not of Israel' (8:7-8), 'of the people of Israel Solomon made no slaves for his work; they were soldiers, and his officers, the commanders of his chariotry and cavalry' (8.9). The Queen of Sheba had expressed the situation as the Annalists would want us to see it: 'Happy are your people! Happy are these your servants, who continually attend you and hear your wisdom! Blessed be your god Yahweh who has delighted in you and set you on his throne as king for your god Yahweh. Because your god loved Israel and wished to establish them forever, he has made you king over them, so that you may execute justice and righteousness' (9.7-8). In the Annalists' story-world, the people of Israel had never had it so good as they experienced under Solomon, and they would never have it so good again. Jeroboam's contention that 'Your father made our yoke heavy' must be rejected by readers of the Annals—unless we are to think of the son of Nebat as a spokesperson for the non-Israelite forced labourers, which would be a splendid widening of 'the people' of 'all Israel' to include the subjugated Canaanite peoples. Such empathy for those unfortunate non-citizens who stand oppressed under the picture of Israelite imperialism in the Annals is unlikely to have been in the minds of the Annalists, but nonetheless it is interesting that the 'taskmaster over the forced labour' is stoned to death by 'the people of Israel' a little later in the story (in v. 18). Presumably, though, that incident comes about because of Rehoboam's attempt to implement his announced policy of expanding his father's yoke by sending the said taskmaster among the Israelites.

The counsellors who had attended Solomon during his reign might have been expected to react with some irritation or bemusement to Jeroboam's accusation about how matters stood under the old regime, but they show the kind of wisdom that we imagine them having used throughout the days in which they interacted with the all-wise Solomon himself. They advise the new monarch, 'If you will be kind to these people and please them, then they will be your servants forever' (v. 7). The implication in the Annalists' story-world is that the people at large had been Solomon's servants throughout his entire reign because he had pleased them and lavished good things upon them. Jeroboam may have been unhappy because of his desire to reign (and once he does achieve his desire, his people will become desperately unhappy under the wickedness of his regime and that of his successors), but the people as a whole enjoyed unparalleled wholeness (*šālôm*) under the skilful hand of Solomon (*šělōmōh*; see 1 Chron. 22.9 for the spelling out of this connection). The golden age can continue, if Rehoboam shows himself to be as wise as his father, and accepts the counsel of his father's counsellors.

But it is not to be. Rehoboam fails to see the wisdom in the older men's counsel, and seeks a second opinion, from younger and less experienced heads. With the zealotry of youth, they heatedly urge a policy of real oppression. If people thought that the father's yoke was heavy, then let them contemplate an even heavier yoke from the son; if they felt that they were being whipped, then let them feel as though they are being bitten by scorpions. This recommended response is given to Rehoboam in v. 11, and he gives it to the people in v. 14. He does not repeat to the people his young courtiers' recommended boast, 'My "little one" (*qoṭonnî*) is thicker than my father's loins' (v. 10), a reticence which may show some element of thoughtfulness on the part of this otherwise headstrong new ruler: such imagery for the new king's potency may amuse the young bucks gathered in a privy council, but in the public assembly its youthful arrogance may sound rather less clever.

Nevertheless the jibe concerning a heavier yoke and the use of scorpions is more than enough for the ill-advised Rehoboam to lose out to the rabble-rouser Jeroboam. The people respond with a poetic chant, so well crafted that perhaps we are to think of Jeroboam having scripted it beforehand in full confidence (on account of Yahweh having 'spoken by Ahijah the Shilonite to Jeroboam', v. 15) that Rehoboam would provide the catalyst for the breaking up of the Davidic/Solomonic kingdom: 'What share do we have in David? We have no inheritance in the son of Jesse. Each to your own tents, O Israel! Look now to your own house, O David' (v. 16). It is the undoing of the oath of loyalty that had been proclaimed just two generations previously: 'We are yours, O David; and with you, O son of Jesse!' (1 Chron. 12.18). With a fateful error of judgment, David's grandson has unravelled a good deal of what David had achieved. 'All Israel' had come to Shechem to crown the third Davidide to rule over them, but the designated one had fallen at his first hurdle, and instead of a joyous coronation we find that 'all Israel departed to their tents' (v. 16) and that as a result of those events 'Israel has been in rebellion against the house of David to this day' (v. 19). There is some consolation for the house of David in that 'Rehoboam reigned over the people of Israel who were living in the cities of Judah' (v. 17), and some further consolation later when it is revealed that the tribal area of Benjamin also remains loyal to Rehoboam (note that he marshalled 'chosen troops of the house of Judah and Benjamin' in 11.1 and that 'he held Judah and Benjamin' in 11.12). Most importantly for the Annalists, he continues unchallenged in Jerusalem itself—indeed he will reign 'for 17 years in Jerusalem, the city that Yahweh had chosen out of all the tribes of Israel to put his name there', 12.13)—and so he retains validity in their scheme of things and their focus will remain on the house of David ruling from that city. But at

Shechem Rehoboam 'the Enlarger' loses a vast swathe of territory and shrinks the kingdom to a fraction of its formerly grand size.

Yet the Annals proclaim that this seeming catastrophe which diminishes the size and prosperity of 'the kingdom of Yahweh' (as it is styled in 1 Chron. 28.5 and 2 Chron. 13.8) was in fact 'a turn of affairs brought about by the deity' himself (v. 15). One might well wonder why Yahweh should wish to bring about a situation in which a substantial majority of his former people will be led astray by the insurrectionist Jeroboam. After all, it will not be long before Jeroboam and his sons will be setting up non-Yahwistic religious practices throughout the new northern realm (11.14-15), and Jeroboam will have to be denounced by Rehoboam's successor as a thoroughly bad thing (13.4-12) who leads his people 'against Yahweh, the god of [our] ancestors' (13.12). But the Annalists offer no direct reason for Yahweh handing the north on a plate to this enemy of Yahweh. The deity's purposes in shaping events as he does are perhaps meant to remain simply inscrutable, with the Annalists adhering firmly to a belief that nothing happens in the world that is not in accordance with divine will but without them being always able to feel that they have fully discerned the divine rationale. On the other hand, it may be that the Annalists provide an implied explanation for this turn of events in the divine scheme of things in the very denunciation of Jeroboam by the son of Rehoboam in ch. 13, in that the apostasy of the north under Jeroboam and his sons serves to throw 'the true religion' advocated in these Annals into clearer focus by the contrast with the practices of the northern regime. In particular, the case for Jerusalem as the only legitimate place of worship becomes stronger in the Annalists' world through Jeroboam's policy of driving the divinely-chosen functionaries, the Levites and Aaronites, out of the northern sanctuaries (11.14-15; 13.9-11).

The Annalists' phrasing at 10.15, that 'the king did not listen to the people because it was a turn of affairs brought about by the deity', seems reminiscent of another Hebrew story, namely the tale of the exodus from Egypt, in which we read that 'Yahweh hardened the heart of Pharaoh, and he would not listen to them' (Exodus 9.12, with 'them' being Moses and Aaron). In that tale, the deity explains to Moses that the reason why he ensures that 'Pharaoh will not listen to you' is 'in order that my wonders may be multiplied in the land of Egypt' (Exodus 11.9). Perhaps the readers of these Annals of the House of David are meant to deduce that the reason why Yahweh ensures that Rehoboam does not listen to the people's request for a light yoke is in order that the ramifications of abandoning Yahweh may be spelled out clearly in the land of Israel.

In any event, when Rehoboam makes a move to implement his announced policy of 'increasing the yoke' by sending in Hadoram, 'who was taskmaster over the forced labour' (v. 18), matters are exacerbated. It might be described as a situation of the man named *rĕhab ʿām* setting about the task of 'broadening' (*rāḥab*) the policy of forced labour to encompass the 'people' (*ʿam*) of Israel in addition to the Canaanites who had been under such conditions during his father's reign, but the people of Israel will not submit to such a policy: they 'stoned [Hadoram] to death, and King Rehoboam hurriedly mounted his chariot to flee to Jerusalem' (v. 18). The golden age of Solomon is at an end.

Chapter 11

Having taken just three days (10.5, 12) to diminish a nation that his grandfather and father had built up over 80 years (1 Chron. 29.27; 2 Chron. 9.30), Rehoboam the so-called 'Enlarger of the Nation' now desperately sets about assembling an army 'to restore the kingdom' (11.1). It turns out that he can call not only on Judah, who had been depicted in the disastrous episode at Shechem as being the only Israelite group to remain under his rule (10.17), but also on Benjamin. It had been Benjaminites and Judahites who had first proved faithful to David (1 Chron. 12.16), and Jerusalem had a substantial Benjaminite presence (1 Chron. 8.28, 32) as well as being defined as the principal Judahite town (2 Chron. 2.7; 11.14), so the combination of these two tribes under the Judahite commander-in-chief is not unexpected. But given that Benjamin was the tribe of which David's predecessor Saul had been a member (1 Chron. 8.33, 40), the loyalty of Benjaminites to Rehoboam can be taken as an indication that the rebellion of Jeroboam son of Nebat is not to be associated with any feeling that the kingdom should be restored to a house that had ruled over Israel before the Davidic monarchy had been instituted.

A 'word of Yahweh' through the prophet Shemaiah states assuredly that the situation in which a huge proportion of Israel has been taken out of the direct control of the house of David is 'from me' (11.4), thus reiterating the storytellers' contention that 'it was a turn of affairs brought about by the deity' (10.15). The national god thus stands firmly against Rehoboam's hurried plans to march against the rebellious northerners and bring them back under his rule: 'You shall not go up or fight against your kindred.' Perhaps surprisingly for a young hothead who had rejected the wise advice of his senior counsellors at Shechem and had chosen instead to follow the foolish advice of his young counsellors, Rehoboam and his commanders accept this 'word of Yahweh', and abandon the planned expedition. It does not mean there will be no future hostilities between the two territories— indeed we are later told that 'there were continual wars between Rehoboam and Jeroboam' (12.15) and then a decisive battle between the troops of Rehoboam's successor Abijah and the troops of Jeroboam (13.2)—but the son of Solomon is persuaded that an invasion of the breakaway territory does not have divine support and would accordingly not succeed, and so he turns back from such a course of action.

Instead, he sensibly puts his energies and resources into building up his defences in the territories of Judah and Benjamin. There is every prospect that the rebel Jeroboam, flushed with his easy success in turning the majority of Rehoboam's erstwhile subjects away from the house of David, will assemble a formidable number of chosen troops from the ten tribes now in open rebellion and launch an invasion of Rehoboam's remaining territory in order to bring the last two tribes also under the control of the house of Nebat. And the king in Jerusalem might well reason that while he is willing to accept the omens proclaimed by a prophet of Yahweh and thus not 'fight against [his] kindred' (v. 4), the new king in Shechem cannot be relied upon to receive or accept the same injunction. This is a man who had apparently received a prophetic word that he would be successful in a revolt against his sovereign (10.15) and there is no telling whether that prophetic utterance—the details of which are not divulged— might be interpreted by Jeroboam as encouragement to seek the complete overthrow of the Davidic monarchy. This is also a man who soon shows himself to be ruthlessly opposed to what the Annalists regard as the true religion of the people of Israel, by preventing the legitimate priests and attendants from serving Yahweh and appointing 'his own priests' instead (11.14-15), and so there can be no confidence that he would heed a 'word of Yahweh' to the effect that 'You shall not go up or fight against your kindred' (v. 4) if it were spoken to him at this time. Accordingly, Rehoboam sets about shoring up his defences, fortifying fifteen strategically important towns in Judah and Benjamin (vv. 6-10) and equipping them with the necessary provisions and hardware to withstand and repel any invasion from their former fellow-countrymen (vv. 11-12).

An 'invasion' of a different sort occurs first, however. 'The priests and Levites who were in all Israel presented themselves to [Rehoboam] from all their territories' (v. 13). Finding themselves ousted by Jeroboam and his sons from their places at the sanctuaries of the north (v. 14), and replaced there by non-levitical personnel engaged in improper practices having to do with 'goat-demons' and sacred 'calves' (v. 15), they move across the new frontier to join their colleagues at the Jerusalem temple. And so too from the general population of the north, 'those who had set their hearts to seek Yahweh, the god of Israel, came after them from all the tribes of Israel to Jerusalem to sacrifice to Yahweh, the god of their ancestors' (v. 16). The unrivalled status of Jerusalem as the location of 'The House for the Name of Yahweh, the God of Israel', as Solomon's temple had been designated at its dedication (6.7, 10), means that even though the son of Solomon has had to cede control over five-sixths of the nation of Israel, nevertheless significant numbers of Israelites from those ceded territories remain faithful to the god of Israel and prove themselves willing to venture into the territory of the custodian of the temple in order to continue 'to seek Yahweh' and 'to sacrifice to Yahweh' (11.16). This will not be something that pleases Jeroboam and his successors—we will read for example that King Baasha of Israel 'built Ramah in order to prevent anyone from going out or coming into [the territory of] King Asa of Judah' (16.1)—but for the Annalists it serves as an indication that Jerusalem remains the centre of true Yahwism. The Solomonic prayer, 'May your eyes be open day and night towards this House, the place where you promised to set your name' (6.20), is shown to remain valid despite the machinations of the upstart Jeroboam. People 'from all the tribes of Israel' cannot be prevented from 'walking in the way of David and Solomon' (11.17).

This idyllic picture will not remain untarnished. We are twice told that matters will change after 'three years' (v. 17), just as matters had changed so dramatically for the kingdom after 'three days' in Shechem (10.5, 12). The Annalists seem to be reconnecting here with a certain fondness for threefold durations of time that they showed in the story of David, in which the great founder of the kingdom enjoyed three days of coronation festivities (1 Chron. 12.39) and the custodian of the sacred ark enjoyed three months of special divine blessing (1 Chron. 13.14), and in which also the king was offered a choice of punishments between one lasting for three days, one lasting for three months, and one lasting for three years (1 Chron. 21.12). In the present situation of David's grandson, there will be three years of blessings while Rehoboam and his people 'walk in the way of David and Solomon' (2 Chron. 11.17).

Now in one respect King Rehoboam does seem to live up to his unique name of 'Expander of the Nation', by setting a royal example of increasing his people through vigorous procreative activity: 'he took 18 wives and 60 concubines, and became the father of 28 sons and 60 daughters' (vv. 18-23). In his efforts in this area he outdoes any other king in the entire Annals. His own son Abijah makes a reasonable show of following the paternal example when 'he took 14 wives and became the father of 22 sons and 16 daughters' (13.21), but thereafter the royal households are rather modest by comparison: Jehoshaphat manages seven sons (21.1-2) and Josiah four (1 Chron. 3.15), and six other kings of Judah are said to have produced more than one offspring (Jehoram at 2 Chron. 21.17; Ahaziah at 22.11; Joash at 24.3, 27; Ahaz at 28.3; Manasseh at 33.6 [though NRSV has the singular 'his son' where the Hebrew text has the plural *bānāyw*]; and Jehoiakim at 36.8, 10). No reference to producing more than their heir is made in the cases of the other ten successors of Rehoboam, so he stands head and shoulders above all his descendants in this achievement.

Perhaps most interestingly, particularly in view of a certain reputation for accumulating wives and concubines that other Israelite traditions have associated with his father Solomon, Rehoboam can be seen in these Annals to be far more active in his efforts in this area than was his father, for according to the Annals the great Solomon had modestly contented himself with just two wives, an Egyptian princess (8.11) and an Ammonite noblewoman (12.13), as well as conducting a dalliance with the Queen of Sheba (9.1-12). The founder of the dynasty, Solomon's father David, comes closer to Rehoboam's levels of marriage and parenting by taking seven wives and producing 19 sons and one daughter, as well as an undisclosed number of concubines and their offspring (1 Chron. 3.1-9), but this still falls well short of Rehoboam's figures. Thus no-one comes close to the efforts of the 'Expander of the Nation' to expand the royal household, even as he reigns over a considerably shrunken kingdom.

Chapter 12

When the anticipated military incursion into Rehoboam's rump state of Judah-plus-Benjamin occurs, it comes not from the expected direction of the north, from the breakaway kingdom of Israel-minus-Judah-and-Benjamin, but from the south, from the overwhelming imperial forces of Egypt. Rehoboam's policy of fortifying and equipping the main towns of his little kingdom (11.5-12) might well have been effective against an Israelite incursion—his son Abijah will be able to repel Jeroboam's forces a decade later when they eventually do attempt such a venture (13.13-20)—but the small Hebrew tribes of Judah and Benjamin are no match for the imperial forces.

At first glance the numbers do not look too ominous for Rehoboam and his troops. He had after all been able to muster '180,000 chosen troops of the house of Judah and Benjamin' (11.1) just three years earlier when he drew up plans—later abandoned under prophetic advice—to mount his own expedition to the north, whereas the figures given now for the Egyptian forces are only a third of that number, at '60,000' plus '1,200' (12.3). However, these are '60,000 *cavalry* and 1,200 *chariots*', and in addition to the Egyptians there is 'a countless army of Libyans, Sukkiim, and Cushites'. Even at the height of Solomonic power and wealth, the then kingdom of all Israel had only possessed 12,000 horses, accordingly to the Annals (at 1.14 and again at 9.25), and only a proportion of these valuable animals were said to have been stabled at Jerusalem, so Rehoboam's Judahite and Benjaminite cavalry and chariots, unable to call upon the resources of five-sixths of the former Solomonic kingdom, would fall far short of the number required to stand against the Egyptian onslaught.

Unsurprisingly, then, King Shishak of Egypt in no time at all 'took the fortified cities of Judah' (12.4) that King Rehoboam of Judah had just 'made very strong' (11.12). The Annalists do not provide figures for the numbers of Judahites killed by the combined forces of Egyptians, Libyans, Sukkiim, and Cushites as the imperial juggernaut overwhelmed hapless defenders and citizens throughout Rehoboam's realm, but nevertheless the reader is again forced to reckon with a situation in which the regal name is proclaiming an enlargement of the people but the actual fate of the nation is quite the reverse.

Of course nothing happens in this story-world by chance, or because of any geopolitical factors that might be analyzed without reference to the religious system advocated by the Annalists.

The imperial forces have been unleashed upon Rehoboam and his people 'because they had been unfaithful to Yahweh' (v. 2). The king had built 'strong fortresses' (11.11) and there had been no invasion from the northern Israelites, and so he had felt himself to be strong (12.1), without further need for full devotion to the Israelite god. Accordingly, 'he abandoned the law of Yahweh, he and all Israel with him'—12.1's dramatic reversal of the earlier picture in 11.16 of 'those who had set their hearts to seek Yahweh, the god of Israel, coming with [the priests and the Levites] from all the tribes of Israel to Jerusalem to sacrifice to Yahweh, the god of their ancestors'.

Such apostasy cannot stand in this realm. The founder of the kingdom, David himself, had set out the fundamental principle to Rehoboam's father in the words 'My son Solomon, know the god of your father, and serve him with single mind and willing heart... If you seek him, he will be found by you; but if you forsake him, he will abandon you' (1 Chron. 28.9). Accordingly, the prophet Shemaiah now proclaims to David's grandson and his officers, 'Thus says Yahweh: "You abandoned me, so I have abandoned you to the hand of Shishak"' (2 Chron. 12.5). A simple and elegant *quid pro quo* is in operation, not entirely unlike the counsel of the elders at Shechem, that if the king would treat the people well then they would treat him well (10.7); on that earlier occasion the son of Solomon had not been able to grasp the beauty and truth of that equation, but at this time he demonstrates a more Solomonic wisdom, humbling himself and declaring 'Yahweh is in the right' (12.6).

In having King Rehoboam and his officers make this declaration in precisely this phrase (in Hebrew *ṣadıq yahweh*, literally 'Yahweh is righteous'), the Annalists have cleverly worked in to the tale of the first king of Judah an allusion to the name of the last king of Judah, Zedekiah (*ṣidĕqiyāhû*, literally 'Yahweh is my righteousness'). The latter monarch will find himself (in 36.11-21) confronted by the imperial forces of the Babylonians, because he and his people abandoned the law of Yahweh just as Rehoboam and his people had done in the earlier scene pictured here at 12.1-12. The telling difference for the Annalists between the two scenes is that Rehoboamic Judah is depicted as 'humbling themselves' (12.6) and declaring that 'Yahweh is righteous', while the king who later bears the name 'Yahweh is my righteousness' would contrariwise 'not humble himself' (36.12) and would not make the confession that his name calls for. The consequences for Zedekiah and the kingdom would of course be absolutely disastrous, while the consequences in the present episode for Rehoboam and the kingdom are concomitantly happy ones: a new word arrives from Yahweh in the nick of time, proclaiming that 'They have humbled themselves; I will not destroy them' (12.7). In the Annalists' world, things are as neat and as straightforward as that.

There is nonetheless a price to be paid by Rehoboam and his people for their erstwhile abandonment of the law of Yahweh. Although they are indeed 'not destroyed completely' (v. 12), they are placed under servitude to the Egyptian empire, 'so that they may know the difference between serving [Yahweh] and serving the kingdoms of other lands' (v. 8). The wealth of Jerusalem, so masterfully and unerringly built up by David and Solomon, is now sucked out of the city by the new Egyptian overlords. Even 'the treasures of the House of Yahweh' (which had been so lovingly described by the Annalists in chs. 3 and 4), as well as 'the treasures of the king's house' (which had been proudly itemised in ch. 9), are carried off to Egypt by the pharaoh Shishak— in short, 'he took everything' (v. 9).

So it is that the son of Solomon is depicted as having squandered his inheritance. He who was supposed to be the expander of his people's fortunes, a veritable *rĕhab ʿām*, had instead overseen the stripping of the national treasuries. First he had lost most of the territory that his grandfather David had moulded into a proud nation, and now he had lost all of the gold and silver with which his father Solomon had adorned the capital. His people were no longer masters of all they surveyed, but were firmly under the thumb of mighty Egypt. All is not lost, since the Egyptians are not given permission by Yahweh to destroy Jerusalem—it remains 'the city that Yahweh has chosen out of all the tribes of Israel to put his name there' (v. 13), and in some respects the conditions in Judah after the imperial army has left can even be said to be 'good' (v. 12)—but the tale of Rehoboam is on the whole a very sorry one indeed. His father had been 'a man of peace' (1 Chron. 22.9) and of unparalleled riches and wisdom (2 Chron. 9.22), but the son had turned out to be a creator of 'continual wars' (12.15) and of impoverishment and foolishness.

Only in one respect has Rehoboam shown himself at all worthy to hold the destiny of his people in his hands. At the crucial time, with Jerusalem on the verge of utter destruction, he had humbled himself and brought about a turning aside of Yahweh's wrath, so that the people were not completely destroyed. That act rehabilitates him in this story-world to some degree, or at least allows the story to continue beyond his time, but, in considering his seventeen-year reign as a whole, the ledger of the Annalists concludes that 'he did evil, for he did not set his heart to seek Yahweh' (v. 14). Without such a setting of the king's heart, the people of Israel were never going to enjoy the increase in blessings that the name 'Rehoboam' might otherwise have portended.

2 Chronicles 13:
Abijah 'the Fatherly'

Despite the allegation that King Jeroboam had 'not set his heart to seek Yahweh' (12.14), he does appear to have bestowed upon his heir and successor a thoroughly Yahwistic name, for the new king's designation, Abijah (*'ăbîyâ*), declares that 'Yahweh is my father'. Such a declaration of devotion to Yahweh would be in keeping with the Annalists' depiction of Rehoboam as someone who maintained proper Yahwistic religion at the temple of Solomon (11.13-16) and who always accepted a 'word from Yahweh' when it was presented to him by a recognised prophet (11.2-4; 12.5-6). It also calls to mind the words of the Davidic oracle that 'I [Yahweh] will be a father to him [the son of David], and he shall be a son to me' (1 Chron. 17.13), and the words of the coronation psalm that speak of 'Yahweh's decree: he said to me, "You are my son; today I have begotten you"' (Psalm 2.7). Abijah's destiny to become king in 'the kingdom of Yahweh' (2 Chron. 13.8) is thus confidently stated in the name that he bears, and indeed we have already been told of Rehoboam having appointed him 'as chief prince among his brothers, for he intended to make him king' (11.22).

Strangely, the man whose name asserts that he has a divine father in addition to his human father seems to possess two human mothers. When we had first learnt of Abijah, we had been told that his mother was 'Maacah daughter of Absalom' (11.20), and indeed we might even have gained the impression that the reason why his father Rehoboam selected Abijah to inherit the throne was because he was the firstborn son of Rehoboam's favourite wife, this very same 'Maacah daughter of Absalom' (11.21). But now when Abijah ascends the throne we are told that 'his mother's name was Micaiah daughter of Uriel of Gibeah' (13.2). The Annalists do not seem to have been able to keep their story straight in this particular. On the whole they are not particularly interested in female characters: there are very, very few mothers to be found in amongst the thousands of fathers listed in the genealogical lists of 1 Chronicles (chs. 1–9), and only half of the mothers of kings of Judah are provided with names in 2 Chronicles (the nine royal mothers that are named, for those who are more interested in such matters than the Annalists appear to be, are to be found at 12.13; 15.16; 22.2; 24.1; 25.1; 26.3; 27.1; and 29.1, in addition to the two discrepant namings of Abijah's mother). Given this lack of regard for female characters in their story-world, it is perhaps not surprising that here in Abijah's case the Annalists have not even taken the care to see to it that the same woman is credited with giving birth to him in the two places where they deign to mention her.

Whatever his precise parentage, the new king comes to the throne of Judah eighteen years after the northern tribes had broken away to form a separate kingdom under Jeroboam (13.1), and it seems that almost immediately a full-scale war breaks out between the two Hebrew nations. It is not clear who initiated the sabre-rattling, whether the northerners have seized a perceived opportunity in the changeover in the southern admin-istration to strike against them or whether the new commander-in-chief Abijah had been harbouring plans to strike against the north as soon as he came to sit upon the throne of David, but a narrative sequence that mentions first that 'Abijah engaged in battle' and then that 'Jeroboam drew up his line of battle against him' (v. 3) and which places Abijah before the battle as standing 'on the slope of Mount Zemaraim that is in the hill country of Ephraim' (v. 4)—that is, in territory that had been under the rule of Jeroboam—suggests that Abijah has taken an offensive rather than defensive position. He has mustered 400,000 men, but meanwhile Jeroboam has twice that number at 800,000 (v. 3). The Judahite forces on this occasion are considerably larger than those which Abijah's father Rehoboam had been able to muster almost two decades previously when he had contemplated marching into the northern realm (11.1), but being out-manned two-to-one still makes the prospects for Abijah's forces look rather bleak.

But the king of Judah, bursting with confidence under the designation that he is Yahweh's son, is not overawed by the sight of an army twice the size of his own. As the new father of the nation, a nation that he sees as encompassing not just his small southern kingdom of Judah but also the northern realm of Israel appropriated by the reprobate Jeroboam, he gives a stern fatherly talk to his people, particularly directed at Jeroboam and his forces. Do they not know that 'Yahweh, the god of Israel, gave the kingship over Israel forever to David and his sons by a covenant of salt' (v. 5)? By tearing up that 'covenant of salt' (an expression denoting a particularly sacred and binding agreement, as in Numbers 18.19), the northerners are attempting to stand against 'the kingdom of Yahweh in the hand of the sons of David' (v. 8). This northern abandonment of Yahweh is further itemised through a reiteration of aspects mentioned in the account of Rehoboam's time, namely Jeroboam's policies of setting up bovine images (v. 8, as in 11.15) and of driving out the Aaronite priests and their Levite assistants and replacing them with non-Yahwistic priests (v. 9, as in 11.13-15). Such apostasy is contrasted with the situation at the temple in Jerusalem, where there are 'priests ministering to Yahweh who are descendants of Aaron, and Levites for their service' (v. 10), who follow the proper regulations of temple service to the letter (v. 11), just as the great David had arranged in Yahweh's name (the full arrangements are set out in 1 Chron. 23). Abijah seems to have forgotten that pharaoh Shishak of Egypt had taken all the gold out of the temple in Rehoboam's time (2 Chron. 12.9), but perhaps when the present king of Judah makes mention of 'the table of pure gold' and 'the golden lampstand' (13.11) we are to imagine either that the pharaoh had graciously allowed those special treasures to remain or that the kingdom of Judah had been able to replace them in the intervening years. In any event, the message is clear: to fight against Abijah is to fight against Yahweh.

In bringing his stirring speech to a close, the king issues the resounding call, 'O Israelites, do not fight against Yahweh, the god of your fathers!' (v. 12)—exactly the kind of saying that ought to be attributed to a man living under the designation 'Yahweh is My Father'. The Annalists then go on to relate that Yahweh 'defeated Jeroboam and all Israel before Abijah and Judah' and that 'the Israelites were subdued at that time, and the people of Judah prevailed, because they relied on Yahweh, the god of their fathers' (vv. 15-18). Abijah has been vindicated by his father-deity, the unquestioned god of his fathers David and Solomon and the god (so acknowledged for at least part of Rehoboam's reign) of his father Rehoboam. The upstart Jeroboam, the one who had 'rebelled against his lord' (v. 6) and who had been assisted by 'certain worthless scoundrels' (v. 7) in tearing a sizeable chunk of the kingdom away from the house of David, is now brought down to size. Abijah recovers some useful territory from him (v. 19), and the northern ruler never recovers his power (v. 20). From a position of having twice the number of troops at his disposal than were available to Abijah (v. 3) and thus being able to set troops both 'in front of Judah' and 'behind them' (vv. 13-14), Jeroboam is brought to a position of utter defeat in which more than half his warriors are killed (v. 17) while the Judahites appear to have suffered few if any casualties. Abijah's words to Jeroboam that 'you cannot succeed' (v. 12) were prophetic, no less than were the words which Yahweh 'had spoken by Ahijah the Shilonite to Jeroboam' (10.15) and which had presumably led Jeroboam to think that he would be successful in rebelling against Rehoboam. Jeroboam's personal defiance of the sons of David, a defiance of Yahweh himself, is now at an end: Yahweh personally strikes him down some time after the battle, and he dies (v. 20), while the son of David in Jerusalem—Yahweh's adopted son—grows strong (v. 21).

As a sign of his strength, the Annalists tell us that Abijah 'took 14 wives, and became the father of 22 sons and 16 daughters' (v. 21). In so doing, he whose name speaks of paternity and patronage fathers more children than anyone in these Annals other than his own father Rehoboam (see the discussion above, under ch. 11). If he achieved all that procreation within his three-year reign (v. 1), then he truly had the strength of the gods, but since his father Rehoboam had earlier been reported as 'finding many wives' (11.23) during his own lengthier reign, the assumption must be that Abijah made a good start on his prodigious fathering activities while he was still the 'chief prince among his brothers' (11.22). His reign when it comes is relatively brief, but it is of importance to the Annalists: through his royal speech to those who had been led astray by his father's nemesis Jeroboam and in the decisive victory that Yahweh grants him over that same nefarious Jeroboam, Abijah articulates and demonstrates the Annalistic notions that the kingdom centred on Jerusalem is Yahweh's kingdom and that the clear choice for the people of Israel or Judah is either 'not to abandon him' (13.10) or 'to abandon him' (v. 11), and if the people choose the latter route then they 'cannot succeed' (v. 12). For the Annalists, Abijah has shown himself to be a worthy father-figure to all Israel.

2 Chronicles 14–16: Asa 'the Healer'

Chapter 14

Quite why Abijah might have bestowed the name of Asa upon his son and heir is not clear. Perhaps there was a resonance to the name in the Hebrew language that is no longer known to us, but the resonance that we do know—and with which the Annalists will make a conspicuous wordplay at the end of the story—is the Aramaic title 'Asa' (in more technical transliteration, *ʾāsāʾ*), meaning a 'physician' or 'healer'. Could it be that the pious Abijah, the one who so earnestly bemoaned the rebellion of the north that had torn apart the covenantal unity of god and people formerly established under the house of David (13.5-7), was hoping that his successor could heal the wounds of that schism and bring the estranged northerners back into the Davidic realm?

If such hopes of repairing the rend in the Hebrew peoples were invested in the royal son, a more Hebraic name such as Raphael, which carries the meaning 'the deity heals' and which in later times is used to good effect as an agent of healing in the Jewish legend of Tobit, could presumably have been employed to portend or pray for such an outcome under the new king of Judah. But the use of an Aramaic name in the Judahite royal family strikes an interesting note at this point in the story of the kingdom. This King Asa of Judah will later send word to King Ben-hadad of Aram, saying, 'Let there be an alliance between me and you, like that between my father and your father' (16.3). There had been no mention of such an alliance when the tale of Asa's father had been related (ch. 13)—the picture there had rather suggested that Abijah needed no help other than pure reliance on the god of Israel to fight his battles and achieve his aspirations for his kingdom—but the bestowal of an Aramaic designation upon the crown prince and the latter man's reference to an alliance with Aram as having existed under the reign of his father rather suggests that a more Aramean-oriented situation pertained in Jerusalem than we might otherwise have thought.

Nevertheless, at first in the tale of Asa no overt reference is made to that neighbouring and powerful kingdom of Aram, despite the apparently Aramaic name borne by the king of Judah. 'King Ben-hadad of Aram' will not come explicitly into the picture until as late as 'the 36th year of the reign of Asa' (16.1-2); before then, the Annalists have other matters to relate.

The beginnings of Asa's reign are auspicious, though also a little puzzling in this story-world. We see the new king doing 'what was good and right in the sight of his god Yahweh' (14.2), and we see him commanding his people 'to seek Yahweh, the god of their fathers' (v. 4), precisely what ought to be enjoined by the son of a monarch named 'Yahweh is My Father' (Abijah, a father who had set the example by calling upon all Israel to be loyal to 'Yahweh, the god of your fathers' [13.12]). The puzzlement comes because we see Asa busily 'taking away the foreign altars and the high places, breaking down the pillars, and hewing down the sacred poles' (14.3), and we wonder how such things come to be in the kingdom when his father Abijah had been depicted as thoroughly devoted to Yahweh. Readers might speculate that the narrative voice could be talking only about the new territory that Abijah had relatively recently annexed from the apostate northern kingdom (13.19), and which accordingly now needed to be brought into conformity with 'the true religion' of Jerusalem, but such an interpretation is ruled out by the specific reference to Asa having to 'remove from all the cities of Judah the high places and the incense altars' (v. 5) and even more so later in his tale when we read that after receiving a forthright prophetic message he 'took courage, and put away the abominable idols from all the land of Judah and Benjamin and from the towns that he had taken in the hill country of Ephraim' (15.8). Apparently Abijah's implicit statement of faith about the Fatherhood of Yahweh was not the sole confession of devotion throughout his kingdom, and it would take his son Asa some time in his own reign to put matters fully right in this regard, though he makes a fine start by undertaking the removal of the 'high places' and associated 'pillars' and 'sacred poles' (*'ăšērîm*, perhaps associated with the cult of the goddess *'ăšērâ* or Asherah, 14.3).

Asa also sets about redoing the work of his grandfather in terms of 'building fortified cities in Judah' by 'surrounding them with walls and towers, gates and bars' (vv. 6-7). After the rebellion of the north two generations before, Rehoboam had 'built cities for defence in Judah' (11.5), only to see an assorted expeditionary force of Egyptians, Libyans, Sukkiim, and Cushites overcome them all (12.3-4), so now his grandson sets about using a time of relative peace and prosperity to shore up the defences once again. And once again the Annalists enjoy providing an accounting of the number of troops at the king's disposal: '300,000 from Judah' plus '280,000 from Benjamin' (14.8), a reasonable increase in the numbers that his father (in 13.3) and grandfather (in 11.1) had been able to muster.

These combined Judahite and Benjaminite forces of just over half a million warriors will soon be put to the test, however, by a new expeditionary force of twice that number, namely 'a million men and 300 chariots' (v. 9), that now invades the little kingdom. This is reminiscent of the situation that Asa's father Abijah had faced a decade previously, when the earlier king's 400,000 men were ranged against twice that number in the Israelite army of 800,000 fighters (13.3), although on that occasion Judah could be seen as the invader of other territory, albeit regarding that territory as rightfully theirs. On this occasion Judah is being invaded, just as it had been in Rehoboam's time, and there is a certain déjà vu in the experience: Rehoboam had been attacked by an imperial force (under Egyptian command, with the pharaoh Shishak calling the shots) that included Cushites (12.4), and now the Cushites return alone but in overwhelming numbers under their own commander, Zerah (14.9). Either they have dispensation from the Egyptian crown to extract booty on the empire's behalf from the territory of Judah, or they have taken advantage of some weakness in Egyptian power to assert their own interests over this small kingdom, but what they have not reckoned with is that this kingdom has Yahweh as its god, and indeed under the 'good and right' leadership of King Asa the Judahites have become even firmer in their dedication to Yahweh alone and thus stand under that god's benevolence at this time. There is no need for Yahweh on this occasion to allow the invading forces any success in order to teach the people of Judah any lessons, as the Annalists believed to be the case in the time of Rehoboam (12.5-8), so the results will be very different in the time of Asa.

Asa takes the initiative, calling on Yahweh to help his people: 'O Yahweh, you are our god; let no mortal prevail against you' (14.11). And Yahweh's help is emphatic: he defeats the Cushites

so thoroughly that not a single one of the million men who had
entered his kingdom escapes with his life intact (v. 13). The
Judahite forces pursue the fleeing troops into formerly Cushite-
held territory, finishing the Cushites off and taking the opportunity to seize from the cities to which they had fled 'a great
quantity of booty' (v. 13), 'much plunder' (v. 14), and 'sheep and
goats in abundance, and camels' (v. 15). Left utterly bereft of
fighting men and of wealth, the Cushites will never again return
to threaten the devotees of Yahweh. Asa 'the Healer' may not
have repaired the breach between Judah and the rest of Israel,
but he has certainly seen off the Cushite menace that had threatened to keep Judah in a weak and unhealthy state. Well might
he summarise the condition of his kingdom under his rule in the
statement that 'the land remains ours because we have sought
our god Yahweh; we have sought him, and he has given us peace
on every side' (v. 7).

Chapter 15

Fresh from his exploits at the head of an all-conquering army,
Asa now receives and acts upon a timely message from his god.

It is not entirely clear which divine spokesman is ultimately
responsible for the wording of the prophetic message: v. 1 says
that 'the divine spirit came upon Azariah son of Oded', while
v. 8 says that 'these words' were 'the prophecy [of] the prophet
Oded'. NRSV decides to bring the latter verse into direct harmony
with the former one by speaking in v. 8 of 'the prophecy of
Azariah son of Oded'. Certainly it is Azariah who is depicted as
speaking the words to Asa, and the lack of the younger prophet's
name in v. 8 might be a mistake made by an inattentive scribe
in the transmission of the text, but it is not impossible that the
Annalists are thinking of a teaching of the older prophet now
presented by his son and successor at the time when Yahweh
has determined that the king needs to hear it, returning as he is
from an overwhelming victory over the Cushites. This is a critical time in the career of a king in the Annalists' view—note
that in a later story King Amaziah decides to include the worship
of Edomite gods in his religious practices after he has defeated
the Edomites (25.14)—so it is vital that the specific message of
absolute fidelity to Yahweh be put before King Asa at this
specific time, irrespective of when the teaching was first formed
in the prophetic family or guild to which Oded and his 'son' (or
'disciple') Azariah belong.

That a prophetic word can be delivered by an individual other than the initiating seer and at a later time than the devising of that message is illustrated in the story of Asa's grandson Jehoram. The Annalists relate that 'a letter came to him from the prophet Elijah' (21.12), berating him for not following the good example of his grandfather Asa and his father Jehoshaphat but instead following the bad example of the northern royal house of Ahab. In that tale the delivery of a letter rather than the appearance of the prophet in the flesh indicates Elijah's unavailability for a personal audience with the king of Judah, but if one understands Elijah as being a prophet active in the northern kingdom and indeed in an earlier period than the time of Jehoram's reign in the south, as other Hebrew traditions indicate even though such details are not explicitly given in these Annals, then one can see that an emissary other than Elijah himself, and presumably some years after Elijah's death, has communicated Elijah's words to Asa's grandson. Something analogous might be in the frame here too in Asa's own tale, with the message being seen as Oded's formulation some time in advance of the occasion of delivery, and then at the right time Oded's son being the divinely-activated agent of delivery to the king.

But whether the words are thought to have originated from 'the prophet Oded' (v. 8) or from 'Azariah son of Oded' (v. 1), the teaching is quintessential Annalistic thinking: 'Yahweh is with you while you are with him; if you seek him, he will be found by you, but if you abandon him, he will abandon you' (v. 2). The slogan is as old as King David himself, according to the Annalists, for they had the founder of the kingdom address his son Solomon and by implication every succeeding monarch with virtually the same words, 'If you seek him, he will be found by you, but if you forsake him, he will abandon you forever' (1 Chron. 28.9). The theme had been continued in the words of the prophet Shemaiah to Asa's grandfather Rehoboam (in 2 Chron. 12.5) and in the prophet-like speech of the monarch himself in the case of Asa's father Abijah's references to abandonment and non-abandonment of Yahweh (13.10-11). The Annalists could hardly be more insistent about the message they want to drive home to their Judahite (or Judean) readers: seek Yahweh and do not forsake him!

The prophetic message on this occasion includes a look back to pre-Davidic times, when the people of Israel had neither 'a true god' (*ĕlōhê ĕmet*) nor 'a teaching priest' (*kōhēn môreh*) nor indeed 'a teaching' as such (*tôrâ*), but lived a precarious existence in which no one could go about their normal activities in safety and in which various ethnic groups were at each other's throats and all the cities of the land were at enmity with each other (vv. 3-6). In those former days the deity was 'troubling them with every kind of distress' (v. 6), presumably—in the Annalists' scheme of things—in order to show the Israelites the consequences of not seeking Yahweh, for 'when in their distress they turned to Yahweh, the god of Israel, and sought him, he was found by them' (v. 4), precisely as the Davidic slogan 'Seek him and he will be found by you' asserts.

Asa readily accepts the message that he should 'take courage' (v. 8), something of an echo of the words of the great David himself to his successor Solomon ('Be strong and of good courage' in 1 Chron. 22.13 and again in 28.20). The choice on this occasion of the additional phrase 'Do not let your hands be weak' (2 Chron. 15.7) seems to suggest some resonance with the royal name, insofar as the word for 'being weak' (*rāpâ*) and the word for 'healing' (*rāpā'*) sound so similar. The precise Hebrew word 'healers' (*rōpĕ'îm*) will be employed by the Annalists later in their account of Asa (16.12), where it clearly functions as a play-on-words with the Aramaic designation 'Healer' of the king's name, but here the sound of *rāpâ* with its similarity to *rāpā'* may be coincidental rather than especially crafted for this context (after all, the verb *rāpâ* also appears in those earlier words of David to Solomon when the founding monarch says that the deity 'will not fail' his son in 1 Chron. 28.20). Even so, it just might be that the Annalists create some room here for the thought that Asa 'the Healer' should have healing hands rather than weak and ineffective ones.

And their man certainly does immediately set about (in 15.8) repairing what needs to be repaired ('the altar of Yahweh that was in front of the vestibule of the House of Yahweh') and excising what needs to be excised ('the abominable idols from all the land of Judah and Benjamin'). It seems that his earlier activities of removing various altars and high places and pillars and poles (as recounted in 14.3-5) had not been as thoroughgoing or as fully effective as they ought to have been, and so renewed efforts are required on that front. And as befits a Davidic ruler, chosen by the god of Israel to oversee true religion for all Israel, Asa finds that 'great numbers' of northerners have rallied to him 'when they saw that his god Yahweh was with him' (15.9), so that he is able to hold in Jerusalem a grand occasion of rededication to Yahweh. Under the divinely-blessed Asa, the people are as one in pledging devotion to Yahweh 'with all their heart and with all their soul' (v. 12), an expression that calls to mind the great Israelite proclamation that 'Yahweh is our god, Yahweh alone; and you shall love your god Yahweh with all your heart and with all your soul and with all your might' (Deuteronomy 6.4-5).

Such absolute devotion to a deity might sound inspiring and stirring, but the very next sentence in the Annals (2 Chron. 15.13) reveals a fanaticism and totalitarianism that seems designed to stop readers in their tracks: a concomitant aspect of this covenant between Yahweh and his people, as understood by the tradents of Judah, is that 'whoever would not seek Yahweh, the god of Israel, should be put to death, whether young or old, man or woman'. This chilling 'oath to Yahweh' is made with 'shouting' and 'trumpets' and 'horns' (v. 14), and 'all Judah rejoiced over the oath, for they had sworn with all their heart' (v. 15)—such a scene of an immense crowd being stirred up into a mass frenzy of murderous zeal is surely a deeply disturbing one to readers of good will, even as it was evidently a scene that gladdened the hearts of the Annalists. For the compilers of these Annals there is presumably nothing untoward in an oath to kill anyone in the kingdom who will not share in absolute devotion to the national god; the Hebrew tradition might include an injunction that 'you shall not murder' (Exodus 20.13; Deuteronomy 5.17), but it also included such classics as 'whoever does any work on the sabbath day shall be put to death' (Exodus 31.15; 35.2) and 'if a man lies with a male as with a woman, both of them...shall be put to death' (Leviticus 20.13). Instructions are given at some length in one of the Israelite law-codes that when anyone is found to have 'transgressed the covenant [with Yahweh] by going to serve other gods and worshipping them..., then you shall bring out to your gates that man or that woman who has committed this crime and you shall stone the man or woman to death' (Deuteronomy 17.2-5). Evidently the Annalists were not alone in ancient Israel in developing an ideology that called for the summary execution of anyone not towing the official religious line.

Thankfully, no full-scale pogrom appears to break out after the covenant-renewal ceremony in 2 Chronicles 15. The only mentioned casualty is the 'queen mother' (*gĕbîrâ*), Maacah, and it is not said that she was put to death, but only that she was removed from her position of honour and that the religious image of the goddess Asherah that she had venerated was destroyed.

Being the king's 'mother' (*ēm*)—or perhaps more exactly in this context his 'grandmother', if 11.20-22 is called to mind—may save her life, but not her lifestyle. A royal lady with a non-Yahwistic agenda is not something that appeals to these story-tellers: they will say of a later king that 'his mother was his counsellor in doing wickedly' (22.3), but here they are relieved to have the cultic wickedness removed from the royal family, and to be able to proclaim that 'the heart of Asa was true all his days' (15.17).

The Annalists will in fact modify that assessment of Asa when it comes to the last phase of his life (in ch. 16), and they already allow themselves here to express some disappointment that not all of the worship sites away from the central temple are done away with (15.17), but nonetheless for the moment Asa stands as an example of fine leadership in Yahweh's kingdom, bringing splendid votive gifts into the temple (v. 18) and being blessed by his god with two full decades of peace (between the covenantal gathering in 'the 15th year of Asa's reign' [v. 10] and the new war to come after 'the 35th year of Asa's reign' [v. 19]). The Annals pass over those 20 years in silence; all may be presumed to be well in the kingdom, in contrast to those earlier times when the deity had felt a need to 'trouble them with every sort of distress' and to 'afflict all the inhabitants of the lands' (vv. 5-6)—under much of Asa's long reign there are calm times, and accordingly these years are 'un-newsworthy' for the Annalists.

Chapter 16

Everything changes in 'the 36th year of the reign of Asa' (16.1), when the northerners, who had been so thoroughly vanquished by Asa's father Abijah (ch. 13), apparently at last feel suffi-ciently recovered to take a stand against the south once again. They block the movement of people between the two Hebrew kingdoms, which if nothing else is a blow against the pretensions of Judah and Jerusalem to be the centre of all Israel and espe-cially to be a rallying place for all from the north who are in any way disaffected by the policies of the northern kingdom (as 11.3-16 and 15.9 had depicted). The new 'King Baasha of Israel' is not prepared to allow that state of affairs to continue, and he is presumably strengthened in his resolve by having forged an alli-ance with 'King Ben-hadad of Aram', ruler of a stronger regional kingdom which had apparently in former times been on Judah's side—to judge from Asa's words to Ben-hadad about the alliance that had existed 'between my father and your father' (16.3), and not from the Annalists' account of the previous reign, which had neglected to mention any foreign assistance in Judah's resounding defeat of Israel in those days.

Asa's response to Baasha's blockade is to seek to turn Aram from its new alliance with Israel back to the former alliance with Judah. Regaining the Arameans as allies is a costly venture: we had only just read of Asa providing the temple with silver and gold (15.18) that had at long last gone some way towards replacing the treasures that his grandfather Rehoboam had lost to the Egyptians (12.9), and now almost immediately after that happy development we read that Asa feels it necessary to take 'silver and gold from the treasures of the House of Yahweh and the king's house' (16.2) and send them to the Arameans. But the tactic is successful: Ben-hadad does indeed break his alliance with Baasha, and instigates a military campaign on the other side of Israelite territory (v. 4), so that the King of Israel must withdraw forces from his southern front with Judah and concentrate on keeping his kingdom more or less intact at other points. This enables Asa and his troops to move into the border area, break down the fortifications that Baasha had been building up, and then re-use the material to build up Judahite fortifications against Israelite incursions (vv. 5-6).

However, such success does not please Asa's god, because it has been achieved in a very different way than the earlier incredible victory against the invading Cushites (ch. 14). On the earlier occasion, when confronted with overwhelming hordes descending upon his tiny kingdom, Asa had 'cried to his god Yahweh, "...Help us, O Yahweh our god, for we rely on you, and in your name we have come against this multitude"' (14.11); but on this occasion the king had neglected to call upon his god but had instead denuded his god's House of its treasures (16.2) in order to achieve an alliance with another kingdom to see off the threat posed by the kingdom of Israel. The seer Hanani steps forward (in v. 7) on Yahweh's behalf to reprimand the king for failing to rely on his god in this later situation and to declare to him that, far from having achieved a meaningful peace, 'from now on you will have wars' (v. 9).

The prophet's words include an intriguing element when he says that 'the army of the king of Aram has escaped you' (v. 7). It had been the army of the king of Israel that had been on Judah's northern frontier and which had had to disengage from there when the Arameans had harassed Israel from the other direction, so we might have expected Hanani to suggest that with Yahweh's help the Judahites could have overcome the Israelites, just as Asa's father Abijah had done, rather than having merely achieved, with the help of the Arameans, a withdrawal of the Israelite army. But the prophet's formulation suggests that Judah might have achieved a victory not only over the forces of Israel but also over the greater forces of Israel's then-ally Aram, had Asa had the good sense to rely again on Yahweh, as he had had on the occasion of the Cushite invasion. That had been a 'huge army', Hanani reminds Asa (v. 8), and it had apparently included 'Libyans' as well as 'Cushites', though this had not been stated in the earlier account of matters, wherein it had exclusively been 'Cushites' that were mentioned (14.9, 12, 13). 'Libyans' were reported as being among the imperial Egyptian forces, which also included 'Cushites' as well as 'Sukkiim', that had attacked Rehoboam's kingdom two generations before, so it is not unreasonable for the prophetic voice to cast the kingdoms of Cush and Libya together for an attack on Asa's kingdom, even though the narrational voice had not done so in the account of that invasion.

Nor is it unreasonable within the sequence of events in these Annals for the prophet to imply that 'the army of the king of Aram' will be a continuing problem for the king of Judah and his successors, for we will read of such Aramean difficulties in the reigns of Jehoshaphat (ch. 18), Ahaziah (ch. 22), Joash (ch. 24), and Ahaz (ch. 28), whereas no king of Judah ever again has to deal with the Cushites or the Libyans (although Jehoram is confronted by 'the Arabs who are near the Cushites' in 21.16). That it will be Jehoshaphat's own fault in making an alliance with the kingdom of Israel against the kingdom of Aram, a folly repeated by his son Ahaziah, after which there is presumably no chance of ever again repeating Asa's achievement of renewing an alliance with Aram, does not seem to be foremost in the Annalists' minds. They will have some words of censure about Jehoshaphat's actions in allying himself to Israel (19.2), but here they lay the blame for ongoing wars at the feet of Asa, by having Hanani proclaim that the king has 'done foolishly' in allying himself to Aram and that as a consequence 'from now on [he] will have wars' (16.9).

No fresh wars do in fact break out in the remaining five years of Asa's life, but the king himself does not have a happy end.

From 'the 39th year of his reign' (v. 12) until his death 'in the 41st year of his reign' (v. 13), the king 'was diseased in his feet, and his disease became severe' (v. 12). We are spared the medical details of this disease, though we might imagine something like chronic gout or lameness, or even a venereal disease—due to the word 'feet' (*raglayim*) sometimes being used in Biblical Hebrew as a euphemism for the genitals (such as in Isaiah 7.20 and 36.12). That the king suffers at the end of his long reign is as it should be in the Annalists' world, because he responds wrongly to the prophet's message. He had responded rightly in the earlier case of Azariah's words (or Oded's words through the mouth of Azariah) in 15.8, when he had taken courage and set about renewing the nation's allegiance to its god, but in this later case of Hanani's words, Asa becomes 'angry with the seer' and 'in a rage with him' about his message (16.10), and has Yahweh's messenger put 'in the stocks' and 'in prison'; and, as if that were not evil enough, the king 'inflicted cruelties on some of the people at the same time' (v. 10). He who had until now deserved a long and happy reign—indeed one even longer than the great David and Solomon themselves, who had each been blessed with 40-year reigns (1 Chron. 29.27; 2 Chron. 9.30)—no longer deserves to have it continue. He should have noted more carefully the second clauses of the earlier seer, who had said that 'Yahweh is with you, *while you are with him*; if you seek him, he will be found by you, *but if you abandon him, he will abandon you*' (15.2); accordingly, the meaningful clause of the second seer, that Yahweh seeks 'to strengthen *those whose heart is true to him*' (16.9) does not apply to the older and less wise Asa. For almost all his days it could be said of Asa that 'his heart was true' (15.17), but towards the very end of his days we see him fallen from his pedestal.

It is a sad demise to an otherwise glorious reign, and yet the Annalists indulge in some evident humour in the telling of the tale, for they relate that 'his disease became severe, yet even in his disease he did not seek Yahweh, but sought help from physicians' (16.12). They do not spell out that the name 'Asa' is a term for 'Healer' or 'Physician' in the Aramaic language, though, as we have seen, the story does bring this disease upon the king as a consequence of his having made an alliance with the king of Aram rather than having relied upon the Hebrew god. One imagines that the early readers of this tale, presumably knowing the Aramaic language reasonably well—as the *lingua franca* of the wider world and a language closely related to Hebrew—and perhaps having consulted an *'āsā'* from time to time themselves, would have chuckled at this pun that juxtaposes the Aramaic word for 'physician' (the king's name *'āsā'*) with the Hebrew word for 'physicians' (*rōpĕ'im*), and such readers would hardly have missed the irony of a so-called physician who cannot heal himself and cannot even find healing from others who are termed physicians, but instead sinks to an ignominious death.

Nevertheless, Asa 'the Healer' does receive an honourable burial, laid to rest with his fathers in the royal tombs, and with 'a very great fire' lit in his honour (v. 14). His 41 years on the throne of Judah will only be outdone by two later rulers, Uzziah (a.k.a. Azariah, with a reign of 52 years [26.3]) and Manasseh (55 years from coronation to death [33.1], though with an unspecified amount of time imprisoned in Babylon in the midst of this period [33.11]). That counts for something, even if 'the Healer' dies unhealed of his 'disease of the feet'.

2 Chronicles 17–20: Jehoshaphat 'the Adjudicator'

Chapter 17

Despite his own Aramaic name and his renewed alliance with the kingdom of Aram (16.2-4), King Asa did not bestow an Aramaic name upon his son; and despite his annoyance at the thoroughly negative judgment that Yahweh had passed upon his seemingly effective international policy (16.7-10), the name which he had placed upon his successor was a proclamation that 'Yahweh judges' (*yĕhôšāpāṭ*). Evidently the name is to be attributed to Asa's earlier period of utter fidelity to Yahweh (chs. 14–15), an attribution borne out by the Annalists' computations that Jehoshaphat 'was 35 years old when he began to reign' (20.31) and that the lapse in his father's seeking of the national god had taken place just five years before the end of Asa's reign (taking the figure of '36' in 16.1 from the figure of '41' in 16.13); these figures would place the birth of the one named Jehoshaphat in the first decade of Asa's period on the throne, a period in which that king was seen as 'doing what was good and right in the sight of his god Yahweh' (14.2) and in which his god was seen as 'giving him peace' (14.6); there are no misgivings about Yahweh's judgments on the part of the monarch at that happy time.

The new royal name will become particularly resonant later in the tale of King Jehoshaphat, when we see 'the Yahwistic Adjudicator' appointing judges to judge on behalf of Yahweh (19.5-7), but already at the beginning of his reign he is implicitly living up to the meaning of his designation. He has evidently decided to 'walk in the earlier ways of his father' (17.3) and to seek 'his father's god' rather than other deities that the northern people of Israel are said to follow (v. 4). Indeed 'his heart was courageous in the ways of Yahweh' (v. 6), just as his father had taken courage after a word from Yahweh (in 15.8), and he sets about renewing and deepening the Yahwisation of the land that his father had begun to undertake at that earlier time, 'removing the high places' (17.6) that Asa had not succeeded in removing

(15.17) and also removing 'the sacred poles' (*'ăšērîm*, 17.6) that Asa must have allowed to reappear after his earlier efforts (14.3) and his especially fine example of cutting down, crushing and burning a particularly prominent such edifice (an *'ăšērâ*-image, 15.16).

In view of the straightforward formula that had been proclaimed to Jehoshaphat's father, that 'Yahweh is with you while you are with him' (15.2), it should be no surprise for readers to find the Annalists now say that 'Yahweh was with Jehoshaphat' (17.3) and that 'Yahweh established the kingdom in his hand' (v. 5). And they are delighted also to say that 'the fear of Yahweh fell on all the kingdoms of the lands around Judah' (v. 10), with even Philistines bringing presents and tribute to the king in Jerusalem (v. 11); such matters are reminiscent of the reign of the mighty David himself, when he comprehensively defeated the Philistines and his fame 'went out into all lands, and Yahweh brought the fear of him on all nations' (1 Chron. 14.17). Jehoshaphat's initial intention had been to 'strengthen himself against Israel' (2 Chron. 17.1) by placing troops in the fortified cities of Judah 'and in the cities of Ephraim that his father Asa had taken' from the kingdom of Israel (v. 2), but he also finds himself in the happy position of facing no threats from any of the surrounding nations. He even receives gifts from a people that had not been mentioned in the stories of his ancestor David, namely 'the Arabs' (v. 11), who bring to him from their extensive flocks no less than '7,700 rams and 7,700 male goats'; perhaps Jehoshaphat might have preferred something like the 'gold and silver' that 'all the kings of Arabia' had brought to Solomon's door (9.14), but nevertheless such a large gift of these invaluable animals will certainly serve the kingdom well.

Although it will be some time before 'the Adjudicator' sends adjudicators throughout his realm, Jehoshaphat engages in something of a dress rehearsal for that policy by already 'in the third year of his reign' sending out various 'officials' (v. 7) and 'Levites' and 'priests' (v. 8). Their mission is 'to teach in the cities of Judah' (v. 7), which they are able to do primarily by means of 'the book of the law of Yahweh' that they have with them (v. 9). Jehoshaphat's father Asa had commanded the people of Judah 'to keep the law [of Yahweh]' (14.4), and now his son has devised a policy that can assist his subjects in such an aspiration. The situation that had once prevailed, of the people being 'without a teaching priest', as the prophetic word had described matters to

Asa (15.3), must not be allowed to repeat itself; the new policy of sending out from Jerusalem these accomplished individuals to 'go around through all the cities of Judah and teach among the people' should see to that.

At the same time as sending a very small band of authorised teachers out from Jerusalem (vv. 7-8 appear to indicate that just 16 individuals are commissioned), Jehoshaphat is gathering a very large band of soldiers in Jerusalem (vv. 14-18 appear to indicate that a force of 1,160,000 men are mustered). Now it may be that the Annalists are not trying to foist so huge a figure upon their readers. After all, that number of soldiers would seem to suggest a total population in excess of three million people for the capital city, and that seems scarcely conceivable even in the Annalists' story-world. Perhaps by 'thousand' (*'elep*) they mean a military unit that notionally contained up to a thousand men but in practice may have contained considerably fewer soldiers than the literal number suggested—but even if they only mean that the king of Judah had stationed in his capital 1,160 of the largest military units that constituted a Hebrew fighting force, it is still an amazingly large figure for the Annals to present, particularly when we see that these are just the troops stationed in the capital, 'besides those [unnumbered soldiers] whom the king had placed in the fortified cities throughout all Judah' (v. 19).

The Annalists are presumably trying to impress readers with this notion of a huge fighting force at Jehoshaphat's disposal. When David had counted the number of soldiers under his command in the full kingdom of all Israel, he had found that he had 1,100,000 fighting men, including—or perhaps in addition to—470,000 Judahite fighters but without taking into account the tribes of Benjamin and Levi (1 Chron. 21.5-6), so Jehoshaphat's ability to muster a similar number of soldiers, and not even including those he had stationed outside of Jerusalem, from just a fraction of David's territory five generations later is an impressive statistic. But in placing such gargantuan figures in the Annals, the compilers seem to undermine their own picture. Jehoshaphat's massive army conjures up an image either of a king who expects his kingdom to be invaded at any moment, thus belying the trust in Yahweh that previous verses have appeared to portray, or of a king who needs a militarised state to keep his people in check, thus belying the bucolic image of Levites and priests teaching the people from Yahweh's law-book that the earlier part of the chapter had appeared to portray. Equally ominously, it could herald a dangerous situation in which the king will need to find something with which to occupy his troops and to get them out of Jerusalem, perhaps by launching an ill-advised assault on another kingdom, and indeed we will not have long to wait before just such a development takes place.

Chapter 18

'The Adjudicator' now makes a serious error of judgment in the Annalists' world: 'he made a marriage alliance with Ahab' (16.1).

Not a great deal is said about King Ahab of Israel in the Annals, but what is said about the northern monarch makes it clear that he is to be regarded as the lowest of the low. The present chapter reports the prophet Micaiah proclaiming that Yahweh has decreed disaster for Ahab (v. 22). Later it will be reported that Jehoshaphat's son Jehoram, king of Judah after his father, 'walked in the way of the kings of Israel, as the house of Ahab had done, for the daughter of Ahab was his wife; he did what was evil in Yahweh's sight' (21.6); and then that Jehoram's son Ahaziah 'also walked in the ways of the house of Ahab, for his mother was his counsellor in doing wickedly; he did what was evil in Yahweh's sight, as the house of Ahab had done' (22.3-4). The fall-out will even include an attempt by the daughter of Ahab, the infamous Athaliah, wife of Jehoram and mother of Ahaziah, 'to destroy all the royal family of the house of Judah' (22.10). All of this has been set in train by Jehoshaphat's making of a marriage alliance with Ahab.

Since no details are given about the particular marriage which Jehoshaphat contracts with the house of Ahab, and no later reference is made to the particularities of Jehoshaphat's own wife or wives but reference is made to the principal wife of his son being a daughter of Ahab (21.6), the Annalists are presumably thinking here in 18.1 in terms of Jehoshaphat arranging a marriage between the heir to his throne and the daughter of the northern king rather than in terms of Jehoshaphat himself marrying a daughter or sister of Ahab. We had read of Rehoboam 'finding many wives for his sons' in 11.23, so Jehoshaphat finding a wife for his son, and in so doing forging a bond between the two Hebrew kingdoms, might be seen as a highly accomplished act. It has certainly transformed the relationship between the two kingdoms: where once there had been 'continual wars' between north and south (12.15), with especially significant outbreaks during the reigns both of Jehoshaphat's grandfather (ch. 13) and of his father (ch. 16), and he himself had had to begin his reign by 'strengthening himself against Israel' (17.1), we now find him sitting convivially with the king of Israel in the northern capital, talking of a possible war that the two can fight side by side against a common enemy rather than of any continuation of the previous warfare between their two kingdoms. It would seem a splendid contract to have entered into—except for its evident potential to compromise the earlier situation that had described the king of Judah as one who 'sought his father's god and walked in his commandments, and not according to the ways of Israel' (17.4).

And who is the common enemy that the two Hebrew kings are contemplating a strike against? None other than the kingdom which had aided the former king of Judah in his desire to shake off the unwelcome attentions of the former king of Israel, namely the kingdom of Aram. At first we are simply told that the present king of Israel has plans to launch an attack on the city of Ramoth-gilead (vv. 2, 3, 5). This place had been mentioned in the genealogies at the beginning of the Annals as a Levite settlement within the territory of the Israelite tribe of Gad (1 Chron. 6.80), so it seems a legitimate aspiration of the king of Israel to bring this area back into Israelite hands—though it is unlikely that he has any plans to return the settlement to the Levites and thus to undo what his predecessors had achieved when 'the Levites had left their common lands and their holdings [in the northern kingdom] and had come to Judah and Jerusalem, because Jeroboam and his sons had prevented them from serving as priests of Yahweh' (11.14). But it soon becomes clear that Ramoth-gilead is currently held by 'the Arameans' (v. 10), and that it is 'the king of Aram' (v. 30) against whom the king of Judah is being asked to fight alongside the king of Israel. Jehoshaphat is being called upon to break the alliance that his grandfather and father had had with Aram (16.3), and to help reverse the Aramean incursion into former Israelite territory (16.4-6). In itself the idea of no longer being in alliance with the Arameans might have appealed to the Annalists, who seemed distinctly unhappy about the arrangement (16.7-9), but standing against Aram will bring no good for either Judah or Israel.

The invitation to mount an attack on his kingdom's erstwhile ally, in league with his new ally, seems entirely right and proper to Jehoshaphat. His response to Ahab is, 'I am as you are, and my people as your people; we are with you in the war' (v. 3). He seems rather eager to cement the new status of brothers-in-arms or kings-in-law that the Judahite–Israelite royal marriage had secured, and eager to find an outlet for that staggering amount of military energy that has been cooped up in Jerusalem (17.13-19). Nevertheless he has the presence of mind to call for a prognostication from Yahweh so as to be sure that the omens are favourable for embarking on the campaign (18.4), and Ahab accordingly assembles the kingdom's prophets to solicit the divine will. No less than 400 prophets are gathered before the two kings, and they all prophesy that the deity views the operation favourably and will give victory to the Israelite forces, but this display of unanimity seems to raise some unease or curiosity in Jehoshaphat's mind and he asks whether there is any other prophet of Yahweh who might be consulted on the matter. Perhaps he has heard of the notoriety of Micaiah son of Imlah, who 'never prophesies anything favourable about [King Ahab], but only disaster' (v. 7), and feels that at least one dissenting voice ought to be heard before the kings proceed to the battle, lest, with nothing but overwhelming proclamations of assured victory ringing in their ears, they be too confident and take insufficient care to secure the predicted victory.

The said Micaiah son of Imlah is produced, and surprisingly he is no dissenting voice after all, but actually prophesies something favourable about King Ahab, with no talk of disaster whatsoever. His message is as one with the 400 other prophets: 'Go up and triumph; they will be given into your hand' (v. 14; cf. vv. 5, 11). Ahab cannot believe his ears, and suspects that Micaiah is simply aping the other prophets rather than speaking his own mind. And indeed, when the king challenges Micaiah, he breaks ranks with his fellow-prophets and delivers the disaster-talk that has come to be expected of him: Israel will be 'scattered on the mountains, like sheep without a shepherd' (v. 16). The apparently prophetic words about Ahab achieving a great victory at Ramoth-gilead, Micaiah now reveals, were specifically designed by the deity to fool Ahab into mounting a doomed expedition, because Yahweh wants to entice the king of Israel to his death at the hands of the Arameans; a 'lying spirit' had been dispatched from the heavenly council to inspire all Ahab's prophets with the false notion that victory was decreed, when the truth is that 'Yahweh has decreed disaster for you' (v. 22).

This is an extraordinary scene in several respects. For one thing, if it is Yahweh's intention that all the prophets should speak only of victory so that Ahab will proceed to his death, it seems strange that a prophet should be permitted by Yahweh to reveal the devious plan to the two kings and their counsellors. Presumably the deity foresees that Micaiah's testimony will be dismissed, and perhaps the 'lying spirit' (of vv. 21 and 22) is at work in prompting the prominent prophet Zedekiah son of Chenaanah to immediately challenge Micaiah (in v. 23), thus ensuring that the king sees Micaiah's words as the product of the man's hatred for the king rather than as indisputably the genuine word of Yahweh. But that is the other intriguing aspect of the scene: that prophets such as Zedekiah are deceived by their god. Zedekiah's name (*ṣidĕqîyāhû*, 'Yahweh is my righteousness', vv. 10 and 23, the same name as will be borne by the last king of Judah), his formula of revelation (*kōh ʾāmar yahweh*, 'Thus says Yahweh', v. 10, the same formula as is used countless times in the Hebrew Bible), and his belief that he possessed 'the spirit of Yahweh' (*rûaḥ yahweh*, v. 23) characterize him as a Yahwistic prophet and not a devotee of another god. All along Jehoshaphat and Ahab have been seeking 'the word of Yahweh' (v. 4) from 'the prophets of Yahweh' (v. 6), and have been hearing from the prophets that 'Yahweh will give [the city] into the hand of the king' (v. 11). Micaiah's vision has the prophets receiving a message that has been sent to them from Yahweh's heavenly council; a false message it may be, to serve the divine purpose, but it is not a message being made up by the prophets themselves or being received from another deity or from a non-heavenly realm. The stark implication of Micaiah's vision is that Yahweh deceives his own prophets when it suits his purposes, and even having 400 prophets all convinced of Yahweh's will is no guarantee that that will has been discerned.

Of course the two kings do not recognize the true divine will, since Yahweh does not wish it to be recognized at this point. The story of Micaiah's vision will vindicate the deity after the outcome of the battle, when, were it not for that lone spokesman's revelations, the accusation that Yahweh had wrongly predicted a great victory for the combined forces of Israel and Judah might be flung at the heavens. But insofar as Jehoshaphat was faced with two competing 'witness accounts' about Yahweh's stance on the Ramoth-gilead project and he chose to accept the wrong one, heading off to the front apparently under the misapprehension that the omens were favourable for battle, we see a king of Judah hardly living up to his name of 'Yahweh's Adjudicator'.

And when he then agrees to Ahab's suggestion that he attend the battlefield in full royal regalia while Ahab himself goes in disguise (v. 29), one wonders if Jehoshaphat is so overawed with his northern counterpart that he will accept anything the king of Israel proposes.

It turns out that the king of Aram has instructed his troops to pin-point the king of Israel and focus all their efforts on him. It is as if the Aramean monarch is aware of Micaiah's prophecy that Israel is to become 'like sheep without a shepherd' (v. 16) on this day, and he apparently has no concern about the king of Judah, even though the latter is the one breaking an alliance with Aram. But with the Arameans concentrating their military efforts on the conspicuous royal presence on the battlefield, it is Jehoshaphat who comes under fiercest attack, and it is only Yahweh's protection that keeps him from succumbing to the onslaught (presumably when he 'cries out' in v. 32, we are to understand this as a plea to his god for help, because Yahweh immediately helps him by drawing the attackers away from him). Contrariwise, there is no divine protection on Ahab, whose disguise-strategy comes horribly unstuck when quite by chance—or by divine design?—an Aramean arrow 'struck the king of Israel between the scale armour and the breastplate' (v. 33). The wounded king is carried from the field of battle on his chariot, and dies at the going down of the sun.

King Ahab of Israel had 'faced the Arameans' (v. 34), and lost. He had wanted to believe that Zedekiah's prophecy 'you shall gore the Arameans until they are destroyed' (v. 10) would prove true and that Micaiah's counter-prophecy that 'Yahweh has decreed disaster for you' (v. 22) would prove false. Ahab had boasted that he would 'return in peace' from Ramoth-gilead (v. 26), but Micaiah had responded, 'If you return in peace, Yahweh has not spoken by me' (v. 27). At the end of the episode, it is clear that Yahweh has indeed spoken by Micaiah son of Imlah, and the disaster that he had decreed for King Ahab is accomplished. Perhaps surprisingly, though, King Jehoshaphat of Judah, his accomplice in the folly of the battle of Ramoth-gilead, is able to 'return in peace to his house in Jerusalem' (19.1). Micaiah's words had not been for Jehoshaphat, who lives to fight another day.

Chapter 19

It is in this chapter that the name of Jehoshaphat (*yĕhôšāpāṭ*, 'Yahweh Judges') comes especially to the fore. After a reprimand from the prophet Jehu for having gone on the ill-fated expedition with the northern kingdom's King Ahab—a 'wicked' man who 'hates Yahweh' (v. 2)—the southern monarch sets about justifying the prophet's words that Jehoshaphat himself is generally someone who has 'set his heart to seek the deity' (v. 3). He begins a particular policy initiative in which the elements of his name echo and re-echo: 'He appointed *judges* (*šōpĕṭîm*) in the land in all the fortified cities of Judah, city by city, and said to the *judges* (*šōpĕṭîm*), "Consider what you are doing, for you *judge* (*šāpaṭ*) not on behalf of human beings but on behalf of *Yahweh*; he is with you in giving *judgment* (*mišpāṭ*). Now, let the fear of *Yahweh* be upon you; take care what you do, for there is no perversion of justice with our god *Yahweh*, or partiality, or taking of bribes." Moreover in Jerusalem *Jehoshaphat* appointed certain Levites and priests and heads of families of Israel, to give *judgment* (*mišpāṭ*) for *Yahweh* and to decide disputed cases' (vv. 5-8).

This is not an entirely new venture for Jehoshaphat, for very early on in his reign he had sent out various officials, including Levites and priests, to 'teach in the cities of Judah' (17.7-9). The present arrangements, which also charge the priests and the heads of families to 'instruct' the people (19.10), are a deepening and furthering of that earlier policy, but now, with the particular element of 'judging' that has been introduced with the appointment of personnel called 'judges', the particularity of the destiny implied in the king's name is at last fulfilled. And when it comes, it is tinged with a certain irony due to what has happened in between the two episodes of royal appointments: all this judging and instructing is 'so that [the people] may not incur guilt before Yahweh, and wrath may not come' upon them, says the king (v. 10), presumably chastened by the prophet's words that 'because of this [cooperation with Ahab], wrath from Yahweh is upon you' (v. 2). The king ends his charge to the appointees with the prayerful expression, 'May Yahweh be with the good!' (v. 11), no doubt grateful for the prophetic judgment in his own case that 'some good is found in you' (v. 3).

The prophet who makes that judgment is 'Jehu son of Hanani' (v. 2), who goes out to meet Jehoshaphat after the king has escaped amazingly unscathed from the battle at Ramoth-gilead. As a southern prophet, Jehu had not been among the 401 prophets consulted before the battle; all of those practitioners, including the unique voice of Micaiah, had been northern personnel, and although Jehoshaphat had had the presence of mind to call for the local prophets to be consulted before he fully committed the Judahite troops to Ahab's misadventure, and proceeds only after the prophetic vote is 400-to-1, it would seem that he had not consulted any Judahite prophets before he had gone to the festive occasion in Samaria at which Ahab proposed the assault against the Arameans. Indeed, the fateful 'marriage alliance with Ahab' that Jehoshaphat had made some years before (18.1), and which will have such severe repercussions for the kingdom of Judah in the following generations, seems to have been contracted without the benefit of prophetic advice, judging from Jehu's depiction here of the house of Ahab as being composed of 'those who hate Yahweh' (19.2).

Jehu himself is a member of a house of some repute. He is the son of Hanani, the seer who had castigated Jehoshaphat's father Asa for re-establishing the alliance with the kingdom of Aram and who had been thrown into prison for his trouble (16.7-10). Jehu might have feared a similar result in his generation, but Jehoshaphat gives no direct response to the son of Hanani; the royal efforts at Yahwistic adjudicating that begin immediately after the seer's proclamation provide an appropriate response to the divine words. Meanwhile the implication that the prophetic mantle can be passed from father to son, or that the task of prophesying is seen as belonging to certain families, is not encountered here for the first or last time in the Annals. At the founding of the kingdom, David had 'set apart for the service the sons of Asaph, and of Heman, and of Jeduthun, who were to prophesy with lyres, harps, and cymbals' (1 Chron. 25.1); accordingly, the notion that the prophetic arts are to be passed in an hereditary line not unlike that operating for kingship and priesthood, and indeed that it is within levitico-priestly ranks that such arts are to be practised (and to some degree controlled?) is there from the beginning of the kingdom. We will not have long to wait in Jehoshaphat's story to hear of 'the spirit of Yahweh coming upon Jahaziel son of Zechariah, son of Benaiah, son of Jeiel, son of Mattaniah, a Levite of the sons of Asaph' (20.14), and a few generations later we will read of 'the divine spirit taking possession of Zechariah son of the priest Jehoiada' (24.20). Although the Annalists do not explicitly say that the divine spirit had been upon Zechariah's father before him, that implication seems very clear in the tale that is told concerning Jehoiada's actions on the deity's behalf (ch. 23). In any event, a prophet being the son of a prophet should not surprise us in these

Annals, even if we are familiar with a particular Hebrew prophet from elsewhere in the traditions of ancient Israel famously claiming that he was 'no prophet, nor a prophet's son' (Amos 7.14).

This prophet's son, Jehu son of Hanani, has an ominous word for Jehoshaphat: 'wrath is coming upon you from Yahweh' (v. 2), despite the 'good [that] is found in you' (v. 3). After setting up his splendid scheme of Yahwistic adjudicators throughout his kingdom, Jehoshaphat's statement 'May Yahweh be with the good!' (v. 11) sounds a hopeful note, but the king knows that the 'wrath from Yahweh' will have to take its course, and that he and his kingdom will have to face up to it.

Chapter 20

Jehoshaphat is both punished and tested by a new invasion of the land of Judah, this time by a combination of at least 'the Moabites and Ammonites' (v. 1), two eastern neighbours of Judah who had reportedly been under David's thumb in earlier times (1 Chron. 18.2; 20.1-3), and some other groups either with them or standing behind them. Verse 1 appears to speak of the Ammonites twice (*běnê ʿammôn wěimmāhām mēhāʿammônîm*, literally 'the sons of Ammon and with them some of the Ammonites'), and then later v. 10 refers to 'the people of Mt Seir' as being the third party to the invasion, while meanwhile messengers report that the army is coming 'from beyond the sea, from Aram' (*mēʿēber layyām mēʾărām*, v. 2). NRSV emends the third party in v. 1 to 'some of the Meunites' and also emends the reference in v. 2 to 'from Edom', since Meunites and Edomites might be thought to be likely partners to Moabites and Ammonites, given that all of these groups were located more or less 'beyond a sea' from Judah, namely on the eastern side of the Dead Sea and the great rift valley. The latter emendation is attractive in view of the connection which the Annals make on a later occasion between 'the people of Seir' and 'the Edomites' (25.14), but perhaps we should not be too quick to change 'Aram' to 'Edom' here at 20.2, since Jehoshaphat has not long returned from fighting against the Arameans at Ramoth-gilead (19.1) and it may be that the Annalists have in mind that the real instigator behind this incursion into Judahite territory is the kingdom against which the king of Judah had so recently and foolishly dared to strike.

But whether or not Aram is calling the shots, the invading forces are described by Jehoshaphat's scouts as 'a great multitude'

(v. 2), more than enough to make the king 'afraid' (v. 3). Since this is the king who had previously stationed more than a million fighting men in Jerusalem, to say nothing of the additional soldiers that he had stationed in the other fortified cities of his kingdom (17.13-19), readers are invited to imagine either that the ill-fated expedition against Ramoth-gilead to which Jehoshaphat had committed troops (ch. 18) had thoroughly decimated his forces or that the Moabites and Ammonites are able to assemble an even larger number of troops than the staggering numbers which the king of Judah had been reported to have assembled in and around Jerusalem.

Jehoshaphat's judgment on this occasion is impeccable: 'he set himself to seek Yahweh' (v. 3). As his father Asa had done when the Ethiopians invaded Judah with an army of a million men (14.9-11), the king cries out to the national god to defend his people. In the earlier case, the Annalists had reported a relatively short petition to Yahweh, but here they represent a detailed prayer from the lips of Jehoshaphat, and they picture 'all Judah standing before Yahweh, with their little ones, their wives and their children' (20.13), the king having proclaimed a fast throughout the kingdom and having gathered a full assembly of the nation before the temple (vv. 3-4).

The prayer asserts that the god of Israel has power over 'all the kingdoms of the nations' and that 'no one is able to withstand' him (v. 6). It includes some aspects of Israel's foundation legends that are not generally developed in the Annals, namely that Yahweh had 'driven out the inhabitants of this land before your people Israel, and gave it forever to the descendants of your friend Abraham' (v. 7), and notes that the present invaders were peoples 'whom you would not let Israel invade when they came from the land of Egypt' (v. 8)—such an assertion calls to mind a Hebrew tradition that Yahweh had commanded Moses not to engage the Moabites or the Ammonites in battle, since the deity was not intending to give the descendants of Abraham any of those lands as a possession (see Deuteronomy 2:9, 19). In Jehoshaphat's prayer, then, the Moabites and Ammonites are depicted as breaking a divinely-ordained arrangement in that they are now 'coming to drive us out of your possession that you have given us to inherit' (2 Chron. 20.11); he conveniently neglects to mention David's expansion of the Israelite realm into Moab and Ammon, and he makes no reference to his own abortive breaking of the alliance with Aram that may have precipitated the present incursion into Judahite territory. But he does allude to the great prayer that his ancestor Solomon had made at the dedication of the temple, when he represents the people as saying, 'If disaster comes upon us, the sword, judgment, or pestilence, or famine, we will stand before this House, and before you, for your name is in this House, and cry to you in our distress, and you will hear and save' (v. 9)—echoing the repeated refrain of Solomon's prayer, that 'if there is famine in the land' or 'if your people go out to battle against their enemies' or if some other calamity is upon them, 'may you hear from heaven' and 'maintain their cause' (6.22-39).

Solomon's prayer of dedication had ended 'O my god, let your eyes be open and your ears attentive to prayer from this place' (6.40). And in the present episode, the god of Israel shows himself to be fully open and attentive to such a prayer, for 'in the middle of the assembly' one of the Levites has 'the spirit of Yahweh' come upon him (20.14), and he proclaims a prophetic word, reassuring king and people that their god will indeed maintain their cause and that tomorrow they will 'see the victory of Yahweh on [their] behalf' (v. 17). Worship and praise ensue (vv. 18-19).

Heartened by the prophecy of a decisive victory, Jehoshaphat assembles the troops early the next morning, not neglecting to position in a prominent role some morale-boosting musicians, who, with their refrain 'Give thanks to Yahweh, for his steadfast love endures forever' (v. 21), replicate an earlier procession organized by the great David himself (1 Chron. 16.14). The king's pre-battle slogan is also poetic (though the NRSV mysteriously avoids the full parallelism by not including the last clause): 'Believe in your god Yahweh, and you will be established; believe in his prophets, and you will succeed' (2 Chron. 20.20). Victory is assured.

The Judahites do not even have to engage in actual battle against the invading hordes, who turn out to be such an incoherent combination of forces that they end up fighting each other to the death before Jehoshaphat's troops have set eyes on them. This is Yahweh's doing, say the Annalists: Judah's god had 'set an ambush' against the enemies of his nation, 'so that they were routed' (v. 22) at their own hands. All that the people of Judah have left to do, after the rag-tag band of Ammonites, Moabites, and 'inhabitants of Seir' (as the third party is now styled, v. 23) have destroyed one another, is to gather up booty—'livestock, goods, clothing, and precious things' (v. 25)—left behind by the would-be conquerors. And since it had been 'a great multitude' that was coming against Judah (v. 2), there is now a great 'abundance' of booty (v. 25) to be gleaned from the dead corpses lying on the battlefield and from the camps of the utterly destroyed armies. The enemies from the east had doubtlessly planned to carry great booty away from Judah after their anticipated conquest of the kingdom, but they had not reckoned on Judah's god sowing utter confusion among them and handing their own possessions on a plate to the people of Judah. Well might the Judahites 'bless' (*bĕrak*) their god and rename the strategic valley in which the intentions of the enemy were turned to dust as the 'Valley of Blessing' (*'ēmeq bĕrākâ*, v. 26), and well might they return to Jerusalem with rejoicing and further musical celebrations in honour of Yahweh (vv. 27-28).

After this dramatic turnaround, all seems well in Jehoshaphat's realm. Fear of his god falls on all the surrounding nations, and his kingdom can live in peace—a reiteration of the situation that had pertained earlier in his reign, before he had become mixed up in Ahab's warfare plans (compare 17.10 and 20.29-30). He reigns for a full quarter-century (v. 31), 'walking in the way of his father Asa and not turning aside from it, doing what was right in Yahweh's sight' (v. 32). And yet there are two niggling aspects that the Annalists note concerning his legacy: there were still 'high places' left in the kingdom in competition with the central temple in Jerusalem, a feature casting doubt on whether the people were fully committed to a thoroughgoing Yahwism (v. 33), and the king persisted in cooperating with the apostate kingdom of the north, this time 'joining with King Ahaziah of Israel, who did wickedly' (v. 35). Jehoshaphat should have taken to heart the message he had received from the prophet Jehu after the disastrous joint war-project with King Ahab of Israel, that venturing with the northern monarchy was 'helping the wicked and loving those who hate Yahweh' (19.2), but it seems that he must be taught the lesson one more time. On this occasion it is a prophet named Eliezer who steps forward to proclaim that Yahweh will not allow this latest joint venture to be any more successful than the earlier one. Building ships in Ezion-geber on the Red Sea might be seen in itself as a noble enterprise akin to the exploits of Solomon at his grandest (8.17-18), but the continued friendship with the house of Ahab that the scheme represents is too much for Yahweh, and he sees to it that no such trading enterprise, which would have benefited the kingdom of Israel along with the kingdom of Judah, can be established. 'The ships were wrecked and were not able to go to Tarshish, and Jehoshaphat [died] and was buried' (20.35–21.1). Thus did Yahweh decisively judge the Yahwistic judge-maker for joining with the apostates of the north.

2 Chronicles 21:
Jehoram 'the Exalter'

Jehoshaphat had brought his people 'back to Yahweh, the god of their ancestors' (19.4); when danger threatened, his rallying cry had been 'Believe in your god Yahweh and you will be established' (20.20), and after the great victory he had led the nation in 'blessing Yahweh' (20.26). It is little surprise, then, that he called his firstborn son Jehoram (*yĕhôrām*, 'Yahweh is exalted'). Jehoshaphat had seven sons in all—the others are listed in 21.2 as 'Azariah, Jehiel, Zechariah, Azariah, Michael, and Shephatiah' (the two Azariahs have slightly different spellings to their respective names, the first given the shorter form *'ăzarĕyâ* and the latter the longer form *'ăzarĕyāhû*, but even so the repeated name suggests either that the Annalists have made an error or that the earlier Azariah had died before the younger one was born)—and he ensured that they all benefited from the wealth of his kingdom, 'but he gave the kingdom to Jehoram, because he was the firstborn' (v. 3).

When the Davidic genealogy had been set out in 1 Chronicles 3, the name of Jehoshaphat's successor was given as 'Joram' (*yôrām*, 1 Chron. 3.11), but in the telling of his tale here in 2 Chronicles 21 the fuller form of 'Jehoram' is consistently used (vv. 1, 3, 4, 5, 9, 16; so also in 22.1, 6, 11; though the Annalists do use both forms of the name when they narrate about the northern king bearing the same moniker, referring to the latter as 'Jehoram' in 22.5*a*, 6, 7*b*, but as 'Joram' in 22.5*b*, 7*a*). The two forms of the name are eminently interchangeable, merely giving the element that signifies 'Yahweh' in either a shorter ('Yo') or a longer ('Yeho') style, together with the unchanged verbal element of 'ram', which is also a component of one of the names borne by the great ancestral figure of the Hebrew peoples, namely 'Abram [= "Exalted Father"], that is, Abraham [= "Father of a Multitude"]' (1 Chron. 1.27).

But the present Joram or Jehoram is no Abram or Abraham. As soon as he has power in his hands, 'he put all his brothers to the sword, and also some of the officials of Judah' (2 Chron. 21.4). Such reprehensible actions have not been seen in the Annals before this event. Solomon had had many brothers (1 Chron. 3.1-9; 14.3-7), yet the Annalists presented no tales of any jostling for power in his time; rather, as befits the quintessential man of peace (1 Chron. 22.9), he was depicted as having ascended the throne smoothly and ruling wisely and benevolently. Abijah had also had many brothers (2 Chron. 11.18-23), yet there had been no difficulties in the royal family over his father appointing him to be the successor. And Asa too had been one of very many sons of the previous monarch (13.21), yet the succession in his case too had apparently been a smooth and harmonious affair. But Jehoram introduces a devastating new element into Judahite politics in these Annals, in making sure that any rival claimants to the throne—his own flesh and blood—are eliminated, along with any officials who might oppose his rule or his methods.

The reason given for Jehoram's appalling behaviour, so out of keeping with the former ways of the kingdom of Judah, is that 'he walked in the way of the kings of Israel, as the house of Ahab had done, for the daughter of Ahab was his wife' (21.6). We will later see this same woman 'setting about to destroy all the royal family of the house of Judah' (22.10), after she had acted as the 'counsellor' of her son Ahaziah 'in doing wickedly' (22.3), so the implication seems to be that it is she who is the devisor of all such wickedness that begins to infect the palace as soon as her husband Jehoram has been placed on the throne. She herself will not be named until later, when we will discover that she is 'Athaliah, a granddaughter of Omri' (22.2), but already her presence is becoming ominous. The ramifications of Jehoram's father Jehoshaphat having 'made a marriage alliance with Ahab' (18.1), which presumably referred to the marriage of his son Jehoram to Ahab's daughter Athaliah, and which had been part of the policy that the prophet Jehu had labelled as a 'love of those who hate Yahweh' (19.2), are now beginning to be seen. Were it not for 'the covenant that [Yahweh] had made with David', in which the deity 'had promised to give a lamp to him and to his descendants forever' (21.7), the Davidic dynasty would be doomed as a result of the Ahabite virus that has been let in through the foolishness of Jehoshaphat.

The damage done to the Davidic legacy is already seen in that 'in [Jehoram's] days Edom revolted against the rule of Judah and set up a king of their own' (v. 8). This reads as though the

Edomites were regarded by the Israelites and Judahites as being rightfully under Hebrew rule ever since Edom had been placed under subjection by David (1 Chron. 18.13). That territory was still reported as part of Israel's domain in the time of Solomon (2 Chron. 8.17), and if its inhabitants are now reported as revolting against Judah then the picture so presented is that Edom was southern territory which Rehoboam managed to hold on to when the northern Israelite tribes broke away from the house of David under the rebellion led by Jeroboam son of Nebat (ch. 10). Edom may have been among the group of formerly subjugated nations that lashed out against Judah in the time of Jehoshaphat (NRSV reads 'Edom' rather than 'Aram' in 20.2), but if not then this is the first concerted efforts by the Edomites to reinstate their former independence—they had after all had their own kings before Israel had produced a king (1 Chron. 1.43-54), so now at last, six generations on from their first subjugation by David, they see their chance. With Jehoram having concentrated his energies on in-fighting within the royal family and having damaged his army by executing various 'officials' as well as princes (v. 4), now is the perfect time for a revolt by a subject people.

The Edomites are not alone in their revolt from Jehoram's rule. The territory of Libnah also shakes him off, or at least attempts to do so. When we recall that 'Libnah with its pasture lands' had been decreed by divine lot as being dedicated to the support of the Aaronite priests (1 Chron. 6.57), its revolt is particularly pertinent: we are told that they 'revolted against his rule because he had forsaken Yahweh, the god of his fathers' (2 Chron. 21.10). Perhaps we can assume that they remained an integral part of the Hebrew realm, even if they declined to give their allegiance to Jehoram, but it is noted that 'Edom has been in revolt against the rule of Judah to this day' (v. 10). No details are given of the outcome of the battle at which Jehoram's chariots are surrounded by Edomites (v. 9), but it would seem that Jehoram managed to escape but did not manage to re-subjugate the Edomites; perhaps an uneasy stand-off between Judah and Edom ensued from that time, until a more decisive battle two generations later (25.14).

A unique prophetic communication now takes place: 'A letter came to [Jehoram] from the prophet Elijah' (v. 12). The delivery of a letter rather than the appearance of the prophet in the flesh, as all other prophets appear in these pages, is curious, but the Annalists give no further details about this Elijah. If we were to enquire into other Hebrew traditions we would find legends about him being a prophet active in the northern kingdom and in an earlier period than the time of Jehoram's reign in the south, and we might accordingly speculate that he sent a letter because he was unable to travel to Jerusalem to deliver his message orally and in person—perhaps because he was imprisoned in the north, as was done to the prophet Micaiah in the time of King Ahab (18.25-26), and as King Asa of Judah had done to the seer Hanani (16.10), or perhaps more dramatically because Yahweh instructed him to write down his message so that it could be taken to King Jehoram of Judah when it would become relevant some years after Elijah's own death. But as intriguing as such a storyline is, the Annalists do not flesh any such details out; they simply report that this prophet's communication to this king came in epistolary form, perhaps leaving it to the prophet's particular references to 'the way of the kings of Israel' and of 'the house of Ahab' (v. 13) to suggest that these words come from a northern prophet who has seen the Israelite kings at close hand.

The message so delivered, perhaps all the more powerful and unchangeable for being in written form, is that Jehoram will in a sense reap what he has sown: he has killed his brothers, and now he will see his own sons destroyed, along with his wives and his possessions, and he himself will suffer from a long and painful disease. Some kind of 'plague' or 'pestilence' (*maggēpa*, v. 14) will also fall upon the people as whole, since their monarch has 'led Judah and Jerusalem into unfaithfulness, as the house of Ahab led Israel into unfaithfulness' (v. 13).

After the quotation of Elijah's message, the narrative does not really relate a 'plague' on the people at large, other than what misfortune for the inhabitants of the country and the city might be imagined in the brief reference to an invasion by 'the Philistines and the Arabs who are near the Cushites' (v. 16). We are not told of the invaders doing any damage apart from 'carrying away all the possessions they found that belonged to the king's house, along with his sons and his wives, so that no son was left to him except Jehoahaz, his youngest son' (v. 17). Of course in those words there is a very clear match with Elijah's prophecy concerning the king's own household, and so too in the description that follows of Jehoram's long and painful disease: the excruciating 'day after day' that the prophet had foretold (v. 15) turns out to be for an agonising period of 'two years' (v. 19), at the end of which 'his bowels came out because of the disease' (v. 19, echoing the prophecy of v. 15 but now adding for extra effect that 'he died in great agony').

Thus the reign of Jehoram 'the Exalter', who so dismally fails to live out the meaning of his name and to exalt the god Yahweh, is brought to an ignoble end by the deity—it is after all 'Yahweh [who] aroused against Jehoram the anger of the Philistines and the Arabs' (v. 16) and it is 'Yahweh [who] struck him in his bowels with an incurable disease' (v. 18). Had he exalted Yahweh, then Yahweh would surely have exalted him, and he would have enjoyed a longer and happier life, but for this kind of king eight years on the throne is more than enough, and there are to be no fires in his honour or any regrets for his passing. His murderous ways have left the kingdom in a terrible state, and worse is yet to come.

2 Chronicles 22:
Ahaziah 'the Seized'

The name of the sixth king of Judah is presented in two different forms in this narrative. It had been reported that 'no son was left to [the previous king] except Jehoahaz, his youngest son' (21.17); but now, when the tale of that son is taken up, the narrators say that 'the inhabitants of Jerusalem made the youngest son Ahaziah king as his successor' (22.1), and from then on the name 'Ahaziah' is consistently used during the telling of his tale (vv. 1*b*, 2, 6, 7, 8*a*, 8*b*, 9*a*, 9*b*, 10, 11*a*, 11*b*), though later in the Annals he will again be referred to as 'Jehoahaz' (25.23, where NRSV emends the name to 'Ahaziah'). There is also a much later king of Judah known as 'Jehoahaz' (see 36.1-4), though the later one is listed as 'Johanan' in the initial genealogical list (1 Chron. 3.15) while this earlier figure is listed there as 'Ahaziah' (1 Chron. 3.11), the name used throughout his story in 2 Chronicles 22. Meanwhile, these characters are not to be confused with the northern King Ahaziah with whom Jehoshaphat did business (2 Chron. 20.35, 37) nor with the northern King Jehoahaz who will be mentioned in due course (25.17, 25).

That the names 'Ahaziah' and 'Jehoahaz' are readily interchangeable can be understood when it is noted that they are essentially the same name, with the two constituent elements—an abbreviation of the divine name and a verbal element—simply in reverse order, the one being ʾăḥazĕyāhû (that is, the verb ʾāḥaz, 'to grasp or seize', plus 'Yahu', a form of 'Yahweh' used at the end of compound expressions) and the other yĕhôʾāḥāz (that is, 'Yeho', a form of 'Yahweh' used at the beginning of compound expressions, plus the verb ʾāḥaz, 'to grasp or seize'). Thus they are two ways of saying the same thing, namely that 'Yahweh seizes' (in fact the form 'Ahaz-Yahu' rather than 'Yeho-ahaz' represents the normal order of things in a Hebrew sentence, though that is of no consequence when it comes to names welding together the

verb and the subject into a compound form). So let us call this
present king 'Ahaziah', and let us see how Yahweh seizes him.

We will not have long to wait, for Ahaziah reigns for only one
year (v. 2), as befits a king who 'did what was evil in Yahweh's
sight' (v. 4). He is thoroughly compromised by the infiltration of
northerners into his court: his mother, Athaliah daughter of
King Ahab, was 'his counsellor in doing wickedly' (v. 3), and it
seems that other members of 'the house of Ahab' were similarly
'his counsellors, to his ruin' (v. 4). Under their counsel, he even
repeats the very same error of judgment that his grandfather
Jehoshaphat had made in joining the northern kingdom in a
military adventure against the Arameans at Ramoth-gilead.
Jehoshaphat had gone arm in arm with the notorious Ahab
himself (18.3), and Ahaziah tries the same misadventure with
Ahab's grandson Jehoram (22.5*a*, a name abbreviated to 'Joram'
in vv. 5*b* and 7*a*). Yahweh had allowed Jehoshaphat to escape
with his life from that episode, because 'some good is found in
you', as the prophet Jehu son of Hanani had said (19.3), but since
no good is found in Ahaziah, his 'downfall' in this episode has
been 'divinely ordained' to take place at the hands of another
Jehu, 'the son of Nimshi, whom Yahweh had anointed to destroy
the house of Ahab' (22.7).

At first it seems that Ahaziah has repeated the good fortune
of his grandfather in that he is not wounded at the battle, as the
northern monarch is (Jehoram, like Ahab at the earlier battle of
Ramoth-gilead, is injured on the battlefield, although the later
king is able to return to his own territory to seek treatment for his
wounds—not that he will be able to avoid the divinely-appointed
Jehu's destruction of his dynasty). But whereas Jehoshaphat
had been permitted by the deity to 'return in safety to his house
in Jerusalem' (19.1), Ahaziah does not return to his own city but
instead remains in the north to show further solidarity with the
temporarily recuperating King Jehoram of Israel. It is worth
bearing in mind that the two men are represented as cousins, in
that the Annals imply that they are both grandsons of Ahab:
Ahaziah's mother Athaliah is the daughter of Ahab (21.6) and
Jehoram's father Ahaziah of Israel is presumably the son of
Ahab (20.35)—indeed the appearance of the name Ahaziah as a
brother of Athaliah suggests that the man born to be king of Judah
was named after his uncle, the man born to be king of Israel and
destined to become the father of King Jehoram of Israel (unless
the Annalists' expression 'son of Ahab' as applied to Jehoram

[22.5, 6] is taken more narrowly to mean that he was not a later descendant of Ahab's but was rather a younger brother of Ahab's son Ahaziah). In any event, the Annals present King Ahaziah of Judah as a close relative of King Jehoram of Israel, so it could be a touching scene that Ahaziah visits his wounded cousin (or uncle) and brother-in-arms, Jehoram.

But this is no tale of happy families. Indeed, it is almost the end for the family of David, since it has become entwined with the family of Ahab, which Yahweh is determined to destroy. It seems that the national god has commissioned Jehu son of Nimshi not only to wipe out all of the descendants of Ahab in the northern kingdom, but also to execute as many of Ahab's descendants in the southern kingdom as he can find, without actually going to Jerusalem itself. Thus when Jehu encounters 'the officials of Judah and the sons of Ahaziah's brothers who attended Ahaziah, he killed them, and he searched for Ahaziah, who was captured while hiding in Samaria and was brought to Jehu, and he put him to death' (vv. 8-9). Yahweh's plan appears to be that everyone in the royal family of Judah who has grown up under the influence of the royal family of Israel is to be wiped from the national plate, so that Judah can start afresh with a new descendant of David who has imbibed no such influence in his formative years. This individual will be the infant Joash, who is secreted away with his nurse to await a later day (v. 11), but for the moment the Davidic dynasty has 'no one able to rule the kingdom' (v. 9) as a result of the thoroughgoing extermination policy of Yahweh's 'anointed' one (v. 7), Jehu son of Nimshi. It is not just Ahaziah 'the Seized' who is comprehensively seized by Yahweh, but all of his nephews and officials are likewise caught up in this divinely-ordained clear-out of the royal houses of the Hebrew kingdoms.

Yet the house of Ahab has one last nefarious attempt at winning the day in Yahweh's own city, for 'when Athaliah, Ahaziah's mother, saw that her son was dead, she set about to destroy all the royal family of the house of Judah' (v. 10), and she would have succeeded, were it not for the quick and brave thinking of 'Jehoshabeath, daughter of King Jehoram and wife of the priest Jehoiada' (v. 11), who is able to steal away the young Joash 'from among the king's children who were about to be killed' and to hide him and his nurse from Athaliah. On any reckoning, the scenario put forward at this point of the Annals is an astonishing one: the queen mother systematically killing her own grandchildren, but foiled in the full accomplishment of such an horrendous activity by the actions of her daughter (or stepdaughter). The saviour of the Davidic line, Jehoshabeath, as a daughter of Jehoram and sister of Ahaziah, is clearly an aunt of the child she rescues, but is she the daughter of the very queen mother who has set about destroying the royal family? It may be that we are to think of her as having been born of a different mother than the murderous Athaliah, and thus of her being the half-sister of Ahaziah and the stepdaughter of a wicked stepmother. Perhaps it is her status as a woman, and therefore her lack of eligibility to inherit the throne, or perhaps also her status as 'wife of the priest Jehoiada', that protects Jehoshabeath herself from Athaliah's ruthless and heartless campaign to have all of the royal children exterminated, and it would seem that the priestly couple's hiding away of Joash 'in the House of God' (v. 12) is entirely successful, either because Athaliah does not think to look for her missing grandson in such a location or because she is unaware that one of her grandsons and his nurse are not among the bodies of the children and their carers that she had had killed.

If Athaliah does not even know how many grandsons she had, and is unaware that Joash has survived her purge, this is a further indication of her thorough wickedness, but in any case her attempt to wipe out her own flesh and blood should be evidence enough that this daughter of Ahab, no descendant of the saintly David, is no fit queen of the kingdom of Judah. Accordingly, the Annalists do not give her the standard formulations that they use for the legitimate rulers of Judah, of the style 'he was so-and-so-many years old when he began to reign, and he reigned for so-and-so-many years in Jerusalem' (e.g. 12.13; 13.1-2; 20.31) or 'the rest of his acts are written in such-and-such records' (e.g. 12.15; 15.22; 20.34). Instead the kingdom is placed in abeyance for six years, while the wicked Athaliah calls the shots in the palace but the rescued Joash is kept safe in the temple complex.

2 Chronicles 23–24:
Joash 'the Healed'

Chapter 23

The infant called Joash is kept 'hidden in the House of God' for 'six years' (22.12) and he will be just 'seven years old' when he is placed on the throne (24.1). Was it his wicked father Ahaziah who named him, and if so, what was Ahaziah wishing to portend in such a name? As noted in the earlier Survey of Judah's Kings, 'Joash' (yôʾāš) and its variant 'Josiah' (yōʾšiyāhû) are the only names on the king-list of Judah that are not easily interpretable, so it may be that the apostate Ahaziah had some less than wholesome thought in mind which we are no longer able to discern. But given that Ahaziah had been on a campaign in league with King Jehoram of Israel against King Hazael of Aram, and that that foolish venture was extended into a period of recuperation leave in the northern kingdom followed by a period of hiding from the regicide who tracked him down and killed him (22.5-9), we could think of the former king of Judah never laying eyes upon or giving thought to the child born to Zibiah of Beer-sheba (who is recorded in 24.1 as Joash's mother).

Accordingly, we might think of the boy's name as coming not from his father Ahaziah but either from his mother Zibiah or perhaps even more likely from his aunt Jehoshabeath and her husband Jehoiada, as the latter couple were the ones who rescued the infant from his nursery and raised him in the temple precincts (22.11-12), and it is that same Jehoiada, high priest at Yahweh's temple, who will arrange for this Joash to sit upon the throne of the kingdom and to restore the temple. Under such a scenario, the possible meaning of the name identified in the earlier Survey, namely that it proclaims that 'he [i.e. the deity] heals', would be very apt. It is clearly Jehoiada's intention that the boy-king, instructed by his uncle-in-law the chief priest, will be the agency of casting out the infection that Queen Athaliah represents and of renewing a right relationship between the people and their god. It is to be through Joash, Jehoiada would wish to signify, that the deity will heal the open wound in the nation that Athaliah has wrought by means of her wicked counsel during the two previous reigns (21.6; 22.3) and by means of her own subsequent illegitimate rule (22.10, 12).

Jehoiada bides his time, but then in the seventh year of the interregnum he takes steps to place Joash openly on the throne that is his inheritance. The arrangements are elaborate and thorough, and they are effective. It seems that not only the priests and Levites, who might be expected to side with Jehoiada against Athaliah, but also 'the heads of families of Israel' (23.2) and 'the captains who were set over the army' (v. 14) are with the chief priest in his plan, and not a single person turns informant to the queen. It is as if 'all Judah' (v. 8) stands with Jehoiada, and Athaliah alone knows nothing of the venture until she 'heard the noise of the people running and praising the [newly-crowned] king' (v. 12). The tables have been turned on her, and she who had 'set about to destroy all the royal family of the house of Judah' (22.10) is now put to death by an execution squad at the entrance of the Horse Gate of the king's house (23.15). Jehoiada stages a covenant-renewal ceremony, declaring that the people of Judah should be Yahweh's people (v. 16), and the mob immediately goes out to kill their chief priest's rival for religious leadership in the kingdom, 'Mattan, the priest of Baal' (v. 17). Yahweh's temple is put back into good order, everything just as it should be 'according to the order of David' and 'as it is written in the law of Moses' (v. 18). No one 'who was in any way unclean' would henceforth be permitted to enter Yahweh's house; no doubt Jehoiada hopes that no Athaliah will ever again enter Yahweh's kingdom and seek to contaminate it. The Davidic descendant Joash has now been 'set on the royal throne' (v. 20) that was his by right all along, and 'all the people of the land [can now] rejoice, and the city [can be] quiet, after Athaliah had been killed with the sword' (v. 21).

Chapter 24

The hopes invested in the boy-king are well realised while he remains a boy and his uncle-in-law as chief priest calls the shots in the kingdom. We are told that 'Joash did what was right in Yahweh's sight all the days of the priest Jehoiada' (24.2), with the most important manifestation of this rightness being a substantial repair-and-renovation programme for Yahweh's house. Arrangements are made for temple taxes to be collected from across the realm, and, although the Levites are a little slow to become active again after their years of inactivity during the interregnum and have to be cajoled by the king and the chief priest to become effective tax-gatherers, once the system is fully operational we see that 'all the leaders and all the people rejoiced' to be paying their taxes for such a worthy cause (v. 10), and the coffers are soon overflowing. This allows the restoration work to proceed apace, and in no time at all the temple has been brought back 'to its proper condition' (v. 13); there is ample tax revenue to fashion new utensils and vessels for the services of the temple, so that all the Davidic rounds of rituals can be conducted as regularly as they had been conducted before the interruption to the temple's well-being.

After the death of Jehoiada, however, it is a different story. Other officials, sidelined while the all-powerful uncle was around, are now able to gain access to the king's ear, and the king, no longer a boy beholden to the father-figure that had raised him and trained him, listens to these counsellors. He begins to neglect the very temple that he had so assiduously restored, and becomes attracted to other forms of religion. Among the prophets that Yahweh sends to redirect the king, Jehoiada's son Zechariah proclaims the basic principle that prophets of former times had enunciated to former kings: 'Because you have forsaken Yahweh, he has forsaken you' (v. 20; compare the words of the prophet Shemaiah to King Rehoboam in 12.15 or the words of the prophet Azariah to King Asa in 15.2). But rather than heed the words of his cousin Zechariah as he had once obeyed every word of the man who had been a father to both of them, Joash allows or even perhaps orders the death of Yahweh's messenger. The prophet's dying words, 'May Yahweh see and avenge!' (v. 22), are soon acted upon by the deity, who brings the Aramean army to destroy 'all the officials of the people' (v. 23)—presumably every last 'official of Judah' who had so reprehensively turned the king from the ways of Jehoiada and Zechariah (v. 17)—and to strike against the king himself.

By the end of the Aramean attack, the 'few men' from Aram had decimated the 'very great army' of Judah (v. 24), and King Joash is left severely wounded. As king, he would have looked to his servants to give him the best care possible and to do all that they could to bring him back to a robust condition in which he might rally his remaining troops to defend the kingdom. But no, instead of aiding the king in his wounded state, 'his servants conspired against him because of the blood of the son of the priest Jehoiada, and they killed him on his bed' (v. 25). Yahweh had seen, of course, as Zechariah had implored, and in allowing Joash to wallow on his sick-bed and be a prone target for the finishing blow administered by the king's own servants—shadowy figures from foreign parts, one an Ammonite and the other a Moabite (v. 26)—Yahweh had indeed decisively avenged the killing of the chief priest's son.

Later in the Annals (in chapter 35) we will read of a king called Josiah embarking on a disastrous policy of confronting the Egyptian pharaoh, refusing to be dissuaded from his action by a heaven-sent message, and then suffering mortal wounds in battle. The impression there too will be of a story containing an ironic spin on the king's name, if indeed 'Josiah' means 'Yahweh heals', for the deity will not heal that later king either, after he is left severely wounded, on account of his not having listened to the divine word that was proclaimed to him by the pharaoh. The parallels between his fate and that of his ancestor Joash are too marked to be entirely coincidental in this story-world. The Annalists appear to have conformed the dénouements of the two kings on the basis of their names having the same essential meaning: those names appear to proclaim that their god is a god of healing, and yet in both cases that god refrains from performing such an act, since both men are being justly recompensed for their rejection of a clear divine word prior to the commencement of battle. Meanwhile it is noticeable that no other king of Judah is depicted in the Annals as being fatally wounded in battle, yet one notorious king of Israel is so depicted, namely the arch-villain King Ahab. Certain echoes of Ahab's ending are particularly strong in the later case of Josiah (see the discussion under chapter 35), whereas here in chapter 24 such echoes are some-what fainter: there is, for example, no depiction in the account of Joash of any disguise-on-the-battlefield strategy, nor is Joash quoted as giving instructions to his charioteers to carry him from the heat of the battle after he has been wounded, but the same essential outcome that Ahab and Josiah share of being left severely wounded by the battle yet only dying some time later is brought out in Joash's tale too.

For more detailed comments on the Annalists' apparent tactic of presenting the fates of Joash and Josiah in terms of the fate of Ahab, the reader may consult the comments in due course on the tale of Josiah, where the echoes of Ahab are loudest. But in essence, the black-and-white ideology of the Annalists is clear: a king might have been protected by the god of Judah through a dangerous interregnal period so that he could ascend to the throne and restore the temple, but if, after the restoration has been accomplished, the king's head is easily turned away from Yahweh and what's more he comes to feel so headstrong as to ignore a word from Yahweh, then he has sunk to the depths of notorious King Ahab of Israel, and deserves to die his death. The name of the king of Judah might designate him as Joash 'the Healed', but the telling of his tale has branded him as a leader who in the end made himself unworthy of the deity's healing touch.

2 Chronicles 25:
Amaziah 'the Strong'

Since the new king comes to the throne at the age of 25 (25.1), we can assume that he was born and named during his father's lengthy period of devotion to the national god, before Joash and his people 'abandoned the House of Yahweh, the god of their ancestors, and served the sacred poles and the idols' (24.17), and so the bestowal of the name Amaziah (*ʾămaṣĕyāhû*), 'Yahweh is strong', upon the prince was a proclamation of the faith by which Joash had lived in the earlier part of his own reign.

And the new king too starts reasonably well in office, 'doing what was right in the sight of Yahweh—though not wholeheartedly' (*raq lōʾ bĕlēbāb šālēm*, NRSV 'yet not with a true heart', 25.2). Indeed essentially the same change that the Annalists had traced in the case of Joash, from following the godly counsel of the priest Jehoiada (24.2-14) to dismissing the equally godly counsel of Jehoiada's son Zechariah (24.20-22), will be set out in the career of Joash's son Amaziah, from accepting and acting upon the first prophetic word that is delivered to him (25.7-10) to rejecting and acting against a subsequent prophetic word (25.15-16). But his very first act upon becoming king is to see that justice is done to the murderers of his father, at the same time being careful not to unleash vengeance upon the children of the regicides. The Annalists note that there is a law of Moses that 'parents shall not be put to death for the [transgressions of their] children, nor shall children be put to death for the [transgressions of their] parents, but only for their own transgressions shall people be put to death' (v. 4); this is a principle that may also be read in Deuteronomy 24.16, but it is not one that was always held to in ancient Israel, nor one that was always followed by the deity himself in certain Israelite stories outside of these Annals, but the god depicted in the Annals is fastidious about it and it speaks well of Amaziah that he follows it too.

The new king's second activity is to assemble troops for a battle. At first the identity of the enemy is not disclosed, and only a little later does it emerge that it is 'the people of Seir' (v. 11) or 'the Edomites' (v. 14) that Amaziah has in view. This is a people who had 'been in revolt against the rule of Judah' ever since the time of King Jehoram (21.10), having previously been subjugated in the time of King David (1 Chron. 18.13), so presumably the new Davidic monarch feels that the time has come to suppress their independence once more. But he finds that he only has some 300,000 soldiers at his disposal (2 Chron. 25.5). This is some 100,000-odd fewer troops than the Judahite forces (not to mention the other tribes of Israel) that David had had at his disposal in the days when he first conquered the Edomites (1 Chron. 21.5), so Amaziah calculates that he needs to hire '100,000 mighty warriors from Israel' at the grand cost of '100 talents of silver' (2 Chron. 25.6), in order to bring his troop strength up to the requisite level.

But this is not the time of King David, when all Israel was basking under Yahweh's blessing. Amaziah should have taken note of the stories of his more immediate ancestors, subsequent to the northern tribes breaking away from the house of David and appropriating the name of Israel for themselves. He should have been mindful of the various divine proclamations that the northern kingdom had abandoned Yahweh, and he should have been aware that Jehoshaphat and Ahaziah had both come unstuck in cooperative military ventures with the northern kingdom. He needs a new spokesman for the deity to step forward and tell him that 'Yahweh is not with Israel' (v. 7) and that if he proceeds in league with Israelite troops then the deity 'will fling you down before the enemy' (v. 8); instead, he should lead out his Judahite forces into battle without the northerners, 'for the deity has power to help'. In other words, he should remember that his name means 'Yahweh is strong', and he should not worry about the 100 talents of silver that he could have saved if he had not thought that he needed help from the north—after all, 'Yahweh is able to give you much more' than the amount of money he had needlessly given to the army of Israel (v. 9).

Amaziah heeds the words of Yahweh's unnamed messenger. He sends the 100,000 Israelite warriors away, and leads out his 300,000 Judahite troops to confront the Edomite resistance without the contaminating presence of the northerners among his forces. And the 300,000 are more than enough to overcome the small numbers of 'men of Seir': 10,000 of the latter are killed on the battlefield in the Valley of Salt (v. 11), and a further

10,000 are marched or dragged to the top of a cliff, from where they are thrown to their deaths (v. 12). It is hardly an attractive picture, but for the Annalists it is an indication of the deity being with the men of Judah against the men of Seir.

How bizarre, then, that the king of Judah, when he returns from the successful campaign, brings with him 'the gods of the people of Seir', not to destroy their images as symbols of false gods (as David had done to the gods of his defeated enemies in 1 Chron. 14.12) nor to parade them as defeated rivals of his national god Yahweh, but rather to 'set them up as his gods' and to 'worship them, making offerings to them' (2 Chron. 25.14). Another unnamed messenger is dispatched by an angry Yahweh, demanding to know from Amaziah, 'Why have you resorted to a people's gods who could not deliver their own people from your hand?' (v. 15). In his new-found devotion to Edomite deities, the king is seen to be proclaiming that 'the gods of Seir are strong', when they patently are not, but instead of drawing the obvious conclusion that his own royal name and his manifest victory over Edom demand from him, that 'Yahweh is strong', Amaziah reacts badly to this second divine message, and prevents the messenger from speaking on in public, though the anonymous prophet does manage to express the conclusion that Yahweh 'has determined to destroy you, because you have done this and have not listened to my advice' (v. 16).

This divine plan to destroy Amaziah unfolds in two stages, spread over two decades (it would seem that the deity has patience when it comes to teaching lessons). The first, and more immediate, stage is occasioned by a new battle, this time between Judah and Israel. The antecedents for this may lie in Amaziah's earlier fateful decision to have hired troops from Israel and then to have discharged them before the battle in the Valley of Salt, thus denying the northern warriors the easy opportunity of gaining booty from the massively outnumbered Edomites. As compensation for the rich pickings that they were denied, the Israelite warriors on their way back to the north had attacked a number of Judahite towns, killing thousands of people and 'taking much booty' (v. 13). It may therefore be that incident that prompts Amaziah, after taking counsel from his advisors, to send a message to King Joash of Israel, saying, 'Come, let us look one another in the face' (v. 17). However, the narrative does not make a direct connection between those two events—in fact the two episodes are separated in the narrative by the account of

Amaziah's devotion to the gods of Edom and rejection of the message from Yahweh—and Joash's cryptic parable about a thorn bush saying to a cedar tree, 'Give your daughter to my son for a wife' (v. 18), might suggest that Amaziah is proposing a marriage alliance between the two kingdoms. Such an alliance, if it is what the present king of Judah has in mind, would be a repetition of the marriage alliance that had been formed in the union of a son of the south and a daughter of the north three generations earlier in the marriage of Jehoram of Judah and Athaliah of Israel, and that had had disastrous consequences for Judah, but on this occasion the present king of Israel is in no mood to associate with the south. Indeed despite his parable about a ludicrous marriage proposal among unequal plants of Lebanon, he appears to understand Amaziah's call for a face-to-face encounter as a hostile gesture, a declaration of an intention to engage in battle, and advises the king of Judah to stay at home or it will be his undoing.

Amaziah is not persuaded that he ought to stay at home. Flushed with his success against the Edomites, he now feels that he can take on the Israelites, but given that he has become a devotee of the Edomite gods rather than remaining exclusively devoted to Yahweh, he has no chance of success in this encounter. In fact his determination to 'look Joash in the face' is Yahweh's doing, because the god of the Hebrews intends 'to hand [Judah] over, because they had sought the gods of Edom' (v. 20). And sure enough, Judah is defeated by the northern forces, Jerusalem's defences are broken down, its treasuries are raided, and captives are taken away to the northern kingdom. Amaziah is left on a much reduced throne, able to contemplate over a dismal 15 years (v. 25) what his name should have told him all along, that Yahweh is indeed stronger than the gods of Edom. He could look upon the temple, denuded of its gold and silver and all its vessels (v. 24), pose the question 'Why has Yahweh done such a thing to this house?' and answer with the visionary words from the story of Solomon, 'Because they abandoned Yahweh, the god of their ancestors who brought them out of the land of Egypt, and they adopted other gods, and worshipped them and served them; therefore he has brought all this calamity upon them' (7.21-22).

The final stage of the divine plan to destroy Amaziah involves the internal Judahite reaction to the national shame and impoverishment that his ill-fated entanglement with the northern kingdom has brought about. A conspiracy against him is hatched in Jerusalem—the Annalists say that it has been brewing ever since 'the time that Amaziah turned away from Yahweh' (v. 27)—and eventually he has to flee Jerusalem in fear of the conspirators, but he is tracked down and killed in the town of Lachish. Thus the man who had begun his reign by executing the conspirators who had killed his father is himself killed by conspirators. It is an ignoble end to a reign that had enjoyed the early success of defeating the Edomites, but had then sought to absorb the gods of Edom into the religious life of Judah. The prophetic principle 'If you abandon Yahweh, he will abandon you' (15.2) has been amply illustrated in the Annalists' account of King Amaziah.

2 Chronicles 26:
Uzziah 'the Mighty'

When the list of David's descendants had been presented near the beginning of the Annals, the son of Amaziah and father of Jotham was listed as 'Azariah' (1 Chron. 3.12), but when it comes now to the telling of his tale, the name is consistently given as 'Uzziah' (2 Chron. 26.1, 3, 8, 9, 11, 14, 18*a*, 18*b*, 19, 21, 22, 23; 27.2). No explanation is given for this difference. Perhaps we are meant to think of the individual in question as having reigned under a different throne-name than the name he had been given as an infant. Later in the story of Judah we will read that 'the king of Egypt made Eliakim king over Judah and Jerusalem, and changed his name to Jehoiakim' (36.4), so an analogous situation may be implied here, although quite who the current imperial power is and why they might wish for a different name for the king of Judah is unclear—in fact Judah appears to be rather independent and successful under the reign of Uzziah, so we might perhaps rather reckon with the prince formerly known as Azariah adopting under his own volition a new regal name when he succeeded his father. Two other kings also have different names in the genealogical list than they carry in their tales (Johanan a.k.a. Jehoahaz [1 Chron. 3.15 versus 2 Chron. 36.1-2] and Jeconiah a.k.a. Jehoiachin [1 Chron. 3.16 versus 2 Chron. 36.9]), and the Annalists provide no explanation of those differences either, so the case of Azariah a.k.a. Uzziah is not unique in this respect.

As the story of King Uzziah unfolds, we will see him in dispute with his chief priest, named Azariah (26.17, 20), over what tasks and responsibilities are proper to a king and what duties and functions are proper to the priesthood, so the slippage of the king's name between Azariah (in the genealogical list) and Uzziah (in the story) can be taken to symbolize the king's own mixing up of the roles of king and priest, while keeping his name as Uzziah in the telling of the tale helps to keep the reader from mixing him up with the character of Azariah the chief priest. Perhaps there is some narrative cost in running with the name of Uzziah for the king, since there are two points in the earlier part of the story that appear to resonate with the other name of the monarch—'Azariah' (*ʾăzarĕyāhû*) means 'Yahweh helps', and the narrative says that the deity 'helped' him and again that he was much 'helped' (the verb *ʾāzar* appears in both cases, namely vv. 7 and 15)—but such a positive resonance would likely not have appealed to the Annalists, who seem to prefer an ironic twist on the royal names. Accordingly, the name 'Uzziah' (*ʿuzzîyāhû*), meaning 'Yahweh is my strength', comes into its own when the king had 'become strong' (the normal verb for this, *ḥāzaq* ['be(come) strong'] appears in vv. 8, 15, and 16, while it is the noun *ʿuzzî* ['my strength'] that appears in the royal name), for then he needs to be taught a decisive lesson that Yahweh's strength is greater than his.

So it is Uzziah 'the Mighty' (rather than Azariah 'the Assisted') who now ascends to the throne of Judah, to begin what will turn out to be the second-longest reign, a period of no less than 52 years (v. 3). This breaks by a considerable margin the previous record of 41 years set by King Asa (16.13), and in the future only King Manasseh with 55 years (33.1) will outdo this new record, but Uzziah will not exercise full governance throughout his half-century of notional rule, on account of his mightiness being taken away from him by the truly mighty Yahweh later in the story, with the result that 'his son Jotham was [placed] in charge of the palace of the king, governing the people of the land' (26.21).

At first, though, Uzziah goes from strength to strength. In accordance with the Annalistic formula that we have met many times, it is noted that 'as long as he sought Yahweh, the deity made him prosper' (v. 5). Indeed the Annalists seem so keen to portray him as an especially blessed character that they use another of their regular formulations in the style 'he did what was right in Yahweh's sight, just as his father Amaziah had done' (v. 4), a specificity that seems rather misplaced when one considers that the Annals had recorded a divine word against Amaziah to the effect that 'the deity has determined to destroy you, because you have done this [wicked activity of turning to other gods] and have not listened to my advice' (25.16). If the formulation of 26.4 is to make sense in this context, readers need to suppose that the narrators are referring to the early period of Amaziah's rule, when he was pictured as acting in accordance with the instructions of Moses (25.4) and paying close heed to the words spoken to him on Yahweh's behalf (25.7-10), and not to the sizeable portion of his reign that unfolded after 'the time that Amaziah turned away from Yahweh' (25.27). In the Annalists' analysis of matters, many of the reigns of the kings of Judah fall into two distinct periods, in one of which the king is faithful to the national god and in the other of which his devotion slips; both father and son here, Amaziah and Uzziah, are depicted in chapters 25 and 26 respectively as following such a pattern, and again in Uzziah's case the earlier exemplary period will be sufficient for the formulation to be used again in the story of his son, Jotham, that he too 'did what was right in Yahweh's sight, just as his father Uzziah had done' (27.2). However, in that later case the Annalists do add a rider, 'except that he did not invade Yahweh's temple' (27.2, alluding to the tale told in 26.16-21), so we might have expected in the present case an analogous phrase such as 'except that he did not turn away from Yahweh to other gods', to express reservations about the second half of Amaziah's reign. However, no such hedging of the expression that father and son 'did what was right in Yahweh's sight' is slipped into the formulation at 26.4.

This god-pleasing activity pertains 'in the days of Zechariah, who instructed him in the fear of the deity, and as long as he sought Yahweh, the deity made him prosper' (v. 5). No information is given about this Zechariah, but since he is instructing the king on religious matters we might postulate that he was the chief priest in the earlier part of Uzziah's reign, performing a similar role to that accomplished in the time of his grandfather by the then holder of the high-priestly office, for we were told that 'Joash did what was right in Yahweh's sight all the days of the priest Jehoiada' (24.2), and only 'after the death of Jehoiada' did the king and his officials start to do things that were not right in Yahweh's eyes (24.17). When we come to the time in which the chief priest is a certain Azariah (26.17, 20), we will find Uzziah doing something of which the deity does not approve, and thus receiving a compelling physical reprimand from Yahweh. But during Zechariah's term of office, all is well, with the king restoring territory that had been recently lost, defeating traditional enemies that had become nuisances once again, building up the fortifications and wealth of Jerusalem, and

putting the army of Judah on a better footing than it had
recently been.

The restored territory is that of Eloth (v. 2), an Edomite area
which Solomon had once controlled (8.17), but which had
presumably been lost in the time of Jehoram during the Edomite
revolt against the rule of Judah (21.8); Amaziah's successful
battle against the Edomites (25.11-14) had created the circumstances in which his son could now have Eloth rebuilt as a
Judahite settlement once again. And that old enemy, the
Philistines, whom Solomon had easily controlled (9.26) but who
had also become restless and powerful again in the time of
Jehoram (21.16-17), are also put back in their place by the
mighty Uzziah (26.6), along with the Arabs (v. 7) and the
Ammonites (v. 8). We are given details of the improvements
that the king brought about both in the capital (v. 9) and in the
countryside (v. 10), and of a reorganization and re-equipping of
the army (vv. 11-15), and we are told—and then told again—
that 'his fame spread' as he continued to 'become strong' (both
phrases appear in vv. 8 and 15).

'But when he had become strong, he grew proud, to his destruction' (v. 16). Uzziah 'the Mighty' comes to believe that he has
golden hands, and that he can appropriate to himself the role of
chief priest. He feels bold enough to 'enter Yahweh's temple to
make an offering on the altar of incense' (v. 16), an action that
incenses the actual chief priest, Azariah, as surely as it offends
the Annalists. Already when they had been setting out the foun-
dational genealogies of the people of Israel, the Annalists had
been categorical in specifying that it was 'Aaron and his sons'
who 'made offerings on the altar of burnt-offering and the altar
of incense, doing all the work of the most holy place, to make
atonement for Israel, according to all that the godly servant
Moses had commanded' (1 Chron. 6.49), and they had gone to
elaborate lengths in their account of King David to show the
temple-planner's fastidiousness over arrangements whereby
'Aaron was set apart to consecrate the most holy things, so that
he and his sons for ever should make offerings before Yahweh,
and minister to him and pronounce blessings in his name for ever'
(1 Chron. 23.13). Perhaps Zechariah's instructions in godly ways
to King Uzziah (2 Chron. 26.5) had regrettably neglected to cover
this realm of strict demarcation between the royal and priestly
offices, but more probably we are to imagine that the king had
been so instructed and that he respected such boundaries during

'the days of Zechariah', but now the wise instructor has passed from the scene and the king, having become 'strong' and 'proud' (v. 16), is thinking that he can enter at will a sanctuary which previously only those consecrated to the holy office of priesthood had dared to enter.

The king cannot get away with such outrageous behaviour in this story-world. Azariah and a troop of 80 burly priests ('men of valour', v. 17) confront Uzziah, and instruct him in what he had not learnt or taken to heart from Zechariah, namely that it is not for the king to make offerings to Yahweh, 'but for the priests, the descendants of Aaron, who are consecrated to make offerings' (v. 18). At first the king does not want to give in to the priests, but of course they have the deity on their side, and Yahweh steps in with a decisive gesture, striking Uzziah with 'a leprous disease' on his forehead (v. 19).

This dramatic moment signals the end of Uzziah's proud effectiveness as King of Judah. From this time on, the head of the kingdom is branded as a man whom the national god has struck with uncleanness. For fear that he will infect others with the loathsome disease, he is excluded from normal society, living in isolation and unable to conduct affairs of state. A regency period now ensues, with the crown prince Jotham placed in charge of royal affairs and 'governing the people of the land' (v. 21) until eventually Uzziah 'the once Mighty' dies and Jotham can fully succeed his father as official king of the realm. We are not told how many of Uzziah's grand total of 52 years as 'king' (v. 3) are spent under the condition of being 'leprous to the day of his death' (v. 21), but we can imagine that he had a great deal of time on his once golden hands to contemplate the moral of his story: if only he had remained true to his throne-name, 'Yahweh is My Strength', rather than thinking 'I myself am strong', things could have been very different indeed.

2 Chronicles 27:
Jotham 'the Perfected'

The tale of Jotham is brief and neat. Enclosed within a dual presentation, at the beginning and end of the tale, of the statistics regarding his age at coronation ('25 years old', vv. 1a and 8a) and the length of his reign ('16 years in Jerusalem', vv. 1b and 8b), we are given a short description in terms of the standard signs of a successful reign: building work in the capital (v. 3) and the countryside (v. 4), and a successful military campaign that brought revenue and supplies to his kingdom (v. 5). It may be noted that this latter accomplishment is at the expense of the Ammonites, who had been paying tribute to his father Uzziah (26.8), so it would seem that 'the king of the Ammonites' (27.5) had made an attempt to tear up the arrangements under which Judah received such payments and that Jotham had acted to reinstate or reinforce the situation. We had not been told how much of Ammon's bounty was being extracted by Judah in the days of Uzziah, but statistics are presented in Jotham's case: for at least three years he benefited each year from '100 talents of silver, 10,000 cors of wheat and 10,000 [cors] of barley' (v. 5), so the oppression of the Ammonites was a lucrative business for him and his people.

The succinct account of Jotham's reign, with nothing to blight the positive picture apart from a note that bad practices could still be found among the people despite the excellent example set for them by their king (v. 2), is presumably due to the Annalists' analysis of it as a straightforward tale befitting a monarch called 'Yahweh is Perfect' (yôtām, a combination of the divine element 'Yo' and the verbal element tām which means 'to be complete or whole or perfect'). Such a one 'did what was right in Yahweh's sight' (v. 2) and 'became strong because he ordered his ways before his god Yahweh' (v. 6); the Annalists evidently believe that not much more needs to be said.

2 Chronicles 28: Ahaz 'the Seized'

After the near-perfect reign of Jotham comes the decidedly disastrous reign of Ahaz. Both father and son reigned for 16 years apiece (see 27.1 and 8 for Jotham's statistics and 28.1 for Ahaz's), but in the former case of a happy and successful time the Annalists had little to say, while now, when the successor turns out to be something of an unhappy failure, the report is considerably more detailed.

Perhaps part of Jotham's near-perfection was that he could see into the future, or that he took note of a seer who could, because in naming his son 'Ahaz' (*'āḥāz*, 'he grasps or he seizes') he seems to be foretelling the man's destiny to be seized by the national god. Of course it could be that the father did not intend the name to signify any action by an unnamed deity; he might rather have meant the next monarch's moniker to symbolize the king himself as the one who acts dynamically, taking hold of opportunities or conquering territories or generally acquiring more and more wealth and prestige. But in this story-world, in which a few generations earlier a king was named with fuller forms of this designation, Ahaziah a.k.a. Jehoahaz (the form *'āḥazĕyāhû* combining 'he seizes' with the subject 'Yahu' and the form *yĕhô'āḥāz* performing the same function with the identical verbal element and the alternative divine abbreviation 'Yeho'), and that king had been comprehensively seized by the deity, readers will fully expect that it will again be the deity who will carry out such an action as indicated in the royal name 'Ahaz'.

The Annalists first set a scene that will require the deity to step in decisively. They depict a king who 'did not do what was right in Yahweh's sight' (v. 1), but instead adopted the ways of the northern kingdom, making cast images to represent divinity and sacrificing some of his children (literally 'he burned his sons in the fire', v. 3; NRSV's rendering 'he made his sons pass through fire' suggests a possibility of survival). He may even be outdoing the kingdom of Israel in adopting various 'abominable practices of the nations whom Yahweh had driven out before the people of Israel' (v. 3), but in re-establishing 'high places' throughout the kingdom of Judah (v. 4) he is certainly compromising the status of the Jerusalem temple in a manner that would gladden the heart of the Israelite apostates.

This adoption of northern ways seems inexplicable, given that Ahaz had grown up in a royal household governed by the splendid King Jotham and there is no indication that his mother and/or other significant influences were from the kingdom of Israel. The Annalists had given a very clear indication of such a damaging presence in the case of the earlier king bearing the 'ahaz' element in his name, Ahaziah, whose mother Athaliah, daughter of King Ahab of Israel, 'was his counsellor in doing wickedly' (22.3). Ahaziah was also said to have had other key counsellors who were from the northern court (22.4), all of which provided an explanation for his walking in the ways of the northern kings and doing what was evil in Yahweh's sight. But in the case of Ahaz the Annals are silent on such matters, declining to inform us of the name or lineage of his mother and providing no insights into his decision to follow northern practices. Later in his story we see him adopting Assyrian practices in a time of Assyrian dominance over Judah (28.20-23), so a possibility at this earlier stage of his reign might be that he was adopting Israelite practices at a time of Israelite dominance over Judah, but the Annalists present a different sequence: first 'he walked in the ways of the kings of Israel' (v. 2), and then 'he was given into the hand of the king of Israel' (v. 5).

Handing Ahaz over to those whose syncretistic religious practices he was mimicking no doubt seems a fitting outcome for the tellers of these tales. But while the Hebrew god is happy to arrange for the Israelites to strike decisively against the Judahites in order to teach the latter the lesson that abandoning Yahweh in an Israelite fashion is no way to be safe from the Israelites, he takes issue with the extent to which the northerners ruthlessly exploit their god-given opportunity to crush the southerners, who are still after all dear to his heart. 120,000 Judahite men are killed in a single day's battle (v. 6), and 200,000 Judahite women and children are taken as captives to the kingdom of Israel (v. 8), with the intention that they become slaves to their Israelite captors (v. 10). So Yahweh calls for one of his northern prophets, Oded by name, to issue a divine rebuke to the returning army of Israel. True, Yahweh had given Judah into Israel's hands because he was angry with Judah, Oded tells the troops, but the ferocity with which the Israelite warriors have gone about their killing spree and the reprehensibility of their intention to enslave the Judahite captives that they have brought north now means that Yahweh's anger will be focussed on them instead, unless they abandon their enslavement plans and send the hapless captives back to the kingdom of Judah.

The prophet is supported by four Israelite (specifically Ephraimite) chiefs, who are worried that keeping the captives will 'bring on us guilt against Yahweh in addition to our present sins and guilt; for our guilt is already great, and there is fierce wrath against Israel' (v. 13). It seems that these influential Israelites have finally assimilated the message that King Abijah of Judah had proclaimed in the early days of the division between the Hebrew kingdoms, while the present king of Judah, Ahaz, had abandoned Abijah's principles. Abijah had spoken of the northerners abandoning Yahweh and facing the consequences while the southerners remained faithful to him and received the blessings that flowed from that (13.4-12), and now the Annals set out a rather different equation, in which the southerners have been unfaithful and received a severe punishment while the northerners are becoming mindful of their culpability for having abandoned Yahweh and of what they face if they continue unabashed. These chiefs are not fooled by the present victory over Judah into thinking that the kingdom of Israel has won back Yahweh's good will. Perhaps they have noted a certain differential in the statistics of battlefield losses: 120,000 slain warriors of Judah on this occasion (v. 6) is a considerably smaller number than the 500,000 slain warriors of Israel on an earlier occasion (13.17). In any event they demonstrate that not all northerners are beyond the pale as far as the Annalists are concerned.

The persuasive powers of the four chiefs, in addition to the stern words of the single prophet, turn the Israelite army from their despicable plan of enslaving the Judahite women and children, and even from carrying home the considerable booty that they had brought back from Judah. Thus the chiefs are able to arrange for the discarded booty to be used to provide for the needs of the captives, who are then assisted in journeying back to Judahite territory. No credit for any of this is given to the king of Israel, who had been named as 'Pekah son of Remaliah' at the outset of the episode (v. 6) but who does not seem to take any personal interest in these significant decisions, nor is any credit due to the king of Judah, who as a thoroughly defeated commander plays no part in the internal northern discussions. The good Samaritans who see to it that the naked are clothed, the hungry are fed, the thirsty are given drink, and the feeble are brought to Jericho on donkeys (v. 15) are the ones 'who were mentioned by name' (v. 15) in the narrative, namely the chiefs 'Azariah son of Johanan, Berechiah son of Meshillemoth, Jehizkiah son of Shallum, and Amasa son of Hadlai' (v. 12). These northerners are worthy indeed to have their names recorded in the book of the south, the Annals of the Davidic kingdom.

Meanwhile Ahaz has not yet experienced the full extent of Yahweh's grip. Having been given into the hand of the king of Israel might be bad enough, even if the captives were eventually returned to Judah by the Ephraimite chiefs, and we should not overlook the brief detail that Ahaz had also been given 'into the hand of the king of Aram, who defeated him and took captive a great number of his people and brought them to Damascus' (v. 5)—with no subsequent report of the Arameans being persuaded by a prophet of Yahweh or any of their own chiefs that they ought to return the captives to Judah. But there is yet more to come: the Edomites, too, took their chance to 'invade and defeat Judah, and carry away captives' (v. 17), and the Philistines are up to their old tricks of making raids on Judahite towns and slicing off valuable pieces of Judahite territory (v. 18). And most distressingly of all, when Ahaz looks to the emerging Assyrian empire to be his saviour and to work a loosening of the divinely-ordained grip upon him of all these assorted enemies, he finds that 'King Tilgath-pilneser of Assyria came against him, and oppressed him instead of strengthening him' (v. 20); no matter how much he impoverishes his little kingdom of Judah to hand over tribute to the mighty Assyrians, it is of no avail, because Yahweh had determined to 'bring Judah low' because of the king's faithlessness (v. 19). The one named 'Ahaz' ('he seizes') has been thoroughly and systematically seized by the deity, no less than his more fully-named ancestor 'Ahaziah' ('Yahweh seizes') was caught in a divinely ordained retributive scheme (22.7).

Nevertheless the seized one remains obstinate to the end. Instead of turning back to the national god, he turns to 'the gods of Damascus', reasoning that 'because the gods of the kings of Aram helped them, I will sacrifice to them so that they may help me' (v. 23). He denudes Yahweh's temple of its furnishings and equipment, and even shuts its doors, so that, for the first time since the great King Solomon had dedicated the building eleven generations before Ahaz, the functioning of the complex comes to a halt. The Solomonic arrangements had been 'ordained forever for Israel' (2.4), but they have been momentarily halted by the puny Ahaz, who cannot recognize the Hand of God when it strikes him. Yahweh will see to it that the doors are opened again in no time at all (29.3) under Ahaz's successor the good king Hezekiah, but Ahaz himself goes down in the Annals as a uniquely perfidious king of Judah, one who 'shut up the doors of the House of Yahweh' (28.24).

2 Chronicles 29–32: Hezekiah 'the Strong'

Chapter 29

The Annalists had pictured King Ahaz as a thoroughly apostate monarch who had abandoned Yahweh in favour of the gods of the surrounding peoples. From the very beginning of his reign he had been talked of as 'making cast images for the Baals' (28.2), and later he is said to have 'shut up the doors of the House of Yahweh' in Jerusalem and to have 'made high places to make offerings to other gods' in all the cities of Judah (28.24-25). Yet when it came to the naming of his sons, he gave full official recognition to the national god of Judah, for the two sons of Ahaz that are mentioned in the Annals are called Maaseiah (maʿăśēyāhû, 'Yahweh's Work', 28.7) and Hezekiah (yĕḥizĕqîyāhû, 'Yahweh Strengthens', 28.27 and a further 34 times throughout chs. 29–32, a slight variation on the form ḥizĕqîyāhû that had appeared in the genealogical list in 1 Chron. 3.13 and that also appears in 2 Chron. 29.18, 27; 30.24; 32.15).

That it is Hezekiah and not Maaseiah who succeeds their father is down to the activities of a particular warrior from the north, for during the infamous incursion into Judah of the Israelite forces when thousands of Judahite soldiers were killed and thousands of Judahite women and children were taken captive, 'Zichri, a mighty warrior of Ephraim, killed the king's son Maaseiah, Azrikam the commander of the palace, and Elkanah the next in authority to the king' (28.7). Although it was not said explicitly that Maaseiah was the oldest son or the one who had been designated to succeed his father, the reporting of his death along with 'the commander of the palace' and 'the next in authority to the king' suggests that he was indeed the crown prince at that time. His seizure by the invading army is all part of Yahweh's giving of Ahaz into the hand of the king of Israel, because of the king of Judah's abandonment of the Hebrew god, and it is an interesting touch that Yahweh takes away the king's son when the king had been described as 'burning his sons in the fire,

according to the abominable practices of the nations whom
Yahweh had driven out before the people of Israel' (28.3). The
practice so described suggests that Ahaz may have sacrificed his
firstborn and certain other offspring, perhaps as offerings that
he intended for Yahweh (regrettably the Annalists do not provide
us with the names of any of the sons who were 'burned in the
fire', so we cannot see whether they possessed Yahwistic names)
or as children offered up to another of the gods to whom the
king paid devotion. If Ahaz had performed child-sacrifices, then
Maaseiah had presumably only become first in line to ascend to
the throne because his older brother or brothers had been offered
up to the heavens, but then Yahweh takes Maaseiah and other
key right-hand men of the king as 'sacrifices' that Ahaz had not
intended. The incident does not cause Ahaz to change his syncretistic ways, although he is not mentioned as offering up any more
of his children after that time, but the 'sacrifice' of Maaseiah
after the sacrifices of other unnamed sons does clear the way for
Hezekiah to become king of Judah in due course.

   According to the text, Hezekiah 'began to reign when he was
25 years old' (29.1), but this can hardly be accepted over against
the earlier figures presented for his father Ahaz, who, we were
told, 'was 20 years old when he began to reign, and he reigned for
16 years in Jerusalem' (28.1). Putting the two sets of figures
together yields an age of just 11 for Ahaz at the birth of Hezekiah,
which might mean that Ahaz was not even in double figures at
the time of the conception of his older children, those whom he
had burned in the fire and also the pre-Hezekian crown prince
Maaseiah. It would seem that the Annalists, normally so fastidious on their numbers, even when making outrageous claims
about the size of armies, have slipped up on the figures for the
royal succession at this point.

   Be that as it may, the arrival on the throne of the one whom
'Yahweh strengthens' is certainly a godsend for the kingdom of
Judah, from the perspective of the Annalists. The new man
immediately sets about reversing his father's policies, returning
the nation to devotion to Yahweh, and Yahweh in return will
reverse the fortunes of the nation. Whereas Ahaz from Day One
of his reign 'did not do what was right in Yahweh's sight' (28.1),
Hezekiah from the very beginning of his tenure in office most
assuredly 'did what was right in Yahweh's sight' (29.2). Indeed
as soon as he is on the throne at the age of 25, 'in the first year
of his reign, in the first month, he opened the doors of the House

of Yahweh' (v. 3)—it might even be that he took action already on his very first day in office, for the later detail that the temple personnel 'began to sanctify on the first day of the first month' (v. 17) might be a reference to Hezekiah's regnal period (though it might alternatively be interpreted as indicating that the king's command began to be carried out on 'new year's day'). In narrative space, the indication that Hezekiah 'opened the doors of the House of Yahweh' in 29.3 is a mere six verses after his wicked father had 'shut up the doors of the House of Yahweh' in 28.24, so the unspecified time in which the temple lay barred and silent is not dwelt upon by the Annalists. However, the re-commissioning of the kingdom's religious practices in the manner beloved of these tradents is very much dwelt upon. They now launch excitedly into a lengthy account of the re-sanctification of the sacred precincts and personnel and re-instatement of the sacred activities and functions that are performed there, in a narrative to match their detailed account of the arrangements for temple life that had been laid down at the very beginning of the kingdom by the saintly David himself (1 Chron. 22–29). This is a new beginning after the shameful neglect and even suppression of the temple services by Ahaz, with Hezekiah acting as a kind of *David redivivus* to re-activate the Davidic constitution, setting everything once again 'according to the commandment of David' (2 Chron. 29.25).

The king first addresses the priests and their levitical assistants in a stirring speech, calling on them to re-sanctify themselves and the temple. He deplores the fact that 'our fathers' (*'ăbōtēnû*, NRSV 'our ancestors', v. 6) had been unfaithful to the national god and had turned their backs on Yahweh's dwelling-place. He might have said that it was 'my father', Ahaz, who had been the pre-eminently guilty one in this national shame, but by using the expression 'our fathers' he spreads the blame more generally among the previous generation, and then by speaking as the new father of the nation to the assembled priests and Levites as 'my sons' (*bānay*, v. 11) he wins them over to a new zeal for the traditional ways that their own fathers had presumably lacked or had had beaten out of them by the previous regime.

The king's words stir the inheritors of priestly office into immediate action, and they set about making themselves holy to Yahweh once again and cleansing Yahweh's temple. After a feverish 16 days of unstinting effort (v. 17), all is in readiness for a grand restoration of temple services, which is enacted by means of a ritual slaughtering of four sets of seven animals: 'seven bulls, seven rams, seven lambs, and seven male goats' (v. 21). At first it is said that these are to be 'a sin offering for the kingdom and for the sanctuary and for Judah' (v. 21), but the range of beneficiaries is then extended by royal decree, 'for the king commanded that the burnt offering and the sin offering should be made for all Israel' (v. 24). It seems that Hezekiah is mindful, as custodian of the renewed temple, of responsibilities to the northern tribes as well, and in due course he will issue an invitation to the people of Israel as well as the people of Judah to come to the House of Yahweh in Jerusalem (30.1). Perhaps the words of the Ephraimite chiefs in his father's time have been reported to him, with their acknowledgment of the 'guilt before Yahweh' that lay upon the northern kingdom (28.13), and he reasons that he can help to turn Yahweh's wrath away from that sister-kingdom which had once been part of the realm of his ancestors David and Solomon even as he is working to turn 'the fierce anger of the god of Israel' (29.10) also away from his own kingdom of Judah. Or perhaps the present pan-Israel sentiments are to be read in connection with the later comment about 'the remnant' that has 'escaped from the hand of the kings of Assyria' (30.6) to imply that the northern kingdom is now only a shadow of its former self and has been left by the Assyrian empire without a king of its own, so that Hezekiah feels a need to act in a kingly manner towards all the Hebrew tribes.

Just in case we might miss the point that Hezekiah is reconstituting the practices that had been set in place by David, the narrators employ the name of the dynastic founder no less than four times in quick succession in the description of Hezekiah's arrangements. He stations the levitical personnel 'according to the commandment of David' (v. 25), he has them use 'the instruments of David' in the music they play (v. 26)—equipment that is reiterated as being 'the instruments of King David of Israel' (v. 27)—and he has them use 'the words of David' in the songs they sing (v. 30). This is a case not simply of Hezekiah 'doing what was right in Yahweh's sight, just as his ancestor David had done' (v. 2), but of Hezekiah reinstating the precise arrangements that his ancestor David had intended for the proper functioning of Yahweh's temple.

After the dark night of the previous regime, a bright new day has dawned for the kingdom of Judah, and so we find the people to be 'of a willing heart' (v. 31) to embrace the opportunity of renewal in the national commitment to Yahweh. The new king's vision 'to make a covenant with Yahweh, the god of Israel, so that his fierce anger may turn away from us' (v. 10) has struck a chord not just with the temple functionaries but also with the people at large, so that the assembly now brings forward 70 bulls, 100 rams, and 200 lambs as burnt-offerings and 600 bulls and 3,000 sheep as consecrated offerings, plus unnumbered offerings of well-being and drink-offerings too (vv. 32-35). So many animals are presented for slaughter for Yahweh that there are too few re-sanctified priests ready to perform all the ritual killing, and the levitical assistants, who have been more conscientious than some of the priests in preparing themselves for divine service, have to take on more of a role in the slaughterfest than might normally be the case (v. 34). Despite that small hitch in proceedings, nonetheless all the ritual killing and the throwing around of animal blood in the sacred precincts (note in v. 22 the threefold dashing of blood against the altar) is seen by the Annalists as a wonderful thing, a most fitting way that 'the service of the House of Yahweh was restored' (v. 35). Fittingly in this story-world, 'Hezekiah and all the people rejoiced because of what the deity had done for the people, for the thing had come about suddenly' (v. 36)—that is to say, just 16 days (v. 17) of Hezekiah's rule have wiped clean the filth of 16 years (28.1) of Ahaz's misrule. What Ahaz had torn asunder, Hezekiah has put back together.

Chapter 30
Hezekiah goes further than simply reinstating the temple routines that had been in place before his father Ahaz suppressed them. He sees the role of the temple as once again having an all-Israel dimension, and he sends out a message 'to all Israel and Judah...that they should come to the House of Yahweh in Jerusalem, to keep the passover to Yahweh the god of Israel' (30.1). There has been no previous mention of a passover festival in the Annals, so suspicion may arise that this is a new-fangled custom in the time of Hezekiah, but to allay such thinking the Annalists speak of the people on this occasion being unable to 'keep it at its proper time' (v. 3) as though 'its proper time' had been well known to them despite the current circumstances, and of many having to 'eat the passover otherwise than as prescribed' (v. 18) as though the prescriptions had been laid down well before this time (note also v. 5's reference

to the Hebrew peoples not having previously kept the festival 'in great numbers as prescribed'). The narrative does say that 'there had been nothing like this in Jerusalem since the time of Solomon son of King David of Israel' (v. 26), thus giving the celebration of passover in Jerusalem the official antiquity of the founders of the temple practices, and later the antecedents of the custom are pushed back even further by the comment concerning the passover celebration in the 18th year of King Josiah's reign that 'no passover like it had been kept in Israel since the days of the prophet Samuel' (35.18). Accordingly not even the celebration that Hezekiah organizes will be quite as splendid as the one that Josiah will stage three generations later, but Hezekiah's efforts will nonetheless occasion a time of 'great joy in Jerusalem' (30.26), the like of which had not been seen in the city since the days of Solomon's splendour.

The letters of invitation to Hezekiah's Grand Passover Festival include a significant piece of information about the apparent situation in the northern kingdom. The southern monarch speaks of 'the remnant of you who have escaped from the hand of the kings of Assyria' (v. 6), which implies that a substantial proportion of the Hebrew peoples have been swallowed up by the Assyrian empire. The Annals do not include an account of such events, but only allude to the devastation of the kingdom of Israel in this passover epistle from Hezekiah, supplemented by the expressions 'the remnant of Israel' (34.9) and 'those who are left in Israel' (34.21) in the tale of Josiah. The oppressive presence of the Assyrian imperial forces will be felt in the kingdom of Judah later in Hezekiah's reign (32.1), even more severely than it had been felt in Ahaz's reign (28.20), but the northern kingdom had apparently come off much worse than the southern kingdom under the force of Assyrian might. Evidently the kingdom of Israel had not had at their helm a Hezekianic ruler who devoted himself and his people to the worship of Yahweh and who accordingly turned back the divine wrath and hence will be able to turn away the might of Assyria when it comes in full earnest against him. Instead, the god of their ancestors had made Israel 'a devastation, as you see' (30.7), though all is not lost: there is the prospect that 'your kindred and your children will find compassion with their captors, and return to this land', if only the remnant who have escaped death or capture will first 'return to Yahweh' (v. 9).

Hezekiah's message is not generally well received among the remnant of Israel. His couriers are laughed to scorn and mocked (v. 10), and 'only a few' from just some of the northern tribes 'humbled themselves and came to Jerusalem' (v. 11). At first it is said that pilgrims from the north for this passover celebration come only from three tribes, namely Asher, Manasseh, and Zebulun (v. 11), but later some folk from Ephraim and Issachar are apparently also to be found (v. 18), so in the final accounting it seems that half of the ten northern tribes are modestly represented in the pilgrimage. But there is nothing half-hearted about the response from the Judahites, for 'the deity's hand was on Judah to give them one heart to do what the king and the officials commanded by the word of Yahweh' (v. 12). Accordingly, 'a very large assembly' gathers in Jerusalem for the occasion (v. 13), and, even though not everything is able to be done 'in accordance with the sanctuary's rules of cleanness' (v. 19), nonetheless the efforts of the king and his restored temple personnel are entirely rewarded, in that 'Yahweh heard Hezekiah, and healed the people' (v. 20) and so too the 'voice [of the priests and the Levites] was heard; their prayer came to his holy dwelling in heaven' (v. 27).

This revivification of the temple services is such a success that, after the prescribed week of festivities has been completed, no one is willing to bring the experience to an end. Instead, everyone agrees that they should continue on for a further week. Thanks to the generosity of the king and his officials in providing a sizeable supply of animals for slaughter, and thanks also to the willingness of the priests to 'sanctify themselves in great numbers' (v. 24), the joyous assembly is indeed able to continue for the additional week. In doing so they replicate the otherwise unparalleled experience that had taken place at the very beginning of the temple's life, when King Solomon and the people had 'observed the dedication of the altar for seven days and the festival for seven days' (7.9). Now King Hezekiah has truly put the House of Yahweh back onto its Solomonic footing, and the Annalists are delighted to report that 'there was great joy in Jerusalem, for since the time of Solomon son of David of Israel there had been nothing like this in Jerusalem' (30.26).

Chapter 31

With Yahweh's House back in full functionality, there are two other aspects to rectifying the religious life of the kingdom. The first is to ensure that the Jerusalem temple and the god who dwells therein have no rivals for the devotions of the people, and the second is to ensure that the temple personnel are properly cared for and organized.

To see to the first of these essential elements of Hezekiah's reforming programme, the people who had just enjoyed a full two weeks of festivities and who are now buoyed up with new-found zeal for Yahweh and his House fan out to the surrounding cities to 'break down the pillars, hew down the sacred poles, and pull down the high places and the altars' (31.1). This Jerusalem-sanctuary-only policy is achieved not just 'throughout all Judah and Benjamin' but also 'in Ephraim and Manasseh', areas of the (former) northern kingdom from whence some of the pilgrims to Hezekiah's Grand Passover Festival had come (30.18) and in which there would seem now to be no authority capable of turning back the intentions of the king of Judah. For the first time since the northern tribes broke away from the ambit of Jerusalem after the death of Solomon, the Davidic king is in a sense again the master of all he surveys.

And Hezekiah now acts particularly Davidically in seeing to the second feature of a properly constituted religious life for the Hebrew peoples, as the Annalists understand it. Readers will recall the lengthy descriptions that had been given, in the account of David's formative reign, of the organization of the sacred functionaries into various divisions for various aspects of divine service in the temple that David was planning under Yahweh's direction (1 Chron. 23–26). Hezekiah is now quite clearly depicted as bringing back the Davidic arrangements that the apostate Ahaz had allowed or encouraged to fall into disuse and disorder. The old 'divisions of the priests and of the Levites, division by division, everyone according to his service' (2 Chron. 31.2), are reconstituted, and the old system whereby the lay population must 'give the portion due to the priests and the Levites, so that they might devote themselves to the law of Yahweh' (v. 4), is reinstated.

The renewed arrangements are very effective, and the new chief priest, presumably a man who had not done well under the previous regime, expresses himself as highly satisfied with the bounty that he and his colleagues are now able to enjoy (v. 10). The Annalists delight in setting out a list (vv. 12-15) of the main players in the elaborate system of collection and apportionment and distribution of the tithes of the people, and in noting and re-noting and noting again that the full compliment of holy personnel are once more functioning 'by divisions' (v. 15), 'by divisions' (v. 16), 'by divisions' (v. 17). All is well again in the Annalists' world, in that 'the priests are enrolled' (beginning of v. 18) and 'the Levites are enrolled' (end of v. 19), and all of these enrolments are 'according to their ancestral houses' (v. 17). To have re-set things in this way is for these narrators the supreme example of a king who 'did what was good and right and faithful before his god Yahweh' (v. 20).

Chapter 32

The Assyrian threat that Hezekiah had alluded to in his passover epistle, with his reference to 'the remnant of you who have escaped from the hand of the kings of Assyria' (30.6), now comes to Judah. There is no 'because' about this invasion, as there had been on earlier occasions, such as the reports that 'because they had been unfaithful to Yahweh, King Shishak of Egypt came up against Jerusalem' (12.2) or that the king of Israel came and 'killed 120,000 in Judah in one day, because they had abandoned Yahweh' (28.6). The Assyrian invasion of Judah comes about not after any unfaithfulness on the part of Hezekiah, but quite the reverse, namely 'after these acts of faithfulness' (32.1) that have been described in the previous chapters. Accordingly, the Assyrian assault is not something that Yahweh has brought about in order to punish the people of Judah or to prompt them to return to him, as seems to be so often the case in the Annalists' analysis of events. Perhaps it is a case of the deity wishing 'to test [the king] and to know all that is in his heart', as is explicitly said of a later event in Hezekiah's reign (v. 31), or perhaps the deity is so confident about Hezekiah's heart after all that the king has been doing—the narrators had just reported that 'every work that he undertook in the service of the House of God, and in accordance with the law and the commandments, to seek his god, he did with all his heart' (31.21)—that this invasion is rather staged by Yahweh as a marvellous way to facilitate an outcome through which the present king of Judah will be 'exalted in the sight of all nations from that time forward' (32.23).

The invasion also gives the storytellers an opportunity to engage in some wordplay with the king's name 'Hezekiah' or 'Yahweh Strengthens' (*yĕḥizĕqiyāhû*), for we find him 'strengthening himself' (*wayyitĕhazzaq*) and 'strengthening' (*wayĕhazzēq*) the city's fortifications (v. 5) and calling upon his people to

'Be strong (*ḥizĕqû*) and of good courage...for our god *Yahweh* is with us' (vv. 7-8), and the narrators add that indeed 'the people were encouraged by the words of *Hezekiah* (*yĕḥizĕqiyāhû*), king of Judah' (v. 8). The king's preparations also include blocking up the flow of the springs that were outside the city walls, so that the imperial forces would not have a ready supply of water upon their arrival, and manufacturing an abundant supply of weapons and shields, with which to hold the Assyrians at bay. He does not panic, but keeps a cool head, and in particular keeps his faith in Yahweh as a greater power than King Sennacherib of Assyria: 'Do not be afraid or dismayed before the king of Assyria and the horde that is with him', he tells his people, 'for there is one greater with us than with him' (v. 7).

This is not the view of Sennacherib, of course. He sends messengers to taunt Hezekiah and the Judahites with the boastful words that 'no god of any nation or kingdom has been able to save his people from my hand or from the hand of my fathers, so how much less will your god save you out of my hand?' (vv. 14-15). The Annalists regard this as 'throwing contempt on Yahweh, the god of Israel' (v. 16), and insofar as the boast appears to contain the implication that Hezekiah's god is 'unable' to save his little nation from the imperial juggernaut of Assyria, this would seem a fair reading of Sennacherib's rhetoric. But another, more intriguing, interpretation of the Assyrian message is possible, for the people of Judah are asked to consider the following questions: 'Is not Hezekiah misleading you...when he tells you, "Our god Yahweh will save us from the hand of the king of Assyria"? Was it not this same Hezekiah who took away his high places and his altars and commanded Judah and Jerusalem, saying, "Before one altar you shall worship, and upon it you shall make your offerings"?' (vv. 11-12). Sennacherib is here tapping into an inner-Israelite debate about whether Yahweh would really wish that all of the traditional places that the Hebrew tribes had regarded as sacred to their god should have been swept aside by the Jerusalem authorities, leaving only the royal precincts in the capital as licensed to conduct the ceremonies and receive the privileges that had formerly been enjoyed at other centres too. This understanding places Sennacherib not as Yahweh's opponent but as his champion, brought in by Hezekiah's deity to overturn the god-displeasing centralization policy that the king of Judah has been vigorously pursuing. It is a clever argument, intended to sow seeds of doubt in the minds of the people of

Judah about Hezekiah's claim to be Yahweh's man, and the Assyrian messengers make sure that such points are driven home to the common people by shouting their propaganda 'with a loud voice in the language of Judah to the people of Jerusalem who were at the wall' (v. 18).

But Sennacherib is not Yahweh's champion, and he does not win the day. After such lengthy posturing by the king of Assyria, taking up eleven verses of narrative, Yahweh's response is narrated crisply, in just one verse: 'Yahweh sent an angel who cut off all the mighty warriors and commanders and officers in the camp of the king of Assyria, so he returned in disgrace to his own land and, when he came into the house of his god, some of his own sons struck him down there with the sword' (v. 21). Yahweh's actions speak louder than Sennacherib's words; the repeated bombast of the Assyrian monarch that the god of Judah would not rescue his people from the hand of the Assyrians (vv. 11, 13, 14, 15, 17) is completely and utterly negated, for 'Yahweh saved Hezekiah and the inhabitants of Jerusalem from the hand of King Sennacherib of Assyria' (v. 22). The dramatic reversal could hardly be more decisive, and the Annalists see no need to provide any further details about how such a miraculous salvation unfolded, or what numbers of imperial troops were involved; for the singers of Hezekiah's praises it is a simple matter of Yahweh stepping in to vindicate Hezekiah, and to create the circumstances in which he could enjoy 'rest on every side' (v. 22) and be 'exalted in the sight of all nations' (v. 23). It is as if the days of David—'the fame of David went out into all lands' (1 Chron. 14.17)—and of Solomon—'I will give him peace from all his enemies on every side' (1 Chron. 22.9)—have returned. Hezekiah, the one whom Yahweh strengthens, has been victorious even against the might of the Assyrian empire, and the city of Jerusalem sparkles again as it had done in Solomon's day, with silver and gold and precious stones and spices, and storehouses full of grain and wine and oil, and cattle-stalls and sheepfolds filled to capacity (2 Chron. 32.27-28).

Nevertheless the Annals record two small grey addenda to the otherwise glittering career of Hezekiah. Soon after the stress of the Assyrian invasion, he became sick and was close to death, but he prayed to Yahweh and was given a 'sign' (v. 24), to which he did not at first adequately respond on account of a certain 'pride of heart' (v. 25), and we are ominously told that there might have been serious consequences for the king and his people had they not had a change of heart (v. 26). And then there is a mysterious matter of 'envoys of the officials of Babylon, who had been sent to him to inquire about the sign that had been done in the land' (v. 31), where it is not clear whether 'the sign' they are investigating is the 'sign' that had been given after Hezekiah's illness-induced prayer or is the miraculous victory over the Assyrian juggernaut that had taken place just before the illness, but in this matter of the envoys from the east 'the deity left him to himself, in order to test him and to know what was in his heart' (v. 31). The results of this latter divine testing of the regal heart are not divulged, but presumably the king was found no longer to suffer from the 'pride of heart' that had jeopardised his standing and the good of his nation in the earlier incident. In any event the narrators move on to mention his renown for 'good deeds' or 'acts of covenant loyalty' (*ḥăsādāyw*, v. 32) and, when his near thirty-year reign is ended, they note that 'all Judah and the inhabitants of Jerusalem did him honour at his death' (v. 33). Despite the notes of uncertainty near the end of his life, he stands as one of the most glorious of kings in these Annals, and even when he stumbles slightly, as he did at the time of his illness, it still provides an opportunity for the Annalists to picture him as one whom Yahweh strengthens, through giving him a sign and bringing him back to the circumstances under which he 'prospered in all his works' (v. 30). Whereas the Annalists almost invariably place an ironic twist against the royal names, of Hezekiah 'the Strong' they have overwhelming, if not exclusively, good things to say.

2 Chronicles 33: Manasseh 'the Forgetful' and Amon 'the Craftsman'

Hezekiah had seen himself as having a role not only for the people of Judah but also for the people of the northern tribes that had broken away from Davidic rule many generations earlier but who now found themselves at the mercy of the Assyrian empire. One of the major tribes of the north, and one which included a number of people who responded positively to Hezekiah's invitation to come and keep the passover in Jerusalem and who then acted zealously in pulling down high places and altars in their tribal area, was the tribe of Manasseh (30.1, 10, 11, 18; 31.1). Accordingly, we might think of Hezekiah bestowing the name of Manasseh upon his son and heir as a sign of rapprochement with the northern tribes, and an indication that he wished his successor to continue to lead not just the Judahites but all the remnant of the children of Israel, especially now that the Assyrian tyrant Sennacherib had been so summarily dispatched by the Israelite god.

In naming his son, Hezekiah might also have had in mind the legend concerning that particular son of Israel, Manasseh, the eponymous ancestor of the tribe that bore his name, for the story went that 'Joseph named his firstborn son *Manasseh* (*měnaššeh*), "For", he said, "the deity has made me *forget* (*nāšâ*) all my hardship and all my father's house"' (Genesis 41.51). Since Hezekiah's agenda had been to reverse the policies of his father Ahaz and to turn Yahweh's wrath away from the nation, his own son Manasseh could be seen as a symbol of the new era, in which the abominable practices of Ahaz would be forgotten and any divine plans to visit misfortune upon the people would be shelved.

If this was what the new Manasseh was meant to portend, then it comes sadly wrong in no time at all, for no sooner has he begun to reign at the tender age of 12 (33.1) than the Annals are recording that he reversed the wonderful ways of his father and reinstated the wicked ways of his grandfather. The same kind of language that had been employed to categorize Ahaz as a thoroughly reprehensible ruler is now brought into service again to picture the sins of Manasseh: following the ways of 'the nations whom Yahweh had driven out before the people of Israel' (33.2; cf. 28.3), devoting himself to 'the Baals' (33.3; cf. 28.2), and making his sons (though NRSV alters this to a single 'son') 'pass through fire in the Valley of the Son of Hinnom' (33.6; cf. 28.3). If anything, the grandson outdoes the grandfather in such infamy, since Ahaz had neglected the House of Yahweh in favour of other places of worship of various gods, whereas Manasseh, although he too facilitates the use of other high places for various gods, is also pictured as building altars 'for all the host of heaven' in the two courts of the temple (v. 5) and setting up 'the carved image of the idol' in the temple itself (v. 7), at the very place concerning which Yahweh had said to the founders of the complex, 'In this House, and in Jerusalem, which I have chosen out of all the tribes of Israel, I will put my name forever' (v. 7, partly repeating a sentiment already expressed in v. 4).

It is clear that the king who bears the name 'Forgetting' has forgotten the foundation legends of the temple, and indeed that he has forgotten all the lessons that have been taught over many generations in this story-world and not least in the contrast between his father's and grandfather's reigns. He will need to be reminded, and so we find that 'Yahweh spoke to Manasseh and to his people, but they gave no heed, so Yahweh brought against them the commanders of the army of the king of Assyria, who took Manasseh captive in manacles, bound him with fetters, and brought him to Babylon' (vv. 10-11). Manasseh's father Hezekiah had enjoyed a miraculous escape from the close attentions of the army of the king of Assyria, because Hezekiah had been devoted to Yahweh, but for the son, who presumably had also forgotten about that aspect of his father's reign, there is no such escape until he remembers that it is 'the god of his fathers' (v. 12) who controls his destiny. A period of time spent as a captive in Babylon will allow the muddle-headed one to clear his head and come to his senses. In a kind of individual dress-rehearsal for the captivity of the entire royal family and what is reported to be the entire population of Judah in a few generations' time (36.20-21), and as an example to those later captives as to how they should react to their god sending them into exile in Babylon, Manasseh 'humbled himself greatly before the god of his fathers' and entreated the favour of the deity whom he now acknowledges as his own god too (33.12).

As a result of Manasseh's now exemplary behaviour as a penitent, the deity hears his entreaty and restores him to the throne in Jerusalem, and Manasseh, he who had been so forgetful and careless about the behaviour that the god of Israel expects of those who rule over 'the kingdom of Yahweh' (as this kingdom was called by Abijah at 13.8), now assuredly 'knew that Yahweh was indeed divine' (33.13) and that he alone was to be worshipped in the place that he had chosen out of all the tribes of Israel. Accordingly, the chastened and restored king sets about removing 'the foreign gods and the idol from the House of Yahweh' (v. 15), and he issues a command that Judah should serve Yahweh alone. The high places remain, but at least the people are sacrificing only to Yahweh, and no longer to any of the other gods (v. 17), which is an advance on the situation that had pertained under Jehoshaphat, in whose time, despite the king's own personal piety, the high places also were left functioning but in a context in which 'the people had not yet set their hearts upon the god of their fathers' (20.33). Manasseh had not at first set his heart on the god of his father Hezekiah, but he learned his lesson and he transformed himself into a devoted Yahwist, one who thus in the end deserved to occupy the throne of the kingdom for a record-breaking 55 years (33.1).

His own son, however, never earns the divine favour that Manasseh had attracted through his penitential prayer. Amon, as he is called, starts out as foolishly as his father had done, doing 'what was evil in Yahweh's sight' and devoting himself to those other gods whose worship his father had once promoted (v. 22). But regrettably for Amon, he does not have the good sense to learn from his father's experience—'he did not humble himself before Yahweh, as his father Manasseh had humbled himself, but this Amon incurred more and more guilt' (v. 23)—and so he comes to a sticky end, assassinated by unnamed conspirators who are then themselves quickly dispatched by others. He had reigned for a mere two years (v. 21), so it would seem that Yahweh was not willing to show the same patience again in the very next generation that he had shown to Manasseh; the lesson had been taught very clearly to and through Amon's father, so Amon should not have expected to receive the same indulgence from the heavens to a foolish repetition of Manasseh's condemned behaviour.

The account of Amon's brief reign is itself so brief that there seems to be nothing of the Annalists' customary playfulness with the royal name. The name itself (*'āmôn*) has a meaning in Hebrew, namely 'craftsman' (so used in Proverbs 8.30's depiction of Wisdom as the 'Amon' or 'craftsman' at Yahweh's side during the creation of the world), but King Amon is not seen as crafting any new images but only as taking up again with the images that his father had once made (2 Chron. 33.22). So perhaps, in the context of these Annals, we should think of this particular Israelite king's name in its Egyptian guise as the name of a certain deity, one which coincidentally happens to appear in a rather pertinent way in an Israelite oracle recorded in the book of Jeremiah: 'Yahweh of hosts, the god of Israel, has said: "See, I am bringing punishment upon Amon of Thebes, and Pharaoh, and Egypt and her gods and her kings, upon Pharaoh and upon those who trust in him. I will hand them over to those who seek their life"' (Jeremiah 46.25-26). In serving those non-Yahwistic images and not humbling himself before Yahweh, only to be killed by conspirators seeking his life, King Amon of Judah fits rather neatly into the pattern of that prophetic word from outside the Annals.

2 Chronicles 34–35:
Josiah 'the Healed'

Chapter 34

Like his ancestor Joash, who came to the throne at a tender age after the assassination of his father, the child called Josiah is just eight years old when he is designated king of Judah after the assassination of his father (34.1; cf. Joash's age of seven in 24.1). And as in the case of Joash, whose father Ahaziah had been assessed by the Annalists as a thoroughly wicked man, so too one might wonder in the case of Josiah whether it was his wicked father—in this latter case the image-worshipper Amon—who named the boy, and if so, what the intended portent in the child's name might be. Readers may recall from the discussion in the Survey of Judah's Kings that these two names, 'Joash' (yô'āš) and 'Josiah' (yō'šiyāhû), each a variant of the other, are the only names on the king-list of Judah that are not easily interpretable, so it may be that the evil-minded Amon wished to proclaim in his son's name a meaning which is no longer recoverable by us. However, since one of the possible meanings of the verbal element in these two names is the postulated verb 'āšâ, 'to heal', and we have seen in the tale of Joash that a message of 'the deity heals' makes good sense there, both positively in intention and negatively in the unfolding of the story, it is worth exploring whether a message of 'Yahweh heals' makes equally good sense in the tale of Josiah, whose name shares the same verbal element as that of his ancestor but adds the designation of the specific deity, 'Yahu' (i.e. 'Yahweh').

In terms of the intentions of those who named the child, it is difficult to imagine that Amon, at least insofar as he is depicted as a king who 'sacrificed to all [sorts of] images' and 'did not humble himself before Yahweh' (33.22-23), would have bestowed a Yahwistic name upon his son. Accordingly, as was the case also regarding Joash, we might think that someone other than the boy's father was responsible for the naming. Perhaps those who brought this youngster to the throne after the murder of his father wished him to have such a throne-name as 'Yahweh heals' in order to signal a time of healing and repairing after the wounding of the nation that had taken place during the apostate practices and in the violent end of the previous reign. The young Joash had had the chief priest of the time, Jehoiada, to engineer his ascent to the throne and to counsel a restoration of the temple; we are not told who counsels Josiah, but he too will purge the land and the temple of impurity and infection, so it is easy to speculate that there were pious powers behind the latest boy-king's throne who would have regarded a throne-name proclaiming Yahweh's desire to heal as entirely appropriate at such a time.

At the age of 16 (eight years into his reign, v. 3), the lad named for Yahweh began fully to orientate his devotion to that god, 'the god of his ancestor David', and at 20 years of age (12 years into his reign) he began to purge his kingdom of non-Yahwistic religious practices. Like his great-grandfather Hezekiah, Josiah sees himself as having responsibilities to all the Hebrew tribes over which their ancestor David had ruled, and so his zeal in smashing the altars and shrines dedicated to other gods extends also to the northern tribal areas, 'in the towns of Manasseh, Ephraim, and Simeon, and as far as Naphtali' (v. 6), indeed 'throughout all the land of Israel' (v. 7). He may also, at least in Judah and Jerusalem, have exercised a policy of executing the priests and devotees of deities other than the official national god, but whether the Annalists are taken as implying such a policy depends on whether vv. 4 and 5 are interpreted as involving the killing of current practitioners or merely the desecration of the graves and remains of such people who had already died of natural causes. Josiah's namesake Joash had been associated with the death of the chief priest of Baal in front of his altar at the hands of a zealous mob of Yahwists (23.17), and the other monarch with a 'healing' name, King Asa, had implemented a policy under which 'whoever would not seek Yahweh, the god of Israel, should be put to death' (15.13), so Josiah's policy of burning the bones of the priests of Baal on their altars (34.5) may similarly involve the extraction of life from until-then-very-much-alive bodies before treating the now-dead bodies to further profound disrespect.

After six years of ruthlessly crushing non-Yahwistic religion throughout his realm, Josiah then turns to repairing and renovating the Jerusalem temple. He does not experience the irritating delay that his ancestor Joash had had to overcome (back then there had been some sluggishness on the part of the levitical personnel in getting the temple restoration project up and running, 24.4-9); his swifter success may be because he was a good deal older than Joash and the temple functionaries had been operating under the renewed impetus for many more years than had been the case on the earlier occasion of temple repairs and renovations. This time the money flows in quickly and smoothly, and not only from 'throughout Judah and Jerusalem' as had been the case for Joash's project (24.9) but also 'from Manasseh and Ephraim and from all the remnant of Israel' (34.9), and the restoration work is done 'faithfully' and to the sound of levitical music (v. 12).

The climax of the renovation programme comes with the emergence of 'the book of Yahweh's law' (v. 14). This is reportedly discovered in the temple during the repair work, it is then prognosticated over by the leading prophetess of the day, and it becomes the basis of a covenant ceremony in which the king and the people commit themselves to following the decrees and statutes set out in the book. In this story-world nothing new is devised by a king such as Josiah, but rather what had been in place from the beginnings of the kingdom is rediscovered and reapplied, and here the kingdom's re-acquaintance with the venerable constitutive document comes as a kind of reward from the deity for the renewed attention that has been given to his temple and his service, giving the nation a chance to reinvigorate itself as Yahweh's people and to stave off the implementation of the threats that the deity had made to cast the people out of the land and to cleanse it from the stain they had placed upon it. There had been references to such a book from time to time in the earlier tales: David had instituted temple arrangements 'according to all that is written in Yahweh's law' (1 Chron. 16.40), Jehoshaphat had sent out officials with 'the book of Yahweh's law' in their hands (2 Chron. 17.9), Joash's priests were instructed to follow what was 'written in the law of Moses' (23.18), Amaziah was said to have acted in accordance with what was 'written in the law, in the book of Moses' (25.4), and Hezekiah too had ensured that temple ceremonies were conducted according to the stipulations that were 'written in Yahweh's law' (31.3). The implication is that knowledge of this book had fallen so far from the consciousness of the priests during the brief reign of image-worshipping Amon and the first two decades of Josiah's reign that they had not known where to put their hands on a copy of the document until the chief priest Hilkiah found it during the renovation programme in the temple complex.

When the book is read to the king, he is shocked at the implications of his kingdom having neglected it for so long. His chief concern is that the deity will be pouring out unquenchable wrath upon the kingdom 'because our fathers did not keep Yahweh's word, to act in accordance with all that is written in this book' (34.21). And so he sends his chief priest and his secretary of state and several other top officials to 'inquire of Yahweh' concerning the deity's current intentions over against what he has threatened to do if his people were to neglect his written instructions. Interestingly in such a male-oriented saga as these Annals, the group of men charged with finding out what Yahweh has in store for the kingdom head straight to a woman, 'the prophetess Huldah' (NRSV uses the gender-neutral term 'prophet', but it is worth noting and celebrating that the Hebrew text uses the feminine form *nĕbî'â*, a singular and precious admission from the Annalists that the office and function of a 'prophet' [*nābî'*] was not restricted to men). She tells the officials of Judah that Yahweh will indeed be bringing disaster upon the kingdom. 'Because they have forsaken me', the deity says through his prophetess, 'and have made offerings to other gods, so that they have provoked me to anger with all the works of their hands, my wrath will be poured out on this place and will not be quenched' (v. 25). So the king was right to be concerned about the fate of his kingdom, but for him as king there is a gentler word: because of his penitence, he will not personally experience 'all the disaster that [Yahweh] will bring on this place and its inhabitants' but will 'be gathered to [his] grave in peace' (v. 28). There is a stay of execution, and even though the actual death of Josiah will turn out to be less peaceful than it would have been had he not stumbled in his walking in the ways of Yahweh, the prophetess's essential prediction is assured: the kingdom will not be destroyed during the tenure of the present monarch, but it will not long survive his departure from the throne.

Nevertheless, while he sits on the throne of David, Josiah will do his best to facilitate fidelity to Yahweh's laws. He assembles 'all the people, both great and small', has 'all the words of the book of the covenant' read to them, pledges himself as king to follow Yahweh diligently, makes all the people pledge themselves likewise to 'act according to the divine covenant', and ensures that throughout his kingdom and for the rest of his reign no one turns aside 'from following Yahweh, the god of their ancestors' (vv. 30-33). All of this gladdens the hearts of the Annalists, even as they brace themselves to recount the disaster that Yahweh will be bringing upon Jerusalem and Judah in due course.

Chapter 35

There is yet one last happy episode before the final inexorable decline of the kingdom begins to unfold, and that is that 'Josiah kept a passover to Yahweh in Jerusalem' (v. 1). The only other mention of a passover celebration in the Annals had been in the time of Josiah's great-grandfather Hezekiah, but Josiah's festival occasion is grander than that; in fact 'no passover like it had been kept in Israel since the days of the prophet Samuel' (a seer mentioned in passing in the Annals on a number of occasions in connection with the saintly King David: 1 Chron. 9.22; 11.3; 26.28; 29.29), and indeed 'none of the kings of Israel'—not even that *David redivivus* Hezekiah himself—'had kept such a passover as was kept by Josiah' (2 Chron. 35.18). The statistics, as always in the Annals, make the point: Josiah contributes to Yahweh's altar 30,000 lambs and kids and 3,000 bulls, his officials contribute 2,600 lambs and kids and 300 bulls, and the levitical leaders contribute 5,000 lambs and kids and 500 bulls (vv. 7-9). This compares with Hezekiah on the earlier occasion giving 7,000 sheep and 1,000 bulls, his officials giving 10,000 sheep and 1,000 bulls, and the levitical leaders failing to make a contribution (30.24). While Hezekiah's officials do better than Josiah's officials, the total number of animals provided in the deity's honour at the latter king's event outdoes the earlier occasion by two-to-one (Hezekiah's team had only managed to dispatch 19,000 hapless animals, whereas Josiah and his men had led no less than 41,400 victims to the great slaughter).

The Annalists are keen to show that Josiah's Even-Grander-than-Hezekiah's Passover Festival is operated strictly by the book. The king instructs the Levites that the preparations must be made 'following the written directions of King David of Israel and the written directions of his son Solomon' (v. 4) and that the ritual slaughtering must be performed 'according to the word of Yahweh by Moses' (v. 6), and sure enough the narrators report that the temple personnel did everything 'as it is written in the book of Moses' (v. 12). We are further reassured that the various activities were staged 'according to the ordinance' (v. 13), 'according to the command of David' (v. 15), and 'according to the command of King Josiah' (v. 16). This is a case not simply of Josiah 'doing what was right in Yahweh's sight, and walking in the ways of his ancestor David' (34.2), but of Josiah following to the letter the precise arrangements that his ancestors David and Solomon had committed to writing. It seems that 'the book of Yahweh's law given through Moses' (34.14) was not the only ancient document that had been rediscovered in Josiah's time, and of course the reader is reminded of the frequent use of David's name in the earlier account of Hezekiah's re-establishment of temple practices in his own day (29.25-30). Whenever anything is right or proper in this kingdom, the Annalists can trace it back to the shining example of David.

But after this ultimate of passover celebrations, the scene changes rapidly. The Egyptians are marching through the land of Judah, on their way to a battle elsewhere, and Josiah decides to confront them (35.20). The Annalists offer no explanation for the Judahite king's fateful decision; they are not as interested in geopolitics as they are in theological points, and their theological contention here is not only an implied one that Josiah has not consulted his god before embarking on this course of action— in contrast to David's fastidiousness about inquiring of the deity concerning battle plans and preparations (1 Chron. 14.10-16)— and neither has he prayed to his god to fight for his people—in contrast to Hezekiah's action when he was directly and purposefully invaded by the Assyrians after his own passover celebration (2 Chron. 32.20-22)—but the Annalists' explicitly have Josiah give no heed to a message from the heavens when it is presented to him by the man against whom the king of Judah is determined to fight. He simply and recklessly 'did not listen to the words of Neco from the mouth of the deity, but joined battle in the plain of Megiddo' (35.22). Neco had sent envoys to Josiah, telling him that the Egyptians were on a heaven-appointed mission that had nothing to do with Josiah, and so he should 'cease opposing the deity, who is with [the Egyptians], so that he will not destroy you' (v. 21), but the king of Judah refuses to accept the pharaoh's word for it, and rushes to his doom. Despite adopting a disguise on the battlefield, the king is struck by Egyptian arrows, and, despite being brought back to Jerusalem by his servants, he dies from his wounds. The tragedy could hardly be of more epic proportions; the Annalists note that 'all Judah and Jerusalem mourned for Josiah' and that 'all the singers have sung of Josiah in their laments to this day' (vv. 24-25).

The unfolding of this dramatic episode has significant points of contact with an earlier episode in the Annals, involving Josiah's namesake Joash. We had read in 2 Chronicles 24 of Joash's abandonment of Yahwistic religion and of Yahweh's swift vengeance, with that king suffering a catastrophic defeat at the hands of the Aramean army and then being finished off by certain opportunists. That story seemed to be developing an ironic spin on the king's name, if indeed the name 'Joash' was understood by ancient Hebrew readers as carrying the meaning 'he heals' (that is, 'the deity heals', or in its longer form 'Jehoash' as 'Yahweh heals'), for evidently the deity did not heal the king after he was left severely wounded by the foreign forces, on account of his not having listened to the divine word that had been preached to him by the son of his former mentor. So now when we read in chapter 35 of Josiah, eight generations later, embarking on the disastrous policy of confronting the Egyptian pharaoh, refusing to be dissuaded from his action by a heaven-sent message, and thus suffering mortal wounds in battle, the impression is that here again is a story containing an ironic spin on the king's name, if indeed 'Josiah' means 'Yahweh heals', for the deity does not heal the king after he is left severely wounded by the archers, on account of his not having listened to the divine word that had been proclaimed to him by the pharaoh.

The parallels between the fates of the ancestor Joash and the descendant Josiah are too marked to be entirely coincidental in this story-world. In these Annals, both men are wounded in battle and are manifestly not healed of those wounds by Yahweh. It seems that the Annalists have conformed the dénouements of the two kings to parallel each other on the basis of their names having the same essential meaning: those names appear to proclaim that their god is a god of healing, and yet in both cases that god refrains from performing such an act, since both men are being justly recompensed for their rejection of a clear divine word prior to the commencement of battle. Meanwhile it is noticeable that no other king of Judah is depicted in the Annals as being fatally wounded in battle. Yet one notorious king of Israel is so depicted, namely the arch-villain King Ahab.

The story of Ahab's end went as follows: 'The king of Israel said to Jehoshaphat [king of Judah], "I will disguise myself and go into battle, but you wear your robes." So the king of Israel disguised himself, and they went into battle... But a certain man drew his bow and unknowingly struck the king of Israel between the scale armour and the breastplate; so he said to the driver of his chariot, "Turn around, and carry me out of the battle, for I am wounded." The battle grew hot that day, and the king of Israel propped himself up in his chariot facing the Arameans until evening; then at sunset he died' (18.29-34). The connections between that depiction and the end of Josiah in the present chapter are striking, for in the scene here too we read that Josiah 'disguised himself in order to fight with [Neco]... And the archers shot King Josiah; so the king said to his servants, "Take me away, for I am badly wounded." So his servants took him out of the chariot and carried him in his second chariot and brought him to Jerusalem; there he died' (35.22-24).

Note the evident key features with which Josiah's battle strategy and outcome replicate Ahab's battle strategy and outcome: entering the battle in disguise but being struck nonetheless, instructing the charioteer to take him out of the battle on account of his wounded state but eventually dying nonetheless. There are of course some incidental differences of detail, but clear echoes of Ahab's fate are to be observed in the fate of Josiah. The echoes in the fate of Joash had been somewhat fainter, in that there was no depiction of a disguise-on-the-battlefield strategy nor was that king quoted as giving instructions to his charioteers to carry him from the heat of the battle after he had been wounded, but the same essential outcome of being left severely wounded by the battle yet only dying some time later was brought out in that tale too.

But why is it that the Annals present the fates of Joash and Josiah in terms so clearly reminiscent of the fate of Ahab? At first sight this seems a bizarre choice on the part of the story-tellers, since these two southern rulers were both renowned for being repairers of the Jerusalem temple, while the northern monarch was equally renowned in the received traditions for the depths of his wickedness. The Annalists evidently felt that they must provide a theological explanation for the ignominious deaths of the temple restorers. Accordingly, they created parallel scenarios in which their heroes possessed a fatal flaw: the two kings apparently grew so confident about their own blessedness that they ignored the divine counsel given to them, thus riding foolishly into an identical fate that is inevitable within the strict storytelling conventions of these Annals. Their horrid end is their own doing in this story-world, and they have no one to blame but themselves.

The black-and-white ideology of the Annalists is clear: you might have cleansed and repaired the temple, you might even have renewed the covenant and celebrated the greatest passover of any of the kings of Judah, but if after all that you feel so headstrong as to ignore a word from Yahweh, then you have sunk to the depths of notorious King Ahab of Israel, and you deserve to die his death. Your names may proclaim 'Yahweh heals', but your stories will be made to proclaim that Yahweh ruthlessly destroys those who disobey him. Such is the systematic scheme set out in the Annals, at work in the tales of Joash and now Josiah, those two Ahabs of the south.

2 Chronicles 36:
Jehoahaz 'the Seized',
Jehoiakim 'the Appointed',
Jehoiachin 'the Established',
and Zedekiah 'the Righteous'

After the sudden death of Josiah, the little kingdom of Judah, squashed between the jostling giants of Egypt and Babylon, deteriorates rapidly. At first the people of Judah place one of Josiah's sons on the throne, but the Egyptian overlords remove him after just a few months and put one of his brothers in his place; then after a few years the new Babylonian overlords remove that man and a few months later they do the same with his son, and just a decade later they bring the kingdom of Judah to an ignominious end.

The end-game is so rapid and confusing that not even the Annalists, with their penchant for names and numbers, can seem to get it all straight. They say that the first of Josiah's sons to have a time as king of Judah was called 'Jehoahaz' and that he 'was 23 years old when he began to reign' and that he 'reigned for three months in Jerusalem' (36.2); and that the second of Josiah's sons to sit on the throne was called 'Eliakim' at first and then 'Jehoiakim' later and that he 'was 25 years old when he began to reign' and that he 'reigned for eleven years in Jerusalem' (vv. 4-5). They follow this up by saying that the first of Jehoiakim's sons to have a time as king of Judah was called 'Jehoiachin' and that he 'was eight years old when he began to reign' and that he 'reigned for three months and ten days in Jerusalem' (v. 9); and that the second of Jehoiakim's sons to sit on the throne was called 'Zedekiah' and that he 'was 21 years old when he began to reign' and that he 'reigned for eleven years in Jerusalem' (v. 11). The problem with several of these names is that the genealogical list (at 1 Chron. 3.15-16) which the Annalists had provided for the Davidic kings had named the first of these men as 'Johanan',

not 'Jehoahaz', and the third of them as 'Jeconiah', not 'Jehoiachin';
on the second of them, the genealogical list had gone with the
name 'Jehoiakim' and had made no mention of the alternative
name 'Eliakim'. And the problem with several of the numbers is
that they make Jehoahaz (a.k.a. Johanan) two years younger
than his brother Jehoiakim (a.k.a. Eliakim), even though the
genealogy had explicitly said that the former was Josiah's firstborn son, and they make Jehoiachin (a.k.a. Jeconiah) at least
twelve years younger than his brother Zedekiah, even though
the genealogical list implies that the former was Jehoiakim's
firstborn son.

To resolve the discrepancies with the names, we would have to
suppose that three and not just one of these four kings went
through name changes for one reason or another. The Annalists
do say that 'the king of Egypt made Eliakim king over Judah and
Jerusalem, and changed his name to Jehoiakim' (2 Chron. 36.4),
though they offer no explanation for why 'the king of Egypt'
should prefer the king of Judah to be called 'Yahweh Raises Up'
(yĕhôyāqîm) rather than 'El Raises Up' (ʾelĕyāqîm). Nonetheless,
with two other kings in those topsy-turvy last years of the
kingdom of Judah seemingly also carrying divergent names,
when the genealogical list is compared to the story of the reigns,
readers might extrapolate analogous scenarios in which Johanan
was made king and was renamed Jehoahaz and later Jeconiah
was made king and was renamed Jehoiachin. We had met with a
situation earlier in these Annals of a king whose story was told
under one name (2 Chron. 26.1–27.2 spoke of 'Uzziah') whereas
he had been listed under a different name in the Davidic genealogy (1 Chron. 3.12 thought of that individual as 'Azariah'), and
the Annalists had provided no explanation for that difference, so
such discrepancies are not confined to the final breakdown of
the kingdom.

As for the difficulties with the numbers, readers have a choice
of dispensing with the ordering of the genealogical list in the
case of these particular kings, or of dispensing with the figures
set out in the account of the kingdom's last years. By themselves,
the numbers given might just work, so long as we suppose that,
in each case of brothers having a turn on the throne, the first
brother placed there was not the firstborn son of the previous
king. After all, earlier in the Annals it had not been invariably
the case that the oldest son was elevated to rule: Solomon was
well down the list of David's sons (1 Chron. 3.1-9), and Abijah

was not Rehoboam's firstborn son (2 Chron. 11.18-22). Indeed, it is not too difficult to imagine a scenario in which the 23-year-old Jehoahaz (36.2) could have been preferred in some circles to the 25-year-old Jehoiakim (v. 5, speaking of the situation just three months later than Jehoahaz's elevation), and so the Egyptian action of removing the younger brother and placing the older brother on the throne would then be applying a principle of primogeniture over against allowing the people of Jerusalem to choose their own king. But it is more difficult to imagine that an 8-year-old Jehoiachin (v. 9) would have been made king rather than his 21-year-old brother Zedekiah (v. 11, speaking of the situation three months and ten days after Jehoiachin's elevation). And when we note that the statistics also compute as having Jehoiakim at the relatively tender age of 15 when his son Zedekiah was born, we might suspect that the Annalists have confused the two Zedekiahs to be found in the genealogical list, the one a brother of Jehoiakim (1 Chron. 3.15) and the other Jehoiakim's son (1 Chron. 3.16). Nonetheless, the figure of 15 years old for fatherhood is not impossible, and it is not as hard to accept as the earlier statistics which had suggested that Ahaz was only 11 years old when his son Hezekiah was born (computing 2 Chron. 28.1 and 29.1).

If we accept the details given in the telling of the tales, then the first of this motley band of four final rulers is Jehoahaz, who has a mere three months on the throne of Judah before the Egyptians 'deposed him in Jerusalem' (36.3) and 'carried him to Egypt' (v. 4). In charge of this imperial seizure is Pharaoh Neco, the same man against whom Josiah had foolishly stood at Megiddo, not accepting the pharaoh's instruction to 'cease opposing the deity, who is with me, so that he will not destroy you' (35.21). Now the deity's agent Neco takes hold of Josiah's son, the aptly named Jehoahaz (*yĕhô'āḥāz*, embodying the proclamation that 'Yahweh seizes', a more appropriate designation in this tale than the genealogical name Johanan or 'Yahweh is gracious' would have been). Just as his similarly-named ancestor Ahaziah (a name which placed the divine and verbal elements in the opposite order) had been seized by the divinely-appointed Jehu son of Nimshi (22.7-9), and just as the more succinctly-named Ahaz (a name expressing only the verbal element) had been squeezed by a triple whammy of Arameans, Israelites, and Assyrians (28.5, 6, 20), so too Jehoahaz is comprehensively apprehended by the long arm of the deity.

The second of the Final Four fares somewhat better, in that
he apparently enjoys the support of the Egyptian authorities and
is thus able to reign for as much as a decade. The Egyptians even
insist on him using the name of the god of Judah within his regal
name, changing his ecumenical moniker of Eliakim ('El raises
up') to the locally-specific Jehoiakim ('Yahweh raises up'), a
specificity that the Egyptian king had avoided when he sent
envoys to Josiah some months previously—that is, Neco was not
quoted in 35.21 as saying that 'Yahweh has commanded me to
hurry, so cease opposing Yahweh, who is with me', but now he
calls for a Yahwistic element to be incorporated into the Judahite
king's name, as indeed had generally been the custom among
the kings in Jerusalem (no less than 10 of the previous 16 kings
of Judah had possessed a Yahwistic element in their name).
Perhaps Neco is hoping by such a stratagem to mask Egyptian
hegemony over Judah and make the nation more compliant to
his economic interests in the land, or perhaps he genuinely
believes that the local god is on his side, much as Sennacherib of
Assyria had seemed to imply that he believed when he came
against Hezekiah of Judah (32.11-12). But the Egyptian confidence that Yahweh has raised up or appointed their Judahite
puppet king Jehoiakim to run the kingdom as part of the Egyptian
empire is completely shattered when the new power of Babylon
under the command of the all-conquering Nebuchadnezzar
sweeps into Judah, captures Jehoiakim, and carries the erstwhile ruler along with certain items of booty from the House of
Yahweh off to Babylon. This dramatic reversal of fortune comes
about because Jehoiakim 'did what was evil in the sight of his
god Yahweh' (36.5), including various 'abominations' and other
matters that were 'found against him' (v. 8); such a king might
proclaim in his name that he has been appointed by Yahweh, but
he should not have overlooked the fact that Yahweh can dismiss
from office anyone that he can appoint (or allow imperial authorities to appoint) to office.

The brief reign of Jehoiachin is something of a reprise of
Jehoahaz's experience, in that he reigns for only a few months
before he is taken away to the imperial headquarters and his
brother is put on the throne in his place, except that now it
is the Babylonians who are calling the shots and it is to Babylon
that Jehoiachin is taken, along with further items of booty from
the House of Yahweh. It seems a harsh judgment on the part
of the Annalists to imply that Jehoiachin deserved his fate

because 'he did what was evil in Yahweh's sight', when the lad was only 'eight years old when he began to reign' and reigned for a mere 'three months and ten days in Jerusalem' (v. 9), hardly an age at which or a tenure in which to show one's true worth or worthlessness, but such an analysis is the only way that these narrators can make sense of such events. In any case, the extreme brevity of the reign certainly provides an ironic twist to the name of Jehoiachin (*yĕhôyākin*), with its proclamation that 'Yahweh establishes' or 'Yahweh makes firm'. In fact the same would apply to the genealogical list's version of the name as Jeconiah (*yĕkonĕyâ*), since it too appears to contain the same divine and verbal elements in reverse order. Yet insofar as the line of Davidic descent will continue on from 'the sons of Jeconiah the captive', according to the genealogy (at 1 Chron. 3.17), this boy-king so swiftly wrenched from the throne in Jerusalem can be thought of as having the last laugh in due course, though at this stage of the story the Annalists say nothing about him producing any offspring or having any personal hope.

The end of the line of the Davidic dynasty, at least as regards a descendant of David reigning as king in Jerusalem, comes with the monarch known as Zedekiah. He is the only one of the Final Four for whom the Annals give just one name, and that exclusive designation, *ṣidĕqîyāhû* or 'Yahweh is my righteousness', is the final twist in the tales of the Judahite kings. Far from living up to his name, this king 'did what was evil in Yahweh's sight, did not humble himself before the prophet Jeremiah who spoke from the mouth of Yahweh', and refused to 'return to Yahweh' (2 Chron. 36.12-13). Indeed, under his reign, according to the storytellers, the people of Judah 'were exceedingly unfaithful, ...polluted the house of Yahweh, ...[and] kept mocking the deity's messengers, despising his words and scoffing at his prophets, until Yahweh's wrath against his people became so great that there was no remedy' (vv. 14-16). And so it is that the all-righteous Yahweh terminates the reign of Zedekiah the anything-but-righteous king and indeed suspends the kingdom of Judah altogether. The devastation is total, with 'the king of the Chaldeans' (a more antiquated designation for the Babylonian emperor) 'having no compassion' on any of the people whom the god of Jerusalem placed in his hand (v. 17). Young and old, able-bodied and disabled, all are either put to the sword on the spot or carried off into exile in Babylon. Yahweh is so livid with the nation's rejection of him that he even allows the temple itself to be completely stripped of anything of value and for the once proud structure to be burned to the ground, along with the entire city.

The Annals had presented a precious House of God that could have stood forever (2 Chron. 6.2) and a royal House of David that could have reigned forever (1 Chron. 17.12), if only the king and the people had remained faithful to their god. Zedekiah becomes the last of the kings of Judah and the last of the royal custodians of Solomon's temple because he and his people were completely unmindful of Yahweh's programmatic words to Solomon and his successors at the time of the building's dedication: 'If you walk before me, as your father David walked, doing according to all that I have commanded you and keeping my statutes and my ordinances, then I will establish your royal throne... But if you turn aside and forsake my statutes and my commandments that I have set before you, and go and serve other gods and worship them, then I will pluck [you] up from the land that I have given [you]; and this house, which I have consecrated for my name, I will cast out of my sight, and will make it a proverb and a byword among all peoples' (2 Chron. 7.17-20).

Zedekiah too is something of a byword, his name having been set up in the story of the first king of Judah, Solomon's son Rehoboam. When that man and his people had abandoned the law of Yahweh and then realised the consequences, they humbled themselves and said, 'Yahweh is righteous' (*ṣadīq yahweh*) (12.6). The narrators lay down the message, 'Because he humbled himself, Yahweh's wrath turned from him, so as not to destroy them completely' (12.12). If only King 'Yahweh is My Righteousness' and his people had taken the same attitude in that respect as their ancestors had done, Yahweh would not have felt the need to destroy the nation completely in the latter time.

But as it is, the god who had chosen Jerusalem as his dwelling place on earth has now determined that the city and its environs must 'keep sabbath', lying desolate and fallow for an appropriate period of time, to 'make up for its sabbaths' (36.21). This implies that there was a period in which the regular sabbaths that Yahweh's law required had not been kept. The Annalists give the appropriate time needed for the land to make up for missed sabbaths as a period of 70 years, a figure which is said to have been decreed in a 'word of Yahweh by the mouth of Jeremiah'—and indeed readers can cross-check this figure in the prophetic book that bears Jeremiah's name: 'This whole land shall become a ruin and a waste, and these nations shall serve the king of Babylon for 70 years'; and again, 'Only when...70 years are completed will I visit you, and I will fulfil to you my promise and bring you back to this place' (Jeremiah 25.11 and 29.10).

Such a period of time might be thought of simply as a full generation-span (witness Psalm 90.10's contention that 'the days of our life are 70 years'), and thus as a sufficient passage of time to ensure that no one who is removed from the land can be brought back to it alive at the end of the Great Sabbath. In the Annalists' strict accounting, however, they may well have seen a specifically numbered fallow period as precisely calculated to make up for the actual sabbaths that had passed. Whether they were thinking in terms of 70 years of one-after-the-other rest-days to make up for centuries of unobserved seventh-day-of-each-week rest-days devoted to godly reflection over against the otherwise interminable daily work-patterns (Exodus 20.8-11) or in terms of 70 sabbatical-years to make up for hundreds of years of unobserved seventh-year-of-each-septenary sabbatical-years of agricultural rest for the land over against the otherwise inter-minable seasonal work-patterns (Leviticus 25.3-7), the most straightforward way to calculate the number of years of missed sabbath-rests represented by a 70-year Great Sabbath is simply to multiply by 7, thus arriving at a figure of 490 years. This applies independently of the number of days understood to comprise a year; that is, it does not matter whether the Annalists were working with a solar or a lunar calendar. The working is obvious in the case of a solar year, but calculations become more complicated if numbers of months and days are calculated according to the fundamentally additive paradigm of the lunar calendar. Even so, if the Annalists had any sense of the frequency with which leap months had to be added in order to keep the calendar in synchrony with the seasons (for instance, using the Metonic cycle), then, over a long enough period, even detailed 'long-hand' calculations using the lunar calendar approximate to the solar calendar, to which the lunar calendar is constantly being brought back.

Nevertheless, we might add the quirky observation—for which I am indebted to my colleague Andrew Davison—that if one were minded to use the lunar system to arrive at '70 years of days' (assuming 354 days per year, without leap months) and the solar system for the number of sabbaths per year (52.18 sabbaths), then the number of years for which 70 years of exile would compensate is 474.9 years. This particular combination of solar and lunar measurements would appear to be very unlikely for ancient chronographers to make, since it uses a solar parameter for the shorter period and a lunar parameter for the longer, but it is an intriguing figure to set alongside these Annals, because it just so happens that the figures spread across the pages of the Annals for the reigns of the kings yield a total span of 474 years and some months for the period of the monarchy. The precise number of months would depend on how far into the seventh year of Athaliah's rulership the coronation of the boy-king Joash took place, but the Annalists do not give us a precise figure for that. The details that are set out may be brought together as follows: 40 years of David (1 Chron. 29.27) plus 40 of Solomon (2 Chron. 9.30) plus 17 of Rehoboam (12.13) plus 3 of Abijah (13.2) plus 41 of Asa (16.13) plus 25 of Jehoshaphat (20.31) plus 8 of Joram (21.20) plus 1 of Ahaziah (22.2), then an interregnum for 6 years and some months (23.1) followed by 40 years of Joash (24.1) plus 29 of Amaziah (25.1) plus 52 of Uzziah (26.3) plus 16 of Jotham (27.1) plus 16 of Ahaz (28.1) plus 29 of Hezekiah (29.1) plus 55 of Manasseh (33.1) plus 2 of Amon (33.21) plus 31 of Josiah (34.1) plus a few months of Jehoahaz (36.2) plus 11 years of Jehoiakim (36.5) plus a few months of Jehoiachin (36.9) and finally 11 years of Zedekiah (36.11).

This uncannily close match between the figure of 474 years and some months of the monarchy as set out in the Annals on the one hand, and the figure of 474.9 years of sabbaths being equivalent to 70 sabbath-years in a mixed lunar/solar calculation on the other, is a fascinating matter. However, given the quirkiness that the latter calculation involves, it might be safer to take the more conventional figure of 490 years as the number of years for which 70 years of exile would compensate. The period of the monarchy in the Annals, at around 474 years, falls short of that figure by around 15 years, but we might speculate that the Annalists thought of the initial quasi-king of Israel, Saul, as having ruled the Israelites for that length of time, even though the grudging account that they provide of his leadership (in 1 Chron. 10) gives no such figure. But in any event, we can say that the period of the monarchy, whether calculated down to the last sabbath or merely approximating the desired parameters, looks to be the period of sabbathlessness that the Annalists have in mind when they say that the land 'lay desolate, keeping sabbath, to fulfil 70 years' (2 Chron. 36.21). After almost half a century of king after king endlessly drawing upon the land, that land requires seven decades of rest to recover its pristine status, ready for a fresh start.

The fresh start is made possible through the good offices of 'King Cyrus of Persia', whom Yahweh raises up after the destined 70 years of sabbath-rest for the land of Judah have expired (2 Chron. 36.22). By this time Cyrus has been given 'all the kingdoms of the earth' (v. 23), which obviously includes the Babylonian empire and its subject kingdoms such as Judah, so that the new Persian king of kings has it in his power to release the exiled Judahites and to facilitate their return to their homeland. And he is enthusiastic about this venture: just as Hezekiah had sent verbal and written word to all the scattered Israelites of his time that they should come to the House of Yahweh in Jerusalem (30.1), so now Cyrus 'sent a herald throughout all his kingdom and also declared in a written edict' (36.22) that the scattered children of Israel should return to Jerusalem to raise a temple to Yahweh once again.

As was noted in the Introduction, these Annals are a 'book of beginnings', looking back to a legendary past, and yearning for a bright future in which the lessons of the past, as the Annalists saw them, would have been learnt. By starting out (in 1 Chronicles) with Adam and the generations that were believed to have descended from him, the Annalists had alluded to the very beginnings of humankind and in turn to the beginnings of the great divisions of peoples in the known world and the beginnings of the Israelite people itself. By devoting an inordinate amount of text to their story of King David as founder of the Israelite kingdom and planner of its temple, and (in 2 Chronicles) to their story of the building and dedication of the temple by King Solomon, they showed that they were most interested in getting across a certain view of the regal and religious system they advocate. And by drawing the Annals to a close, after all the tales of blessings upon the kings who were faithful to Yahweh and terrible consequences for the kings who were unfaithful to him, with the invitation from the Persian king for people to 'go up' to Jerusalem, the Annalists end with a new beginning—and an implied challenge for their community, to act in accordance with the way these storytellers envisaged things to have been constituted in the earlier beginning of 'the kingdom of Yahweh'.

Accordingly, these ultimate words of the Annals may be regarded as the climax and the interpretive key of the whole annalistic enterprise. There is the possibility of starting again—and, god-willing, doing better with the Davidic heritage than the generally disappointing sequence of motley monarchs had done. Yahweh remains committed to the project that he had set in train with David half a millennium before, and having granted the land its sabbath-rest he is now at work creating a fresh opportunity for 'whoever is among you of all his people': it is time once again 'to build him a house at Jerusalem, which is in Judah' (36.23). Armed with these Annals, and taking to heart the repeated and reiterated lessons contained within them, the restorers and rebuilders of Jerusalem will surely not sink to the depths of an Ahaz or an Amon or a Zedekiah, but will rise to the heights of a David or a Solomon or a Hezekiah. They will take as their motto the very last word of the Annals: 'Go up!'

Bibliography

Readers seeking further (or alternative) comments on 2 Chronicles may wish to consult the following commentaries:

Coggins, R.J., *The First and Second Books of the Chronicles* (Cambridge Bible Commentary; Cambridge: Cambridge University Press, 1976).

Curtis, E., and A. Madsen, *A Critical and Exegetical Commentary on the Books of Chronicles* (International Critical Commentary; Edinburgh: T. & T. Clark, 1910).

DeVries, S.J., *1 and 2 Chronicles* (Forms of Old Testament Literature; Grand Rapids: Eerdmans, 1989).

Dillard, R.B., *2 Chronicles* (Word Biblical Commentary, 15; Waco: Word Books, 1987).

Japhet, S., *I & II Chronicles: A Commentary* (Old Testament Library; London: SCM Press, 1993).

McConville, J.G., *I & II Chronicles* (Daily Study Bible; Philadelphia: Westminster Press, 1984).

Myers, J.M., *II Chronicles* (Anchor Bible, 13; New York: Doubleday, 1965).

Selman, M.J., *2 Chronicles* (Tyndale Old Testament Commentaries; Leicester: Inter-Varsity Press, 1994).

Tuell, S.S., *First and Second Chronicles* (Interpretation; Louisville: John Knox Press, 2001).

Wilcock, M., *The Message of Chronicles* (The Bible Speaks Today; Downers Grove: Inter-Varsity Press, 1987).

Williamson, H.G.M., *1 and 2 Chronicles* (New Century Bible Commentary; London: Marshall, Morgan & Scott, 1982).

Several recent studies on various aspects of the interpretation of the books of Chronicles may also be of interest:

Graham, M.P., S.L. McKenzie and G.N. Knoppers (eds.), *The Chronicler as Theologian: Essays in Honor of Ralph W. Klein* (Journal for the Study of the Old Testament Supplement Series, 371; London and New York: T & T Clark International, 2003).

Hognesius, K., *The Text* of *2 Chronicles 1–16: A Critical Edition with Textual Commentary* (Coniectanea Biblica, Old Testament Series, 51; Stockholm: Almqvist & Wiksell International, 2003).

Japhet, S., *From the Rivers of Babylon to the Highlands of Judah: Collected Studies on the Restoration Period* (Winona Lake, IN: Eisenbrauns, 2006).

Kalimi, I., *An Ancient Israelite Historian: Studies in the Chronicler, His Time, Place and Writing* (Studia Semitica Neerlandica, 46; Assen: Van Gorcum, 2005).

Kalimi, I., *The Reshaping of Ancient Israelite History in Chronicles* (Winona Lake, IN: Eisenbrauns, 2005).

Schweitzer, S., *Reading Utopia in Chronicles* (Library of Hebrew Bible/ Old Testament Studies, 442; London and New York: T & T Clark International, 2007).

Williamson, H.G.M., *Studies in Persian Period History and Historiography* (Forschungen zum Alten Testament, 38; Tübingen: Mohr Siebeck, 2004).

Index of References

Lightning Source UK Ltd.
Milton Keynes UK
UKOW031424040713

213216UK00001B/2/A